Court and Country Politics
in the Plays of Beaumont and Fletcher

Court and Country Politics in the Plays of Beaumont and Fletcher

Philip J. Finkelpearl

PRINCETON UNIVERSITY PRESS

PRINCETON, NEW JERSEY

Library of Congress Cataloging-in-Publication Data

Finkelpearl, Philip J.
Court and country politics in the plays of Beaumont and Fletcher /
Philip J. Finkelpearl.
Includes bibliographical references.
1. Beaumont, Francis, 1584–1616—Criticism and interpretation.
2. Fletcher, John, 1579–1625—Criticism and interpretation.
3. Political plays, English—History and criticism. 4. Courts and
courtiers in literature. 5. Country life in literature. I. Title.
PR2434.F53   1990   822'.309358—dc20   89-27456

ISBN 0-691-06825-9 (alk. paper)

Publication of this book has been aided by the Whitney Darrow Fund
of Princeton University Press

This book has been composed in Linotron Baskerville

Princeton University Press books are printed on acid-free paper,
and meet the guidelines for permanence and durability of the
Committee on Production Guidelines for Book Longevity of the
Council on Library Resources

Printed in the United States of America by Princeton University Press,
Princeton, New Jersey
10 9 8 7 6 5 4 3 2 1

To Some Old Friends

In appreciation of a lifetime
of support and inspiration:

KITTY
and
Anne and Dave
Bob
Sophie and Jack
Denise and Bob
Susan and Stephen

CONTENTS

ACKNOWLEDGMENTS

THIS BOOK began as an ambitious effort to say everything about the vast canon of work ascribed to the seventeenth-century English collaborative playwrights Francis Beaumont and John Fletcher. Eventually I discovered that this would have been a formidable task even with the assistance of as many additional collaborators as the playwrights themselves had. Thus I have restricted my discussion to the areas in which I differ significantly from the *consensus gentium*, primarily, but not exclusively, regarding the politics of the plays. I avoid many matters (among them the insoluble problem of exactly who wrote what) and do not even mention plays unrelated to my concerns. However, I hope that through my narrow window I have shown something of the importance and fascination of this remarkably neglected subject.

Some parts of this book first appeared as articles, often in very different forms: " 'Wit' in Francis Beaumont's Poems," *Modern Language Quarterly* 28 (1967): 33–44; "Beaumont, Fletcher, and 'Beaumont and Fletcher': Some Distinctions," *English Literary Renaissance* 1 (1971): 144–64; "The Date of Beaumont and Fletcher's *The Noble Gentleman*," *Notes and Queries* 24 (1977): 137–40; "The Role of the Court in the Development of Jacobean Drama," *Criticism* 24 (1982): 138–58; and " 'The Comedians' Liberty': Censorship of the Jacobean Stage Reconsidered," *English Literary Renaissance* 16 (1986): 123–38.

My thanks are due to the Houghton Library, Harvard University, for the reproduction of the title page of the quarto of *A King and No King* (1619).

This book was written with the aid of fellowships from the John Simon Guggenheim Foundation and the National Endowment for the Humanities, for which I hereby make grateful acknowledgment.

I want to thank Teresa Faherty, Susan Sawyer, and Kerry Walk for help in preparing the manuscript, Professor Margery Sabin for constant encouragement, and Dr. Eleanor M. Hight for forcing me to buy my now-beloved computer.

I also want to express my gratitude to Professor Charles Forker of the University of Indiana for his many useful suggestions and above all to Professor Stephen Booth of the University of California of Berkeley for a reading of my manuscript as meticulous, remorseless, and brilliant as one would expect of the author of his notable work on Shakespeare.

Court and Country Politics in the Plays of
Beaumont and Fletcher

INTRODUCTION

Two happy wits, late brightly shone
The true sonnes of Hyperion,
Fletcher and Beaumont, who so wrot,
Johnsons Fame was soon forgot,
Shakespeare no glory was alow'd,
His sun quite shrunk beneath a Cloud.
—Samuel Sheppard (1651)

A STUDY of the writing done together and separately by the Jacobean playwrights Frances Beaumont (ca. 1585–1616) and John Fletcher (1579–1625) must begin by mentioning the position of great importance they once held and its almost complete collapse. If one is to trust the various kinds of evidence—the records of performances, the reprintings of their quartos, the contemporary allusions—they were exceedingly popular in their lifetimes. At his death Beaumont was the third writer, after Chaucer and Spenser, to be placed in what has come to be known as the "Poet's Corner" of Westminster Abbey, apparently out of high regard for his writing.[1] Fletcher by himself also had a strong reputation. But the dominant impression in the seventeenth century was of a joint achievement and equal admiration for the "Parnassus biceps," as they are described in 1647 in a poem on the title page of the First Folio edition of their work.

The folio, with a portrait of Fletcher as the frontispiece (on which it is mentioned that he was the son of the bishop of London), containing thirty-four plays and thirty-five commendatory poems, some by the most important literary figures of the time, appears to have been prepared as a volume to rival the folios of Shakespeare and Jonson. For this there may have been ulterior motives. It has been suggested that the folio, published as it was in the middle of the Civil War, was designed to exploit sentimental associations with the "good old days" before the cohorts of Sir Hudibras began to destroy the great works

---

[1] I state the matter thus because his far less distinguished poet-brother Sir John was also placed there in 1627, but in his case it would seem a result of his connection to George Villiers, duke of Buckingham, whose mother was a Beaumont. Villiers did not achieve his supreme position at court until after Francis Beaumont's death. Evidence for the significance of Francis Beaumont's placement in the abbey is included at the end of chapter 1.

of time. Relying upon Beaumont and Fletcher's popularity among the gentry, the folio may have been produced as "a propagandist reassertion of the Stuart ethic at a crucial moment in the fortunes of the Court."[2] The evidence for this theory includes its production by the royalist publisher Humphrey Moseley, the apparent involvement in the project of the cavalier propagandist Sir John Berkenhead, and the explicit sentiments of some of the prefatory poems, almost all of which were written by avowed royalists. One contributor went so far as to suggest that in the present atmosphere it might even be dangerous to profess admiration for Fletcher, and the omission of the last word in one passage confirms the volatile political atmosphere:

> whether to commend thy Worke, will stand
> Both with the Lawes of verse and of the Land,
> Were to put doubts might raise a discontent
> Between the Muses and the [Parliament].[3]

Another contributor asserted that a stalwart general in one of the plays would have chosen to be "o'th' Better side" in the Civil War.[4] Still another somehow found Fletcher a political philosopher who taught "how kingdomes, in their channel, safely run, / But rudely overflowing are undone."[5]

One can reconstruct personal ties among many of the prefatory poets of the 1647 folio. They were largely cavalier literati who were disposed to see Beaumont and Fletcher from a partisan point of view and to praise them immoderately. Fulsome as was the adulation of many of them, James Shirley set the world record for prefatory blurbs:

> but to mention [them], is to throw a cloude upon all former names and benight Posterity; This Book being, without flattery, the greatest Monument of the Scene that Time and Humanity have produced, and must Live, not only the Crowne and sole Reputation of our owne, but the stayne of all other Nations and Languages.[6]

In 1679 the Second Folio added eighteen more plays. During the Restoration, according to Dryden, two "Beaumont & Fletcher" plays

---

[2] P. W. Thomas, *Sir John Berkenhead (1617–1679): A Royalist Career in Politics and Polemics* (Oxford, 1969), p. 134.

[3] Arnold Glover and A. R. Waller, eds., *The Works of Francis Beaumont and John Fletcher* (Cambridge, 1905–12), 1:xvii. As far as I have been able to determine, Alexander Dyce in his edition, *The Works of Beaumont and Fletcher* (London, 1843–46), 1:xvi, was the first to insert the obvious omitted word.

[4] Glover and Waller, *Works of Beamont and Fletcher*, 1:xxii.

[5] Ibid., xxvi.

[6] Ibid., xi.

were performed for every one by Jonson and Shakespeare. Every age has its inflated reputations, but what is most striking in this case is the quality of the critics—to cite only the greatest, Jonson and Dryden—who took it for granted that these plays would "rise / A glorified worke to Time."[7] It was a judgment about which the age felt as assured as we do about the permanence of Joyce, Yeats, and Eliot.[8]

From these heights the decline of Beaumont and Fletcher was precipitous and swift. With the reformation and sentimentalization of the stage in the eighteenth century, it was natural that performance of their plays, with their frank and often obscene language, would be drastically curtailed. Some vestiges of their high reputation persisted well into the nineteenth century as one can deduce from the appearance of six editions between 1711 and 1846. Keats and Wordsworth expressed admiration for their work, but for the most part Beaumont and Fletcher did not profit from the rediscovery of the lesser Elizabethan dramatists. Lamb found them "an inferior sort of Shakespeares and Sidneys,"[9] and Coleridge used them as whipping boys for the glorification of Shakespeare. He found the form of their plays mechanical, not organic; their characterization defective; and their morality reprehensible. Perhaps most damning was his accusation that their politics were those of "servile *jure divino* Royalists."[10]

Not even the large-scale resurrection of the Jacobean dramatists in the twentieth century restored much of Beaumont and Fletcher's lost glory. T. S. Eliot's assessment played the most important part in their present status. He chose not to devote a separate essay to them in his studies of Elizabethan drama, and with one brilliant phrase in his essay on Jonson he administered the coup de grace: "the blossoms of Beaumont and Fletcher's imagination draw no sustenance from the soil, but are cut and slightly withered flowers stuck in the sand."[11] Today the only play of theirs that is widely admired and performed

[7] Ben Jonson, "To the worthy Author M. *John Fletcher*," in Cyrus Hoy's edition of *The Faithful Shepherdess* for Fredson Bowers, gen. ed., *The Dramatic Works in the Beaumont and Fletcher Canon* (Cambridge, 1966–), 3:492, ll. 14–15.

[8] See the various studies of this phenomenon by Arthur C. Sprague, *Beaumont and Fletcher on the Restoration Stage* (Cambridge, Mass., 1926); Lawrence Wallis, *Fletcher, Beaumont, and Company* (New York, 1947); and John Harold Wilson, *The Influence of Beaumont and Fletcher on Restoration Drama* (Columbus, Ohio, 1928).

[9] "Specimens of English Dramatic Poets" in *The Works of Charles and Mary Lamb*, ed. E. V. Lucas (New York, 1903–5), 4:285n.

[10] *Coleridge on the Seventeenth Century*, ed. Roberta F. Brinkley (Durham, N.C., 1955), p. 655. Coleridge's charge has reappeared in a more sophisticated form in J. L. Danby's statement in *Poets on Fortune's Hill* (London, 1952) that the "declassé son of the Bishop and the younger son of the Judge are James's unconscious agents" (p. 157). The use of "unconscious" puts Danby in an unassailable position.

[11] "Ben Jonson," *Selected Essays, 1917–1932* (New York, 1932), p. 135.

with any regularity is the least characteristic of their work, *The Knight of the Burning Pestle*. On the literary stock exchange Beaumont and Fletcher are generally consigned to the fourth level of Elizabethan-Jacobean dramatists. Not merely excluded from a share of the position just below Shakespeare with Marlowe and Jonson, they are not even granted equality with Middleton, Tourneur, and Webster; it is even questionable whether they are admitted as the peers of Chapman, Ford, and Marston. They have been cast as the Rosencrantz and Guildenstern of Jacobean drama, "deferential, glad to be of use" to king and court.

Eliot's devastating formulation was a characteristic adaptation (unacknowledged) of an adverse criticism of a play of Sir John Suckling's by Richard Flecknoe in his *A Short Discourse of the English Stage* of 1664: "Beaumont and Fletcher first writ in the Heroick way, upon whom Suckling and others endeavored to refine agen; one saying wittily of his *Aglaura* that 'twas full of fine flowers, but they seem'd rather stuck than growing there."[12] The wit whom Flecknoe quotes lived closer than Eliot to the collaborators' blossoms and was, in fact, responding to something he perceived as fresh and vital. But this vitality grew out of the richly rotting soil of the court and country of King James. After the Glorious Revolution of 1688 with Parliament, guided by the common law, in firm control of the kingdom, the crucial political dimension of these plays—as this book argues—was ignored or misconstrued, and with it much of their power withered away in the sandy soil.

Eliot concludes a comparison of a passage of dramatic verse by Beaumont and Fletcher to one by Jonson thus:

> Detached from its context, this looks like the verse of the greater poets; just as lines of Jonson, detached from their context, look like inflated or empty fustian. But the evocative quality of the verse of Beaumont and Fletcher depends upon a clever appeal to emotions and associations which they have not themselves grasped; it is hollow. It is superficial with a vacuum behind it.[13]

Some years ago I responded to Eliot's passage by attempting "to show that Beaumont and Fletcher felt as Eliot did about the rhetoric of their characters. Their plays dramatize a moral vacuum and a hollow center. They are not signs of the decadence of the Jacobean theater; as much as the more blatant examples of Marston and Tourneur,

[12] *Critical Essays of the Seventeenth Century*, ed. Joel Spingarn (Oxford, 1908), 2:92.
[13] *Selected Essays*, p. 135.

they are plays that comment on the decadence of the age."[14] I reached this conclusion from a brief study of the collaborators' family backgrounds, their social placement, their friends and connections, the influences on their plays, and above all the evidence of the plays themselves. I suggested that the playwrights' aims were almost precisely the opposite of those usually assigned to them. By attempting to replant Beaumont and Fletcher in their native garden, I hoped to restore some of the original sheen to their withered flowers. But as Captain Gulliver said about the tepid response to the publication of his voyages, I cannot find that my article "has produced one single effect according to my intentions." The place of Beaumont and Fletcher in the histories of Jacobean drama has remained unchanged. Cyril Connolly once said, "Within every fat man, there is a thin man struggling to get out." I had always felt that leanness was the most desirable and efficient form for all bodies, but the response to my essay has convinced me that in this case the opposite is necessary, that my claims can only be persuasive in a fattened version, one that presents its case as fully and with as many of what John Adams called "stubborn facts" as I can muster. This does not mean that I discuss the entire vast corpus. It will be enough for the case I want to make if I restrict myself to the relatively small number of plays Beaumont and Fletcher wrote in collaboration, and to enough of Fletcher's solo plays to demonstrate that he adhered to the same attitudes and convictions when writing alone.

To substantiate my belief that political criticism of court and king was a central urge in the most important plays of Beaumont and Fletcher, I found it necessary to write two separate essays, to which I frequently refer here. The first denies to the Jacobean court the central role of patronage and influence toward the drama, particularly that of Beaumont and Fletcher, that it is frequently accorded. The second argues that Jacobean censorship was somewhat less efficient and formidable and that the drama was politically freer than it is usually described.[15] These essays clear the ground for the elaboration of my view that the Age of Shakespeare and Donne and Jonson was not utterly foolish in taking seriously the plays of Beaumont and Fletcher, that their plays are more significant and attractive than they have been portrayed, and that their fundamental thrust is in a radically different direction from that normally accorded them.

[14] "Beaumont, Fletcher, and 'Beaumont & Fletcher': Some Distinctions," *English Literary Renaissance* 1 (1971): 163.

[15] "The Role of the Court in the Development of Jacobean Drama," *Criticism* 24 (1982): 138–58; and " 'The Comedians' Liberty': Censorship of the Jacobean Stage Reconsidered," *English Literary Renaissance* 16 (1986): 123–38.

Chapter One

THE COUNTRY, THE PLAYHOUSE, AND THE MERMAID: THE THREE WORLDS OF BEAUMONT AND FLETCHER

How Angels (Cloyster'd in our humane Cells)
Maintaine their parley, Beaumont-Fletcher tels;
Whose strange unimitable Intercourse
Transcends all Rules, and flyes beyond the force
Of the most forward soules; all must submit
Untill they reach these Mysteries of Wit.
—John Pettus (1647)

THE ASTONISHING consistency of texture of the plays of "Beaumont-Fletcher" has led many to assume a virtual interchangeability of the identities of these writers, as expressed in the couplet, "For still your fancies are so wov'n and knit, / 'Twas FRANCIS FLETCHER, or JOHN BEAUMONT writ."[1] In a famous phrase John Aubrey spoke of a "wonderful consimility of fancy,"[2] for which an admirer suggested a biographical explanation: "Mitre and Coyfe here into One Piece spun, / BEAUMONT a Judge's, This a Prelat's sonne."[3] The Castor and Pollux of the English stage, as Thomas Fuller designated them,[4] in fact had backgrounds so different that friendship, much less harmonious collaboration, might well have been impossible. Theirs is a story of parallels that eventually converged.

BEAUMONT'S FAMILY HISTORY

Thirty years after Francis Beaumont's death, the publisher Humphrey Moseley attempted to obtain the playwright's picture for the

[1] George Lisle in 1647 folio, Arnold Glover and A. R. Waller, eds., *The Works of Francis Beaumont and John Fletcher* (Cambridge, 1905–12), 1:xxii.

[2] *Brief Lives*, ed. Anthony Powell (New York, 1949), p. 53.

[3] Sir John Berkenhead in 1647 folio, Glover and Waller, *Works of Beaumont and Fletcher*, 1:xliv.

[4] *The Histories of the Worthies of England*, ed. P. Austin Nuttall (London, 1840), 2:513.

1647 folio edition of the collaborators' plays. He tried two sources: "those *Noble Families* whence he was descended" and "those Gentlemen that were his acquaintance when he was of the *Inner Temple*."[5] There was a third group he might have tried: surviving colleagues from his days at the Bankside where he lived and worked. But by the time Moseley began his project, this base resource might have been forgotten because in the interval the "nobility" of Beaumont's family had come to be stressed.[6] This development happened to coincide with the ascendancy at court of the handsome George Villiers, eventually duke of Buckingham, whose mother Maria Beaumont Villiers was a poor relation of the branch of the Leicestershire Beaumonts who lived at Coleorton. Moseley's impression of Beaumont's noble descent would seem to be corroborated by the pedigree that Charles Mills Gayley constructed in 1914.[7] There one may discover the most august aristocratic families in England: Cavendish, Talbot, Nevil, Hastings, even Plantagenet. But a close examination will confirm the well-known fact that if one searches far enough, one can discover relationships among almost all the gentry families in Elizabethan England.

Within the Beaumonts' own family—certainly among the leaders in Leicestershire—the branch living at Coleorton seems to have been the most important. It was not until the appearance of Francis's grandfather John (fl. 1529–54) that his immediate family became prominent, or to be exact, notorious. This John Beaumont had a meteoric career as a lawyer and judge that reached its height with his appointment as Master of the Rolls in 1550. In the best Tudor manner he amassed much property from the Reformation, including the eventual family seat, a recently dissolved priory at Grace Dieu, Leicestershire. His second wife, Elizabeth Hastings, was collaterally related to the greatest family in the county, the earls of Huntingdon. Before this marriage (ca. 1540) Beaumont had been involved in a serious feud with George, first earl of Huntingdon. In 1538 John Beaumont wrote to Lord Cromwell, complaining that the earl "doth labour to take the seyd abbey [Grace Dieu] ffrom me; . . . for I do

[5] Glover and Waller, *Works of Beaumont and Fletcher*, 1:xiv.

[6] A poem by Thomas Bancroft speaks of Shakespeare's "height," Jonson's "weight," Chapman's "fame," and Beaumont's "name": *The Jonson Allusion Book*, ed. Jesse F. Bradley and J. Q. Adams (New Haven, Conn., 1922), p. 175.

[7] *Beaumont, the Dramatist* (New York, 1914), tables A, B, C, D. While a valuable study, it must be used with caution. The most reliable material on the background of the Beaumonts appears in the introduction by Roger Sell to his edition of the poems of Francis Beaumont's brother, *The Shorter Poems of Sir John Beaumont*, Acta Academiae AAboensis (Aabo, Sweden, 1974), 49:3–26. Dr. Sell's work expands on Mark Eccles's biographical sketch of Sir John Beaumont.

ffeyre the erle and hys sonnes do seeke my lyffe."[8] After his marriage
to the earl's relative, the relationship became more amicable. Judge
Beaumont's public career ended in shame and scandal when it was
discovered that he had abused his position by engaging in forgery
and peculation on a vast scale. As receiver general of the Court of
Wards he managed to cheat the Crown of no less than twelve thousand pounds. Joel Hurstfield concludes that Beaumont was "a man
of ability, an experienced lawyer and judge, who might have risen
higher but for his failure to recognise that there was a limit to peculation, even in the Tudor age."[9] John Beaumont's punishment involved imprisonment and the forfeiture of all his estates to Francis,
second earl of Huntingdon (his enemy, the first earl, having died).
Probably this arrangement was a legal maneuver or a prearranged
stratagem (perhaps inspired by the family connection), since John's
wife Elizabeth was allowed to regain possession of the bulk of his land
and fortune after his death.[10]

The relative lenity of the punishment is confirmed by the fact that
the dramatist's father, also named Francis, does not seem to have suffered from his father's misdeeds. He too became a lawyer and eventually a judge of the Court of Common Pleas. Unlike his father, he
was described after his death as a "grave, learned, and reverend
judge."[11] Clearly, he was quite affluent by the time he made his will,
which lists estates in ten parishes in Leicestershire and others elsewhere and provides many generous bequests.[12] His marriage to Anne
Pierrepoint of nearby Holme-Pierrepoint, Nottinghamshire, is also a
measure of the Grace Dieu Beaumonts' status since the notoriously
ambitious Bess of Hardwick was willing to permit one of her daughters, Francis Cavendish, to marry Anne Pierrepoint's brother Henry.

THE BEAUMONTS' RECUSANCY

If John Beaumont's peculations did not cause his descendants to live
under a cloud, other activities of the family certainly did. It was

[8] Gayley, *Beaumont, the Dramatist*, p. 13.

[9] *The Queen's Wards* (Cambridge, Mass., 1958), p. 226.

[10] See the entry for John Beaumont in the *Dictionary of National Biography* (hereafter
DNB).

[11] William Burton in *Description of Leicester Shire* (1622), quoted by Gayley, *Beaumont,
the Dramatist*, p. 16.

[12] See his will in Alexander Dyce, ed., *Works of Beaumont and Fletcher* (London, 1843–
46), 1:lxxxix–xc. Another sign of his wealth is his loan in 1584 of two hundred pounds
to his noble relation, the third earl of Huntingdon. The quarrel between the families
was now apparently resolved. See Claire Cross, *The Puritan Earl* (London, 1966), p.
109.

known as long ago as 1914 with the publication of Gayley's book that Anne Beaumont Vaux, the daughter of Judge Francis Beaumont's sister Elizabeth, was intimately involved in the Gunpowder Plot, as were her relatives the Treshams. We now know that the playwright's grandmother (Elizabeth Hastings Beaumont), two of his uncles (the aforementioned Henry and his brother Gervase Pierrepoint), his mother, and even his father before he became a judge were also active recusants. As Mark Eccles describes the situation,

> [Beaumont's] mother Anne . . . denied in 1581 that she had harbored Edmund Campion [the Jesuit priest and martyr], but the [Privy] Council sent for the books and writings found at Gracedieu and ordered the "Massing stuffe" to be defaced. . . . While her brother Gervase Pierrepoint was in prison for having concealed Campion, the government seized letters that Francis [Sr.] and Anne had sent him with two fallow deer pies. Anne Beaumont was again examined at the time of the Throckmorton plot [1583], when the commissioners also described "old Mrs. Beaumont" [the dramatist's mother] . . . as "a recusant and great favourer of papists." . . . Even [the dramatist's father] Francis Beaumont was charged in 1591 with having been hitherto a large contributor to seminary priests, but when he became a justice of the assize he executed the laws and sentenced Walpole and other priests to death for treason.[13]

For punishment, in 1581 Anne Beaumont was put under house arrest, and two prominent neighbors, Adrian Stokes and Sir Francis Hastings, were charged to keep watch over her.[14] The degree of involvement of the Pierrepoints in recusant activities was even greater than Eccles reported. Gervase Pierrepoint was one of Edmund Campion's most trustworthy guides on his hazardous priestly mission through the countryside. Henry Pierrepoint eventually agreed to conform, but Gervase remained an implacable recusant. As late as 1601 he was imprisoned and tortured in the Tower for his activities.[15]

Judge Beaumont and Anne Pierrepoint had four children: Henry, born ca. 1581; John, born ca. 1583–84; Francis, born ca. 1585; and Elizabeth, born ca. 1588. There is no baptismal record for any of them in the parish register of Belton, a fact that leads to the suspicion

[13] "A Biographical Dictionary of Elizabethan Authors," *Huntington Library Quarterly* 5 (1941–42): 294. The Coleorton branch of the Beaumonts was virulently anti-Catholic. See Richard S. Smith, "Huntingdon Beaumont: Adventurer in Coal Mines," *Renaissance and Modern Studies* 1 (1957): 115–53, esp. Beaumont's statement on pp. 149–50.

[14] *Acts of Privy Council*, August 30, 1581.

[15] See Evelyn Waugh, *Edmund Campion* (New York, 1935), esp. p. 177.

of secret baptism by a Catholic priest.[16] After Judge Beaumont's death in 1598, the oldest of the three brothers, Henry (later Sir Henry),[17] succeeded to the estate; upon his death in 1605 John, also a poet, became the master of Grace Dieu. As Lawrence Stone observed, it was the worst possible moment for a recusant, as John proved to be, to acquire an estate: "Elizabethan parliaments had enacted strict laws against Catholic recusants and in 1605 James saw an easy way of gratifying his followers by granting the right to enforce these laws and to take the profits. . . . The most active period of the grants was between 1605 and 1611, the commonest form being the gift to a courtier of the fine and forfeiture of eight or ten recusants."[18]

Thus began the period of persecution for the Beaumonts of Grace Dieu. As Eccles's account describes,

> John Beaumont succeeded to Gracedieu on the death of his brother Sir Henry in July 1605. . . . By October the profits of his recusancy had been allotted to Sir James Sempill, a companion of King James since boyhood. . . . Two-thirds of his lands and all his goods . . . were thereby forfeited to the King and were formally granted in 1607 to Sempill, who was still profiting from them in 1615. . . . [John] Beaumont was now required to live at Gracedieu, . . . "beynge a Recusant Convicted And remayninge confyned to hys house."[19]

Francis Beaumont himself seems not to have maintained the family faith. I draw this conclusion from the Leicestershire clergyman Thomas Pestell's praise of Beaumont's adeptness at confuting Jesuits, many of whom passed through Grace Dieu:

> The Jesuits that trace witt and subtiltye,
> And are mere cryticks in Divinitie;
> Who to the soadring a crackt cause allow
> Sett fees for every new distinction; thou [Beaumont]

[16] Sell, *Shorter Poems of Beaumont*, pp. 4–5. Sell has unearthed a wealth of material to corroborate the family's staunch adherence to their faith.

[17] It is worth noting that both of Francis Beaumont's brothers were knighted but that Francis was not. This is consistent with his character as I try to convey it in this book. Note that the dramatist's brother Henry is not to be confused with his uncle Henry, brother of Francis, Sr., or with Sir Henry of Coleorton.

[18] *The Crisis of the Aristocracy* (Oxford, 1965), p. 440. See also Samuel Gardiner, *History of England . . . (1603–1642)* (London, 1895), 2:18–20, for a graphic description of the persecution of recusants in the years of hysteria just after the Gunpowder Plot.

[19] "A Biographical Dictionary," p. 295. A Sir Henry Hastings was similarly penalized at the same time, the money going to Lady Elizabeth Stuart. Coincidentally, the earlier nemesis, neighbor and relation Sir Francis Hastings, got into trouble for his Puritanism and was confined to his house in Somerset. See Cross, *Puritan Earl*, p. 51.

By a clean strength of witt and judgment wert
Well able to confound, if not convert.[20]

But in assessing the attitude toward princes and courts in Beaumont's
plays, it is useful to recall that during the entire period in which he
was a writer, most of the income from his family's estate was being
siphoned off by the Crown to a Scottish crony of the king while Beaumont's brother John was virtually imprisoned on his own land.[21]

BEAUMONT'S CONNECTION WITH THE INNER TEMPLE

By now it should be clear that it begs many questions merely to label
Beaumont as an affluent member of the gentry with noble relations.
There is a further complication if one considers another group to
which the publisher Moseley connects Beaumont, the "Gentlemen . . .
of the Inner Temple." Of course, many of the gentry passed through
the Inns of Court for a brief time, but the Beaumonts' connection
was different: they were a veritable Inner Temple dynasty. Francis's
infamous grandfather John twice served as reader (a tribute to his
legal scholarship but also to his wealth); he also was the society's leading officer, known as treasurer, for many years. The playwright's father, Francis, Sr., and uncle Henry also rose to eminence at the Temple. Both were readers; Francis, Sr., was also a member of the
governing body known as benchers. All three of his sons spent some
time at the Inner Temple. About the social position of lawyers in
early seventeenth-century English society Wallace Notestein wrote,
"by virtue of their manner of education and discipline, they had become almost a class in society, a class with which the Government had
to reckon as with the nobility and the gentry."[22] If one considers that
every male in the Grace Dieu branch of the Beaumont family for
three generations was a member of the Inner Temple and that in the
first two generations they were successful, important lawyers, judges,
and officers of their Inn, it may be argued that the "class" into which
Francis Beaumont was born was this special subclass of lawyers.

Many of the important participants in the battles between James
and Parliament resided at the Inns of Court; naturally (as one knows
from diaries and memoirs) their attitudes and points of view provoked discussion in the halls and studies of the Inns. The most prom-

[20] These are lines 35–40 of Pestell's elegy on Beaumont, reproduced in full in appendix B.
[21] As I implied earlier, the situation improved greatly for Sir John Beaumont once
his cousin Villiers became King James's favorite.
[22] *The Winning of the Initiative by the House of Commons* (London, 1924), pp. 49–50.

inent member of the Inner Temple at that time, Sir Edward Coke, was surely James's most outspoken opponent; and among the young Francis Beaumont's coevals at the Inner Temple was the great scholar and defender of the common law, John Selden, who was almost the same age as Beaumont and admitted to the Temple in 1603.

An even more direct conduit to the politics of the day would have been the Leicestershire cousins Sir Henry Beaumont of Coleorton, an executor of Francis, Sr.'s, will, and this Henry's brother, Sir Thomas Beaumont of Staunton Grange. Both were members of Parliament,[23] and in his study *The House of Commons (1604–1610)*, Notestein singled out these two Beaumonts as "early English liberals, who stood for the individual."[24] Sir Henry only lived until 1605, but throughout the period when Francis was writing plays, Sir Thomas was a constant, outspoken critic of the king. In a conference between James and thirty members of the Commons in 1610, Thomas made a classic statement on the function of the law. As paraphrased by a reporter, he said, "The walls between the King and his people were the laws. If ministers of state leaped over them and broke them down, what security was there for the subject? Contempt for the law was as dangerous to the Commonwealth as a tormented spirit to the body." Notestein concludes, "Beaumont's words suggest a desperation that may have been affecting many members of the House."[25]

Descended from a family of lawyers, judges, and M.P.s—some prominent opponents of the court, some suffering court-inspired persecution for their religious beliefs—Francis Beaumont was brought up in an atmosphere that could hardly have favored the new Stuart dynasty.

FLETCHER'S BACKGROUND AND LIFE

Few facts are known about John Fletcher's own life, but a great deal of enlightening information exists about his ancestry, background, and social connections. As with Beaumont the story begins with his paternal grandfather. Far from having any Plantagenets (however distant) in his pedigree, Richard Fletcher, Sr., came from humble stock—"honestis parentibus natus," according to the plaque erected in his memory by his sons. He was ordained by the soon-to-be-martyred Bishop Ridley in 1550, made vicar of Bishop's Stortford, Hertfordshire, in 1551, but was deprived of this position under Queen

---

[23] I have been unable to discover whether either was a member of the Inner Temple, although both seem to have had sons who were.

[24] (New Haven, Conn., 1971), p. 507.

[25] Ibid., p. 410.

Mary. It is recorded by Foxe in the *Book of Martyrs* that in this dark period Richard Fletcher and his son Richard, Jr., John Fletcher's father, witnessed in 1555 the burning of the Protestant martyr Christopher Wade. Later in Mary's reign the elder Fletcher was imprisoned for his religious beliefs.[26]

After the accession of Elizabeth, Richard Fletcher, Sr., served as vicar of Cranbrooke, Kent. He produced two distinguished sons. The younger one, Giles (ca. 1548–1611), was a diplomat, member of Parliament, government official, and author of the sonnet sequence *Licia* (1595). His comprehensive account, *Of the Russe Commonwealth*, published after his return from a mission to Russia, is a remarkably perceptive study still cited by historians. Two of Giles's sons were the well-known "Spenserian" poets, Giles, Jr., and Phineas.

John's father, Richard Fletcher (d. 1596), had a brilliant career, at least until its disastrous last chapter. He was educated at Bene't (now Corpus Christi) College at Cambridge and was briefly its chief officer in 1573. During his ministry at Rye, which began in 1574, his handsome appearance, elegant manner, and ability as a preacher brought him to the attention of Queen Elizabeth. He became chaplain to the queen in 1581 and dean of Peterborough in 1583; he also held other rich livings. As chaplain at the execution of Mary, Queen of Scots, he took a prominent part in the proceedings. Possibly his notoriously stern "Amen" at the moment of execution in response to the ritualistic intonement of "So perish all the Queen's enemies" was inspired by his memory of the Protestant martyrdoms he observed in his childhood. His rivals claimed it was a bid for the queen's favor, which certainly followed.

In quick succession Fletcher became bishop of Bristol (1589), Worcester (1593), and London (1595). This last position must have been most convenient for this "praesul splendidus" (as Camden described him)[27] because he already owned a house in Chelsea and spent more time at court than at any of his dioceses. In his petition to Lord Burleigh for the bishopric in London, he mentioned his desire to "be nearer the court, where his presence was accustomed

---

[26] For the lives of Richard Fletcher, Jr., and Sr., see Lloyd E. Berry's introduction to his edition, *The English Works of Giles Fletcher, the Elder* (Madison, Wis., 1964) and the entry for Richard Fletcher in the *DNB*. As with Beaumont's, Fletcher's pedigree by Gayley in *Beaumont, the Dramatist*, table E, headed "Fletcher, Baker, Sackville," is rather misleading. Insofar as John Fletcher had a tie to the august Sackvilles, the earls of Dorset, it could scarcely have been more tenuous, deriving from his father's brief marriage to Maria, the widow of Sir Richard Baker. Maria's late husband's sister was married to Richard Sackville, first earl of Dorset.

[27] Quoted from the *DNB* article on Richard Fletcher.

much to be, and his influence might be of use to serve the court."[28] Later he spoke complacently of the "especiall cumfort seculer that ever I conceyved to have lived in hir highnes gratious aspect and favour now xxty yeres past."[29]

At this point Bishop Fletcher's luck turned. His first wife, Elizabeth Holland, died in 1592. In 1595, shortly after he became bishop of London, Fletcher married Maria, whose husband, Sir Richard Baker, had died only a few months before. Not only was the marriage overhasty; Maria was notorious for her loose morals. Inevitably, the bishop's timing and choice of second wife provoked public outrage and cruel amusement. John (later, Sir John) Davies wrote five poems,[30] privately circulated, that plainly called the bishop's wife a "whore."[31] In typical Elizabethan fashion he satirized the bishop as much for his lowly origins as for his unseemly actions. In one poem Davies writes, "the match was equall, both had Common geare."[32] In another he asks,

> How can a viccars sonne a Lady make?
> And yet her ladyshipp weare greatly shamd'
> If from her Lord she should no tytle take;
> Wherfore they shall devide the name of Fletcher:
> He my Llord F, and she my Lady Letcher.[33]

Davies wrote these poems to Richard Martin while they were both resident at the Middle Temple. After holding three bishoprics it was still possible to be ridiculed for one's humble origins by an Inns of Court wit.[34]

The more tragic consequence of the bishop's marriage was the queen's instant, violent displeasure. She banned Fletcher from her presence and suspended him from his episcopal functions. After six months the suspension was lifted, and eventually the queen was willing to receive him. But his own brother Giles attributed Fletcher's death soon afterward in 1596 to the queen's actions. In a letter seek-

---

[28] Dyce, *Works of Beaumont and Fletcher*, 1:ix.

[29] Ibid., 1:xii.

[30] The poems were recently and persuasively attributed to him by Robert Krueger in *The Poems of Sir John Davies* (Oxford, 1975). The address of one of the poems to "Martin" led earlier editors to suspect that it was a Martin Marprelate work. Krueger shows that Davies is referring to his friend Richard Martin.

[31] Ibid., p. 177, no. 12, l. 10.

[32] Ibid., p. 178, no. 16, l. 8.

[33] Ibid., no. 15, ll. 10–14.

[34] Ironically, Davies was similarly sneered at in the Middle Temple revels of 1597–98 because his father was supposedly a tanner. See my *John Marston of the Middle Temple: An Elizabethan Dramatist in His Social Setting* (Cambridge, Mass., 1969), p. 53.

ing financial aid for the family, Giles wrote, "He hath satisfied the errour of his late marriage with his untimely and unlooked for death, which proceded spetially from the conceipt of her Highnes displeasure and indignation conceived against him."[35]

At his death the bishop left debts of fourteen hundred pounds, partly the result of his rapid advancement with an attendant crippling succession of "first fruits" payments. In addition, for the London episcopacy Fletcher had to pay—in the corrupt manner such matters were effected—no less than twenty-one hundred pounds in "*douceurs*" to various courtiers.[36] Along with his debts—eventually forgiven through the intercession of the earl of Essex—the bishop consigned his eight children to the guardianship of his brother Giles, who had nine of his own and very slim financial resources.

The dramatist John Fletcher, the fourth of the bishop's children, was born in 1579 in Rye.[37] Of his early years not much is known with certainty. It is claimed that he attended his father's college, Bene't, Cambridge, starting in 1591, receiving a B.A. in 1595 and an M.A. in 1598.[38] After his father's death in 1596 John apparently lived with his uncle in what could only have been a very crowded London house for some years; he was almost certainly still living there in 1601.[39] His uncle's troubles were compounded by a nearly fatal complicity in the Essex conspiracy, after which the all-powerful and indispensable Burleigh and his son never completely trusted him. He received no significant preferment thereafter. Giles and his children blamed their poverty directly on King James. The king had made Giles great promises before he came to England, but as his son Phineas Fletcher wrote in 1610, "his promise [was] writ in sand."[40] Richard and Giles Fletcher's families had good reasons for believing that they had been mistreated by personal acts of commission and omission by both Eliz-

---

[35] Dyce, *Works of Beaumont and Fletcher*, 1:xiv–xv.

[36] See Christopher Hill, *Economic Problems of the Church* (Oxford, 1963), p. 16.

[37] The house of his birth survives; it is now a tearoom.

[38] J. and J. A. Venn, comps., *Alumni Cantabrigienses* (Cambridge, 1922), part 1, 2:149.

[39] In *English Works of Giles Fletcher*, Lloyd Berry lists all of Giles's children. In 1601 five were still alive. At the same time eight of Bishop Fletcher's were alive. Since his oldest son, Nathaniel, brought suit against Giles in 1600 claiming that he had mismanaged the bishop's estate, it is most unlikely that he would have been living under the same roof. The presence of John at his uncle's home would therefore be required to make true Giles's statement of 1601 that his family consisted of "a wyfe and 12. poor children" (p. 404).

[40] "Piscatorie Eclogues" in *The Poetical Works of Giles Fletcher and Phineas Fletcher*, ed. Frederick S. Boas (Cambridge, 1909), 2:178. The identification of "Amintas" in the first eclogue with King James has been demonstrated by Lloyd E. Berry, "Phineas Fletcher's Account of His Father," *Journal of English and German Philology* 60 (1961): 258ff.

abeth and James, and some members of both families responded bitterly. There is no direct evidence that John Fletcher felt similarly, but
certainly nothing in his early life made him any more enthusiastic a
proponent of the monarchy and the court than Beaumont. For both
writers the provocations to alienation were many and strong.

Fletcher's social placement is thus paradoxical. Presumably, he
spent his childhood in sumptuous bishop's palaces. For at least twenty
years his father was a familiar figure at court. Queen Elizabeth may
once have paid a visit to his home in Chelsea, for which according to
legend a special entrance was constructed.[41] Since Fletcher was sixteen at the time of his father's death, the memories of a glamorous
early life must have been vivid. Perhaps no professional English playwright had as much opportunity as Fletcher to learn about and see
the workings of a court. Nonetheless, when he began to associate with
Beaumont in the early 1600s he must have resembled the indigent
Cambridge graduates in the "Parnassus" plays. Writing was his only
alternative to the sort of meager country parsonages to which his
brother Nathaniel and his cousins Giles, Jr., and Phineas were bitterly
rusticated.

BEAUMONT AS INNS OF COURT WIT

Of course, Beaumont never became a lawyer. He may have entered
the Inner Temple with the family vocation in mind, but he did not
complete his legal studies. After a brief period along with his brothers at Broadgates College, Oxford, in 1596–1597, he apparently left
college after the death of his father in 1598. Both older brothers were
admitted to the Inner Temple in 1597, and Francis was admitted in
1600.

A shaft of light into Beaumont's youthful sensibility has survived
in the form of a speech he delivered at the Christmas revels of the
Inner Temple around 1605.[42] Cast in the form of a "grammar lec-

---

[41] Dyce, *Works of Beaumont and Fletcher*, 1:xii, n.x.

[42] Mark Eccles, "Francis Beaumont's *Grammar Lecture*," *Review of English Studies* 16
(1940): 402–14. The precise date of the speech is unclear. It must have been delivered
between 1600, when Beaumont was admitted, and the period when he presumably left
the Temple to write, sometime around 1606. I lean toward the later date, "ca. 1605,"
assigned it by the *Oxford English Dictionary* (hereafter *OED*), simply because Beaumont
sounds much older than the "young students" whom he is treating with much condescension, and his observations sound as if they were based on years of experience in
London. The later this speech is dated, the more likely is it that Beaumont started at
the Inner Temple with the intention of studying the law and that his playwriting began
(ca. 1606) when he (like Marston) abandoned the law. His legal studies would then

ture" delivered between comparable efforts by other students on
arithmetic and music,[43] his speech burlesques the grave tones of a
college pedant, willfully misuses grammatical terms, and satirizes the
manners of the four groups into which he divides his audience.
These, as Beaumont labels them, are the "ancients," the practicing
lawyers who live at the Inn during the legal term and help to train
aspirants to their profession; the "plodders," students studying to
qualify for admission to the bar; the "young students," those who
have just arrived at the Inn and are still "soft imytating peeces fitt for
the impression of eyther plodder or Reveler"; and the "revelers,"
youthful gentry who have come to London to sample the many pleasures of the city and only incidentally to learn something about the
law. What is revealing is how much at home Beaumont appears in his
ancestral Inn of Court while standing outside all the groups and
viewing them with a distant, satiric eye. He offers for a price to teach
the young students how to trick parents into sending them more
money, how to cheat tailors, and how "to see a play att the banck side
with Templarian credit enough." He knows the plodder's shady legal
tricks for augmenting his income as well as the reveler's preference
for "naples silke stockinges" and habit of "pronouncing betwixt dancing measures to night his yesterday pend speech to his Mistris."

Beaumont observed London and his colleagues closely, showing
the satirist's eye for telling detail. His speech is also an exercise in
controlled tone, in "solemn foolery" (as John Evelyn called a similar
one) that rivals John Hoskins's better-known effort in the same
genre. Hoskins devised his speech, delivered at the revels of the Middle Temple in 1597/98, to include in brief space most of the figures
of rhetoric; his aim was to ridicule excessive linguistic artifice and fus-
tian speech.[44] Beaumont, under the pretext of expounding on the
etymological aspect of grammar, was more interested in establishing
himself as a cynical wit:

> Admitt there were a compound to be Etimologis'd as money; for the
> purpose I will shew out of . . . what simples and by what meanes every
> particular sort . . . ought to derive this compound mony: Out of What

---

account for the gap between his poem *Salmacis* (1602) and his first play, *The Woman
Hater* (1606).

[43] The "arithmetic lecture" delivered by Heneage Finch is part of the same manuscript as Beaumont's; the "music lecture" is lost. Compared with Beaumont's, Finch's
speech is a feeble effort. But in view of the question of the politics of Beaumont's circle,
it is worth noting that as an M.P. in 1607 Finch delivered a notable attack in Parliament
against the king's power to lay impositions. See Notestein, *House of Commons*, p. 384.

[44] Printed in *Directions for Speech and Style*, ed. Hoyt Hudson (Princeton, N.J., 1935),
pp. 108–13.

shall he derive it? out of the Country. from what simples shall he derive yt? from two simples, his simple father and his simple mother. by what meanes shall he derive yt? now yt will appeare as playne as in speech how necessary his orthography is for him, for the cheefe meanes whereby he must etemologise this compound money from the simples aforesaid must be by writing a true orthographicall letter wherein yt shall not be amisse for him to complayne of the changeablenes and fog-gynes of the citty ayre at his first comeing, whereby he was driven to take phisicke which has strucke him a litle into debt, whereupon his father cannot chuse but send him five pound extraordinary and his mother a duble soveran for a token, and so much for etemology.[45]

As with most parodies, its continuation eventually feels self-indulgent and protracted, but the inventive, unpredictable nature of the wit almost excuses the excessive pleasure he takes in his superiority and knowingness.

It is not known with certainty how long Beaumont remained in residence at the Temple. The publisher Moseley's reference in 1647 to his affiliation with the Inn, his commission as late as 1613 to write a masque for the Inner Temple, and certain statements in the Temple's revels speech suggest that he had some kind of connection with the Inner Temple (if only as an attendant at the Christmas revels) for most of his adult life.

BEAUMONT'S ELEGIES

In trying to comprehend a writer whose main body of work is the impersonal form of the drama, one seizes whatever random bits of writing reveal something of the manipulator of the stage puppets. Beaumont's "Grammar Lecture" is one such document; another is the small group of occasional poems, most of them elegies, he wrote at various times in his life. One expects elegies, particularly ones written about neighboring country noblewomen, to be formal and decorous. Curiously, Beaumont chose to use his as vehicles for his irreverent, sometimes uncontrollable Inns of Court wit. The one on Lady Markham, who died in 1609, deserves particular attention. Since Beaumont says that he never saw her, he must have written it at the request of her first cousin, the earl of Huntingdon, either as a favor or for pay.[46] According to her epitaph and everything said about her

---

[45] Eccles, "Beaumont's *Grammar Lecture*," p. 408. I have retained the capitalization but altered the punctuation to make reading easier.

[46] Lady Markham, née Bridget Harrington, was the daughter of Sir James Harrington, whose sister Sarah was Huntingdon's mother. Beaumont was, of course, a distant relative of Huntingdon and hence of Lady Markham.

at her death, Lady Markham was a learned, pious, innocent woman, loved by her husband and children; there is no reason to believe that she deserved posthumous ridicule.[47]

It happens that the very model of an Inns of Court wit, John Donne, also wrote an elegy on Lady Markham under precisely the same circumstances: he too did not know her and his most important benefactress, Lucy, countess of Bedford, also was a first cousin of the dead lady. During this period, according to Bald, Donne was acting "almost as if he were Lady Bedford's officially appointed laureate."[48] Donne's poem is a contrived production that idealizes Lady Markham even beyond his usual level of exaggeration on such occasions. He claims that death will not have the same effect on her flesh as it does on others':

> In her this sea of death hath made no breach,
> But as the tide doth wash the slimie beach,
> And leaves embroder'd workes upon the sand,
> So is her flesh refin'd by deaths cold hand.
> As men of China, 'after an ages stay,
> Do take up Porcelane, where they buried Clay;
> So at this grave, her limbecke, which refines
> The Diamonds, Rubies, Saphires, Pearles and Mines,
> Of which this flesh was, her soule shall inspire
> Flesh of such stuffe, as God, when his last fire
> Annuls this world, to recompence it, shall,
> Make and name then, th'Elixar of this All.[49]

Beaumont's elegy takes the opposite tack from Donne's hyperbolic veneration. It is so extreme in its disrespect that Dyce called it "outrageous" and Donne's editor Grierson found it in "execrable" taste.[50] The comic indecorum of the opening gives a broad hint of what the poet is going to do:

> As unthrifts groan in straw for their pawn'd beds:
> As women weep for their lost Maiden heads;
> When both are without hope or remedy,
> Such an untimely griefe I have for thee.[51]

[47] Her epitaph appears in a note in Dyce, *Works of Beaumont and Fletcher*, 1:xxx–xxxi.
[48] R. C. Bald, *John Donne* (New York, 1970), p. 177. Donne was also patronized by Huntingdon's wife.
[49] *Poems of John Donne*, ed. H.J.C. Grierson (Oxford, 1912), 1:280, ll. 17–28.
[50] Dyce, *Works of Beaumont and Fletcher*, 1:xxxi, and Grierson, *Poems of Donne*, 2:209.
[51] "An Elegy on the Lady Markham" in Francis Beaumont, *Poems* (London, 1653), sig. D8r–E1r. This was the first appearance of the poem in print. References in the text are to this edition. C. H. Herford, Percy Simpson, and Evelyn Simpson, eds., *Ben*

Anyone casting about for metaphors to express regret for lost oppor-
tunities could readily find more appropriate vehicles. The unthrift
and the exvirgin are traditionally comic and seem carefully chosen—
with the rhyme of "beds" and "Maiden heads"—to prepare for the
sexual theme that follows. Beaumont proceeds to underline the nature of his role as elegist by stating the situation frankly and then
inventing a patently absurd, pseudological consequence:

> I never saw thy face, nor did my heart
> Urge forth mine eyes unto it whilst thou wert,
> But being lifted hence, that which to thee
> Was deaths sad dart, prov'd Cupids shaft to me.

(sig. D8ʳ)

As opposed to Donne's claim that the lady's flesh will become an
elixir, Beaumont insists that her body is now a rotting, odoriferous
corpse overrun by worms. In a fit of extravagant wit more appropriate for his Inner Temple friends than the grieving family, he claims
that he now loves the dead lady whom he has never met because she
is incapable of making the demands and enforcing the tortures that
his other mistresses have:

> Know he, that when with this I do compare
> The love I do a living woman beare,
> I finde my selfe most happy: now I know
> Where I can find my Mistris, and can go
> Unto her trimm'd bed, and can lift away
> Her grasse-greene Mantle, and her sheet display,
> And touch her naked; and though th' envious mould
> In which she lies uncovered, moist and cold,
> Strive to corrupt her, she will not abide
> With any art her blemishes to hide.[52]

After pursuing this conceit for many lines, the poet develops yet another fantasy worthy of note by Kraft-Ebbing:

> You Wormes (my Rivals) whil'st she was alive,
> How many thousands were there that did strive
> To have your freedome? for their sake forbeare
> Unseemly holes in her soft skin to weare:

Jonson (Oxford, 1925–52), 8:426, similarly appalled, believe that the "poem was intended as a satire or joke."

[52] Sig. D8ʳ. Some years later, in *Bonduca* (5.2), Fletcher portrays a hard-bitten Roman
soldier, until then immune to love, who becomes smitten with a young woman *after* she
has committed suicide heroically. He is viewed as a comic madman.

But if you must (as what Worms can abstaine
To taste her tender body?) yet refraine
With your disordered eatings to deface her
But feed your selves so as you most may grace her.

(sig. D8ᵛ)

He concludes in proper elegiac form with directions to his epitaph-carvers, the worms:

upward roule
Your little bodies, where I would you have
This Epitaph upon her forehead grave.
Living, she was young, faire, and full of wit:
Dead, all her faults are in her forehead writ.

(sig. E1ʳ)

Isolated from the rest of the poem the epitaph would sound like a carefully weighed, civilized verdict. Living, Lady Markham doubtless possessed the sorts of faults the poet ascribes to his former mistresses, faults one would expect of a young, fair, and witty lady of the queen's bedchamber as she was. But when she is dead, such faults seem venial.

Perhaps Beaumont felt that the civil sentiments of the epitaph excused the rest of the poem. In fact, one scarcely notices the ending amid the stench of a moldy, worm-filled corpse and the fantasies of necrophiliac adultery and cannibalism. Perhaps there is a work more repellent by the Marquis de Sade or Genet, but not in the English Renaissance. It would be comforting to believe as I once did that Beaumont designed the Markham poem as a witty attack on the commercial elegy. Beaumont's worms seem a direct challenge to Donne's claims about Lady Markham's impermeable flesh. At the Temple, where the antielegy would have taken a welcome place beside Sir John Davies's antisonnets and where a jab at Donne would have caused a minor sensation, the Markham poem as I envisioned it would have enhanced Beaumont's reputation as one of London's Bright Young Men.[53] Unfortunately, knowing her close family ties to the Hastingses, I can no longer believe that Beaumont would have used Lady Markham as a vehicle for literary parody. In fact, some evidence suggests that this elegy and two others by Beaumont were viewed as serious, impressive tributes. In his elegy on Beaumont referred to earlier, Thomas Pestell, an acquaintance of Beaumont's and a beneficiary of the earl of Huntingdon's patronage, says to Death,

[53] See my " 'Wit' in Francis Beaumont's Poems," *Modern Language Quarterly* 28 (1967): 33–44.

I yet must judge
Thou slewst him [Beaumont] for a spitefull grudge,
'Cause those quick lines from his live Muse did passe
Have marble shedd and everlasting brasse
Over three ladies [Markham, Rutland, and Clifton],
    which still fresh shall be,
And live to thy disgrace in memorie.[54]

Pestell was a sober clergyman, and the Hastingses were (at least) Puritan sympathizers. That they would not find this poem grotesque requires one to acknowledge a shift in a sense of the decorous beyond what is normally admitted.

Nothing in the elegies about two other nearby country neighbors, the ladies Rutland and Clifton, matches the extremes of the Markham poem, but both have similar moments. In the elegy on Lady Rutland, Beaumont describes her as having led a life more "like a betrothed virgin than a wife," not as one might expect because of her unworldly virtuousness but because her husband, the notorious Roger Manners (who was dead by the time Beaumont wrote this), "if we may trust to fame, / Could nothing change about thee but thy name."[55] In the Clifton elegy there is an address to Death in the same repulsively witty vein:

For such her beauty was, that, if thy loath'd
And naked self were with such garments cloth'd
Of flesh and blood, cover'd with such a fair
And tempting skin, adorn'd with such a hair,
Stuck with such eyes, —although I know who brings
Thee in his company shall be to kings
But an unwelcome guest, —yet, in despite,
Thy hated self would prove a favorite,
And that same lady think herself divine
That could but draw thee for her Valentine.[56]

It is a bright and witty conceit to have Death mask as Lady Clifton, but the Petrarchan cataloging of the parts of her body in an elegy, her transformation into the favorite of kings, and her re-creation as a Valentine lead one to feel that the poet was willing to sacrifice almost everything for a witty device.[57]

---

[54] Lines 109–14 of Pestell's elegy, which is reproduced in full in appendix B.

[55] Dyce, *Works of Beaumont and Fletcher*, 11:508, ll. 40, 35–36. Jonson also mentions her husband's impotence in his elegy on Rutland.

[56] Ibid., ll. 49–58.

[57] Drayton's orthodox "Elegy to Lady Clifton" helps to confirm Beaumont's aberrant elegiac impulses.

In his Mermaid Tavern poem Beaumont speaks critically of "the wit of our young men, fellows that show / No part of good, yet utter all they know."[58] Astonishingly, Beaumont maintained his amoral wittiness beyond the moment when he could feel "young": he completed the Clifton poem, his last piece of writing, *after* he had suffered the debilitating stroke in 1613 that eventually killed him.[59] One of the most frequent assertions by Beaumont and Fletcher's contemporaries was that "Mr. Beaumont's maine Businesse was to lop the overflowings of Mr. Fletcher's luxuriant Fancy and flowing Wit."[60] There may have been an element of truth in this, but from all external evidence, Beaumont required at least as much "lopping" as Fletcher.

FLETCHER'S "COUNTRY" PATRONS

It is not certain precisely when Beaumont and Fletcher first met; it may have been earlier than usually thought, as early as 1602.[61] Fletcher's commendatory verses for *Volpone* suggest that by the time of its composition in 1606 he had become acquainted with the most important literary figures in London, and on the basis of internal evidence some have detected Fletcher's hand in Beaumont's work in 1606–7. According to Dryden, they wrote several plays together before the very successful *Philaster* appeared around 1610. From then on the worst of Fletcher's financial problems must have ended. With his great productivity and popularity, and his position, formally or informally, as chief playwright for the King's Men after Shakespeare's retirement, he must have achieved reasonable economic security, if not the level of affluence reached by company shareholders like Shakespeare.

[58] Herford, Simpson, and Simpson, *Ben Jonson*, 11:374–77, ll. 70–71.

[59] The evidence for this once again comes from Pestell's invaluable elegy on Beaumont: "But even in midst of most infirmitie / It crown'd his last worke with so faire an end, / 'Twould puzzle the best witts alive to mend" (120–22). That it was the Clifton poem he is referring to is made clear when he says that "the very last words that his quill / Lett fall" (50–51) were those warning against the use of "preservatives" (i.e., quack drugs for prolonging life) in the last ten lines of the poem.

[60] *Aubrey's Brief Lives*, ed. Oliver L. Dick (Ann Arbor, Mich., 1949), p. 21.

[61] I base this on a reference in John Nichols, *The History and Antiquities of the County of Leicestershire* (London, 1795–1815), vol. 3, part 2, p. 659: "Mr. Whalley [the 18th-century scholar] preserves a copy of verses 'on Mr. Frances Beaumont, on his Imitation of Ovid,' signed J.F.; which, he says is undoubtedly by John Fletcher." This may be the poem prefatory to *Salmacis* that is signed "A.F." in the 1602 edition but "J.F." in the 1640. In any case Whalley's Fletcher poem, referring to Beaumont's Ovidian *Salmacis* published in 1602, suggests an acquaintance three or four years before their first known collaboration. It also independently corroborates the fact that Beaumont wrote an Ovidian poem, *Salmacis* having been published anonymously.

However, until the success of *Philaster* Fletcher's financial situation
was precarious. This the prefatory material to the quarto of *The Faithful Shepherdess* (1608–9) makes clear. Along with commendatory poems by Beaumont, Chapman, Jonson, and Nathan Field, Fletcher
also included dedicatory verses to three knights who were obviously
patrons. There can be little doubt about the motive behind Fletcher's
flattering verses to Sir Walter Aston, whose annual income of ten
thousand pounds made him (according to the *Dictionary of National
Biography*) one of the richest men in England:

> (Nor do I flatter) for by all those dead,
> Great in the muses, by *Apolloes* head,
> He that ads any thing to you; tis done
> Like his that lights a candle to the sunne.[62]

It would seem that Fletcher's path to Aston was through Beaumont.
Aston's estates in or contiguous to Leicestershire were close to Beaumont's home. Since 1602 Aston had been Michael Drayton's prime
patron; from that same year, if not earlier, one can date close ties
between Drayton and the Beaumonts.[63]

It is likely that Beaumont also introduced Fletcher to another of
the *Faithful Shepherdess* dedicatees, Sir William Skipwith. Descended
from an old and affluent family, Skipwith lived near the Beaumonts
in Leicestershire.[64] Sir John Beaumont, Francis's brother, wrote
verses for a memorial tablet to him.[65]

[62] "*To that Noble and True lover of learning*, Sir Walter Aston," in Cyrus Hoy's edition
of *The Faithful Shepherdess* in Fredson Bowers, gen. ed., *The Dramatic Works in the Beaumont and Fletcher Canon* (Cambridge, 1966–), 3:494, ll.17–20.

[63] Despite Aston's wealth and apparently good relations with King James, it is noteworthy that Drayton dedicated his undoubtedly anti-James work *The Owle* to him. Aston felt exploited by James as well as by Charles, who forced him to accept a very costly
ambassadorship in Spain. See Bernard Newdigate, *Michael Drayton and His Circle* (Oxford, 1941), pp. 146–57.

[64] Skipwith also had social connections with the earl of Huntingdon, according to the
*Historical Manuscripts Commission Report on the Manuscripts of the late Reginald Rawdon
Hastings*, ed. Francis Bickley, vol. 2 (London, 1930), p. 362, cited hereafter as *HMC
(Hastings)*. It may be noted that Skipwith was a figure of some amateur literary accom-
plishment, known according to a contemporary for "his witty conceits in making fit
and acute epigrams, posies, mottos, and devices, but chiefly in devising apt and fit
impreses" (Dyce, *Works of Beaumont and Fletcher*, 2:14n). It has recently been suggested
that Skipwith was the author of a set of verses that accompanied some gifts during
Marston's "Ashby Entertainment," to be discussed below. See James Knowles, "WS
MS," in *Times Literary Supplement*, April 29, 1988, pp. 472, 485; also Mary Hobbs, "A
W.S. Manuscript," *Times Literary Supplement*, June 10–16, 1988, p. 647, for confirmation
of this attribution.

[65] Fletcher must have known the third *Faithful Shepherdess* dedicatee Sir Robert
Townsend through Ben Jonson, for whom he was an important patron.

Whatever slight reward he obtained for these dedicatory epistles, Fletcher's crucial support in his early years came from Henry Hastings, fifth earl of Huntingdon, of Ashby de la Zouch, Leicestershire. This connection is clear in a verse letter Philip Massinger wrote to the third earl of Pembroke while requesting his patronage:

> I know
> That Johnson much of what he has does owe
> To you and to your familie, and is never
> Slow to professe it, nor had Fletcher ever
> Such Reputation, and credit wonne
> But by his honord Patron, Huntington.[66]

Massinger's poem was written after 1615; a verse letter from Fletcher around 1620 to the countess of Huntingdon confirms the existence and strength of this connection.[67] But patronage on the level Massinger suggests makes no sense once Fletcher had become the most popular playwright in London. It would have been during the period before the triumph of *Philaster* that the noble family from Ashby could have been of crucial help to Fletcher. In a prose post-script to his verse letter to Lady Huntingdon, Fletcher mentions a Sir Thomas Beaumont, a Leicestershire neighbor and like all the Beaumonts of that county, a relative of the countess.[68] This postscript

---

[66] For the entire text of the verse letter, see Percy Simpson's letter to the *Athenaeum*, Sept. 8, 1906, p. 273. Massinger's statement is extremely reliable because no one, except possibly Beaumont, knew Fletcher better than he. There is some evidence that Fletcher tried to get Massinger into the Huntingdon circle via the earl's sister Katherine Stanhope. There is also a possibility that Webster too (via Baron Berkeley, who was connected to the Stanhopes) was helped through this circle of patrons. In this connection perhaps it is worth recording that the earl of Huntingdon purchased a carriage made by Webster's father in 1608 (*HMC [Hastings]*, 1:373). One thinks of Jacobean drama as a London enterprise, but the Midlands aristocracy (perhaps enlightened through frequent trips to London) seems to have given aid to Marston, Beaumont, Fletcher, Massinger, and Webster.

[67] S. A. Tannenbaum, "An Unpublished John Fletcher Autograph," *Journal of English and German Philology* 28 (1929): 35–40. The text in *HMC (Hastings)*, 2:58–59 is slightly more accurate. There it is dated "ca. 1620" without an explanation of how the date was arrived at. I suspect that its position among the Hastings papers makes this evident. In any case, I believe the date "ca. 1620" to be correct because the reference to a rhyming "sculer" requires it to have been written after the appearance of John Taylor's first volume of verse, *The Sculler* of 1612, and because the most important post-1612 Spanish crisis—some sort is mentioned in the poem—was that involving the Palatinate in 1620. Further evidence for a late date is Massinger's assertion that by the time he was writing the epistle to Pembroke Fletcher "had . . . wonne . . . reputation and credit": retrospective language about a writer of assured status.

[68] This was the son of Francis Beaumont's cousin, Sir Henry of Coleorton, not the previously mentioned "liberal" M.P., Sir Thomas Beaumont of Staunton Grange, who

tends to confirm what is altogether likely in any case, that Fletcher's
path to the great seat of the earls of Huntingdon at Ashby de la
Zouch was through Francis Beaumont—who was, as we have seen, a
relation of the earl's and a close neighbor, since Beaumont's home at
Grace Dieu was just a few miles from Ashby.[69]

The image of the younger-son-turned-writer from a distinguished
gentry family introducing for purposes of patronage a new friend of
similar background to his noble relatives and other rich connections
conforms precisely to the conventional picture of Beaumont and
Fletcher. In Marco Mincoff's version,

> the private theatres, by encouraging a more cultivated type of dramatist,
> had attracted young men like Beaumont and Fletcher, whose tastes and
> interests, unlike Marston's, were more in the line of the Court than the
> town. The writers may have become unclassed to a certain extent, but
> Beaumont was after all an amateur, writing for pleasure, and he kept up
> his connections with many of the first families of the land, and even
> Fletcher's "chief bosom friend," as Gayley shows, was Charles Cotton, a
> man both of family and literary tastes.[70]

We know enough about the family troubles of Beaumont and
Fletcher to realize that this description of their social status is inaccurate. A closer look at Fletcher's patron Huntingdon will complicate
many of Mincoff's other assertions.

What becomes immediately apparent from Fletcher's verses to the
countess of Huntingdon is that by 1620 he had achieved a relaxed
intimacy with these grand patrons; he had become so much a habitué
of Ashby Castle that he even knew the name of the cook. His urbane,
self-assured epistle is ostensibly searching for a subject:

> There ys not any Sculler of our Tyme
> inventing nowe, more misbegott with ryme
> Then I am at this Instant: But 'tys so
> that I must write. yett hange mee if I knowe
> of what; or to what End.
>
>   (1–5)[71]

---

died in 1614. The recipient of the message from Fletcher became first Viscount Beaumont of Swords in 1622.

[69] The plausibility of this conjecture is enhanced by the knowledge that the poetical
Beaumont brothers were in the habit, as Drayton reports, of inviting their poet friends
from London to visit them at Grace Dieu: they "oft to Soar the southern shepherds
[from London] bring" (Quoted by Gayley, *Beaumont, the Dramatist*, p. 43, from *Poems
Lyrick and Pastoral*, 1606).

[70] "The Social Background of Beaumont and Fletcher," *English Miscellany: A Symposium of History, Literature, and the Arts* 1 (1950): 15.

[71] Tannenbaum, "Unpublished Fletcher Autograph." I have cleared up the punctu-

Speaking as a knowledgeable denizen of the town, he considers discussing, only to reject, the most interesting topic for a noblewoman living deep in the country, namely court news. In the process he reveals his own politics and values:

> Knights, and Lords
> praye by your Leaves, I will not treate of you,
> Ye are too teachy [i.e., touchy]; nor whether ytt bee true
> we shall have warrs with Spaine: (I wold wee might:)
> nor whoe shall daunce I'th maske; nor whoe shall write
> those brave things done: nor summe up the Expence;
> nor whether ytt bee paid for ten yeere hence.
>
> (16–22)

It comes as no surprise to hear Fletcher, the grandson and son of inveterate papist-haters, express the vain hope that James might go to war with Spain; and it corroborates attitudes implicit in some of his plays to hear his dismay at the frivolity and extravagance of James's court.

But why was Fletcher able to speak in such a sophisticated manner and to raise such "teachy" topics to the daughter of the fifth earl of Derby and the wife of the fifth earl of Huntingdon, two of the most important figures in the English establishment? In fact, Ashby was a well-known center of disagreement with and occasionally of passive resistance to some of the policies emanating from London and the court.[72] This had been true for decades before the fifth earl succeeded to the title. The powerful third earl of Huntingdon, Henry Hastings (1536–95), was a zealous Protestant who turned Leicestershire into a veritable sanctuary for Puritanism, patronizing and protecting some of the most radical Puritan clergymen. He was also widely beloved by his tenants and neighbors for his old-fashioned "country" values, as one may see in this ballad written at his death:

> To poor and to needie to high and to low
> Lord Hastings was friendly, all people doth know,
> His gates were still open the stranger to feed
> And comfort the succorless always in need. . . .
> He built up no palace, nor purchased no town,
> But gave it to scholars to get him renown,

---

ation. Tannenbaum thought "Sculler" was a "unique and unrecorded spelling of 'scholar,' " but it is obviously a reference to the sculler-poetaster John Taylor.

[72] However, it strikes me as something of an exaggeration for Lawrence Stone in *Crisis of the Aristocracy*, p. 401, to describe the fifth earl as an "opponent" of James. While keeping his distance, he did perform services for the Crown and received some rewards and recognition.

As Oxford and Cambridge can rightly declare
How many poor scholars maintained are there.
No graves he inclosed nor felled no wood,
No pastures he paled to do himself good;
To commons and countrie he lived a good friend,
And gave to the needie what God did him send.[73]

To ensure the perpetuation in his family of his beliefs, the childless
third earl sent his nephew Francis Hastings to Geneva to study under
Calvin's colleague and successor, Theodore Beza, and took Francis's
son Henry (Fletcher's patron) into his household ("a Protestant sem-
inary in miniature") to nurture him properly.[74] From the number of
books dedicated to the younger Henry by Puritan-leaning clergymen,
and from the sort of life he led and the education he gave his children, it is apparent that the fifth earl was an active supporter of his
great-uncle's moral, religious, and social views.[75]

In addition to doctrinal and moral differences, the fifth earl had
specific personal reasons for distancing himself from king and court.
Various Protestant factions considered the Hastingses, as descendants
of Edward IV, legitimate claimants to the crown. In 1562 when
Queen Elizabeth was seriously ill, the third earl of Huntingdon
seemed moments away from succeeding her.[76] Within the Hastings
family it was felt that King James paid long visits to Ashby out of a
malign urge to impoverish a potential rival of the Stuarts.[77] The con-
spicuous consumption those visits necessitated must have been particularly annoying to Huntingdon, the heir of a nearly bankrupt estate.[78] One of Huntingdon's neighbors, Charles Stanhope, second

[73] Quoted by M. M. Knappen, *Tudor Puritanism* (Chicago, 1965), p. 411, who adds,
"Though allowance must be made for panegyric on such occasions, there are plenty of
corroborating details."

[74] Cross, *Puritan Earl*, p. 24.

[75] One sign of his radical Protestant beliefs was his sending his son to the Puritan
Emmanuel College, Cambridge.

[76] For details of the Huntingdon claim to the throne, see Cross, *Puritan Earl*, pp. 7–
8; also, Knappen, *Tudor Puritanism*, pp. 183–84.

[77] In 1617, for example, the king stayed for a staggering length of time, variously
reported as from three weeks to two months. It is claimed that a special set of rooms
was erected for the occasion. At dinners for James the earl felt obligated to employ as
servers thirty knights in velvet gowns and gold chains. See Henry N. Bell, *The Huntingdon Peerage* (London, 1821), p. 111.

[78] Among the lordly debtors listed by Stone, *Crisis of the Aristocracy*, p. 778, the Huntingdon family is one of the most heavily burdened: about £38,000 in debt. This may
partly be explained by the fact that life at Ashby was lived with "great hospitality and
munificence" (Nichols, *Leicestershire*, 3.2.777), a view confirmed by Fletcher, who says
in his verse epistle to the countess of Huntingdon that at Ashby he will be feasted with
such delicacies as "Brawne" [boar], "Brackett" [a drink], and "good Swan" (26, 27). In
1609 the cost of running the establishment of sixty-eight persons was nearly £3000.

baron Stanhope of Harrington, had been known to refuse to accord the king the homage expected of nobles on royal progresses. The king reproved Stanhope for his negligence but was willing to excuse him because, as he told him in his abrupt way, he was known to be mad. Stanhope replied, "I may be mad, my Liege Sovran, but I am not half so mad as my Lord Huntingdon here, who suffers himself to be worried by such a pack of bloodhounds."[79]

With so many reasons for aversion, it is not surprising to learn that the fifth Earl advised his son to keep as far from the court as possible: "I would rather wish thee to spend the greatest part of thy life in the country than to live in this glittering misery."[80] On another occasion he said to his son:

> I should be sorry that you should like a court life too well, for it is but *splendida miseria*, and Sir Walter Mildmay, a great courtier and councillor of state in Queen Elizabeth's time, in a little book of his hath this saying (Know the court, but spend not thy time there) and I can say in my own experience, that have tasted of all the waters that have issued from honest delights, that no life for the good of the soul, of the body and estate are answerable to a country life.[81]

Nonetheless, Hastings advised his son for reasons of prudence to attend court "once or twice for some three weeks at a time in the year, as also upon commandment, for the Parliament or great triumphs," but he had so strongly indoctrinated him by precept and example that his son amended his advice in a marginal comment from "three weeks" to "a few days."[82] Whatever qualifications one must attach to the term "country" in seventeenth-century political discussions, Fletcher's patron, the Puritan-sympathizing, county-riveted, court-averted, James-persecuted Henry Hastings, fifth earl of Huntingdon, was a "country" lord.[83] At the same time, as he reveals in this letter of advice to his son, Hastings was a literate, observant man who was very conscious of the danger of lapsing into the parochialism of a country gentleman:

> Endeavor to have a general knowledge in all things, else [you will appear like] a country gentleman that can talk of nothing but of subsidies, the

[79] Bell, *Huntingdon Peerage*, p. 111.

[80] *HMC (Hastings)*, 4:333.

[81] *HMC (Hastings)*, 2:70–71. From as early as 1606 and throughout his life, as registered in the *HMC (Hastings)* papers, one finds innumerable letters of excuse by the fifth earl for not attending court: business, health, weather.

[82] *HMC (Hastings)*, 4:333.

[83] There is no contradiction whatever in discovering that eventually Ashby became a royalist bastion in the Civil War, nor in that Huntingdon occasionally performed valuable services and received rewards from the court.

provision, or petty penal statutes for the punishment of rogues, feeding of oxen or sheep, manuring of land or the changes of seasons, that things are dear or cheap, ploughing of land or inclosure or what price corn bears, such a one if he be not talking of these things that will fall asleep at his meals; unless he hears news from the Court, and then he holds up his hands as if he were at prayers, and, if he hear the King once named, he thinks it high treason.[84]

Here is a "character" of the sort of witless country gentlemen that Beaumont complains about to Ben Jonson in his "Mermaid Tavern" poem. The noble author of this observant bit of satire had matured from the "young and raw" youth that Sir John Holles observed when he contrasted Huntingdon unfavorably to the child bride Elizabeth Stanley, to whom he had been affianced. She was fresh from York House in London, where she had been in daily contact with people like John Donne.[85]

THE DERBY-SPENCER CONNECTION: FLETCHER'S "SPENSERIAN" PATRONESS

It still needs to be explained why a radical Protestant, quasi-Puritan nobleman like Huntingdon, noted for his patronage of clergymen and with no discernible interest in writers or the stage would take up and (so Massinger says) actively support a "stage-poet" like Fletcher. The answer is not hard to discover. In 1601 Huntingdon married his child bride Elizabeth Stanley, daughter of the late Ferdinando Stanley, fifth earl of Derby (1559?–1594), and Alice Spencer.[86] Derby was one of the most important patrons of literature among the Elizabethan nobility as well as—even if not operating under the nom de plume "Shakespeare"—something of a writer. According to Spenser's tribute, phrased in his contorted pastoral manner,

> He, whilst he lived, was the noblest swaine
> That ever piped in an oaten quill.
> Both did he other which could pipe maintaine,
> And eke could pipe himselfe with passing skill.[87]

---

[84] From *HMC (Hastings)*, 4:334.

[85] Hannah Buchan, ed., *The Poems of Thomas Pestell* (Oxford, 1940), p. 106.

[86] Since Elizabeth was thirteen and her new husband but fifteen, she was sent back to her mother in London after the marriage and he to his tutors until 1604, when he would have been a mature eighteen.

[87] "Colin Clout's Come Home Again" in E. Greenlaw, C. G. Osgood, F. M. Padelford, R. Heffner, eds., *The Works of Edmund Spenser: The Minor Poems* (Baltimore, 1943), vol. 1, ll. 440–43.

Derby's commitment to literature went beyond the awarding of a few pounds in exchange for a hypocritical dedication. He himself wrote pastoral poetry, gave assistance to Greene, Nashe, and Chapman as well as to Spenser, and was the patron of an acting company, "Lord Strange's Men," that was a direct ancestor of Shakespeare's company. At the same time Derby had an old-fashioned "country" sense of his responsibilities as a lord that was praised in a piece of doggerel reminiscent of that written about the third earl of Huntingdon:

> Of worldly wealth, he makes no coumpt,
> He wayes his honor more:
> Love to his servants doth surmount,
> And to his tenaunts poore:
> Of country still, he taketh care,
> And for the common wealth prepare:
> Remembring well, that fame will tell,
> What people love to chaunge:
> Therefore I say, this present day,
> He may be called Straunge.[88]

Unless the anti-Stratfordian, pro-Derby forces are correct, however, the more important figure in the history of English literature was Derby's wife, whose many names suggest her status, her longevity, and her pride. Born Lady Alice Spencer of Althorp, her father, Sir John Spencer, was very wealthy. Lady Alice was married to Derby from 1579 until his death in 1594, and after six years of widowhood in 1600 she married Thomas Egerton, Baron Ellesmere (1540–1617), when he was sixty and she twenty years younger. He lived until 1617, long enough to regret a union inspired more by dynastic than amatory considerations. Lady Alice insisted on retaining the august title from her first marriage and was known as the countess dowager of Derby. Perhaps one may attribute her interest in literature to the influence of her first husband. However gained, it is no exaggeration for her most recent biographer to assert that Alice Spencer had "more close associations with more great literary figures than any other single person . . . in the greatest period of English literature."[89]

---

[88] Richard Robinson, *A Golden Mirrour*, Chetham Society, 23 (1851): 17. The heir to the Derby title is titled Lord Strange. The earl of Derby, too, was considered a legitimate candidate for the throne—but by Catholics who were alleged to have murdered him by witchcraft when he refused to cooperate with them.

[89] French R. Fogle, " 'Such a Rural Queen': the Countess Dowager of Derby as Patron," in *Patronage in Late Renaissance England* (Los Angeles, 1983), p. 25; see also Wil-

Direct links either of patronage or acquaintanceship can be traced
between her and Spenser, Donne, Daniel, Jonson, Sir John Davies,
Marston, Fletcher, and Milton.[90]

Of these, Lady Alice's tie to Spenser was undoubtedly the most important. In his dedication to her of *The Teares of the Muses*, Spenser
speaks of a family relationship, "some private bands of affinitie,
which it hath pleased your Ladiship to acknowledge." Spenser repeats this elsewhere, and it is most unlikely that he would have made
such a claim in print unless it were true. Although the link did not
do as much for him financially as he might have hoped, Spenser
seems to have been the crucial influence in the formation of his kins-
woman's taste. At least it is true, as Christopher Hill has observed,
that Lady Alice and her family seemed mainly interested in the so-
called "Spenserian" line of poets.[91]

With such a background it was second nature for the new mistress
of Ashby Castle, Lady Alice's daughter Elizabeth (1588–1633), to add
needy poets like Donne, poetasters like the Leicestershire clergyman
Thomas Pestell, playwrights like Fletcher, and literary camp followers
like Donne's friends Sir Henry Goodere and Sir Thomas Roe to the
other more serious-minded figures whom the earl of Huntingdon
was accustomed to aid.[92] When she came of age this Lady Elizabeth
became a formidable and impressive figure, worthy of comparison to
her more celebrated mother. Almost no Jacobean noblewoman would
have required the advice Pestell gave her, "not to pay so close an attention as she had generally done to reading,"[93] and Lucius Carey,

---

liam Riley Parker, *Milton* (Oxford, 1968), pp. 758–59, and David Masson, *The Life of
John Milton* (London, 1873), 1:551ff.

[90] More dubious if not impossible is Fogle's placement of Shakespeare on this list
through her first husband's patronage of the acting company with which Shakespeare
was eventually affiliated. Nonetheless, there is another possible path to Shakespeare
through Lady Alice's sister, Elizabeth, wife of George Carey, Lord Hunsdon, the Lord
Chamberlain and official patron of Shakespeare's company during some of its prime
years.

[91] *Milton and the English Revolution* (New York, 1979), p. 43.

[92] The fourth earl, George Hastings, maintained a provincial acting company, whose
activities can be detected in 1582–88 and 1595–1604. This company was disbanded
almost immediately after Henry, the fifth earl, succeeded to the title (J. T. Murray,
English Dramatic Companies [Boston, 1910], 2:47–49). The elimination of the company
before Elizabeth's arrival at Ashby and the subsequent payment in 1607 of 20 shillings
to Lord Dudley's Players after she came [*HMC (Hastings)*, 1:372] give further credence
to the hunch that interest in the arts stemmed primarily from the female side of the
family. In Puritan Ashby, Lady Elizabeth seems even to have sponsored morris dances:
see "Verses of the Countess of Huntingdon," in *Poems of Pestell*, ed. Buchan, p. 87, l.
29.

[93] Nichols, *Leicestershire*, vol. 3, part 2, p. 777.

second Viscount Falkland, who was inspired to write two elegies on her, claimed she was "learneder than Hypatia."[94] Worried that readers might think his sentiments hyperbolic, he concludes the first of the elegies with a unique postscript: "By him who saies what he saw.— FALKLAND."[95] Even Fletcher's low-keyed epistle compares Lady Elizabeth to "Eve before the fall." Everything suggests that Fletcher had a strong, intelligent patroness, and a Spenserian one at that.

One can detect in 1607 the influence on Ashby of the Spencers and perhaps also of Beaumont. In that year the Huntingdons commissioned the production of an elaborate "entertainment," part processional, part masque. It was to celebrate a visit by the countess's mother, Lady Alice, to Ashby. For the Derby-Spencers such theatrical events were normal household practice. Even in her second marriage in what was presumably a less "artistic" ambiance, Lady Alice and Lord Chancellor Ellesmere offered "entertainments" during Queen Elizabeth's visits in 1601 and 1602. As late as 1632 at her home at Harefield, for an occasion similar to the one at Ashby, Lady Alice commissioned Milton to compose his *Arcades*.[96]

It indicates something significant about the Huntingdon household in 1607 that the London playwright John Marston was selected to write this entertainment.[97] One would think that his notoriety as a foul-mouthed, licentious troublemaker would have disqualified him for consideration, particularly in the Puritan ambience of Ashby.[98] A Puritan pamphleteer had recently attacked Marston "for bringing in the *Dutch Courtezan* to corrupt English conditions, and sent away *Westward* for carping at Court, Cittie, and countrie."[99] Marston was himself writing, and in his capacity as shareholder in the Children of the Queen's Revels was partly responsible for, irreverent and saucy satiric plays that criticized court and king. Less than a year after the "Ashby Entertainment" he was imprisoned, almost certainly for a satiric play, his acting company was temporarily silenced, and he seems to have

[94] Quoted by Kurt Weber in *Lucius Carey, Second Viscount Falkland* (New York, 1940), p. 287, l. 33.

[95] *The Poems of Lucius Carey, Viscount Falkland*, ed. A. B. Grosart, Miscellanies of the Fuller Worthies' Library (Blackburn, Eng., 1872), 3:419.

[96] Then came *Comus* in 1634, commissioned by her daughter and son-in-law, the earl and countess of Bridgewater. See Fogle, " 'Such a Rural Queen'," p. 11.

[97] The date for the performance of the "Entertainment" has recently been determined by I. A. Shapiro as 1608, although "it may have been commissioned for late 1607." See I. A. Shapiro, "A W. S. Manuscript," *Times Literary Supplement*, June 3–9, 1988, p. 617.

[98] However, his Latin City Pageant of 1606 for the visit of the king of Denmark showed that Marston could write decorously when necessary.

[99] Anthony Nixon, *The Blacke Yeare* (London, 1606), sig. B2^r.

been permanently enjoined from further writing. If not elsewhere, at Ashby Marston ought to have been persona non grata for his acrimonious exchange of satires with Joseph Hall, a celebrated Ashby native and a particular beneficiary of the Huntingdons' patronage.[100] Clearly Marston did not know the Huntingdons before the "Entertainment" because his work displays some elementary confusions about family names.[101]

Nonetheless, Marston was selected. Who would have known and admired Marston's work and been in a position to suggest him to Lady Elizabeth? Naturally it is impossible to be certain, but everything points to the countess's cousin by marriage Beaumont. That Beaumont and Marston were well-acquainted is as certain as such matters can be. Marston came from nearby Warwickshire, he and Beaumont lived for some years in contiguous Inns of Court—Marston at the Middle Temple, Beaumont at the Inner Temple. Both had prominent Inns of Court fathers. The acting company in which Marston was a shareholder, the Children of the Queen's Revels, presented several of Beaumont and Fletcher's plays. Both were intimates of Jonson, and in a verse letter to Jonson (to be discussed shortly), Beaumont seems to be speaking in guarded but concerned tones about the disastrous final chapter in Marston's career as a playwright. Other evidence of a personal connection between Marston and Beaumont and Fletcher is that the collaborators had access to a manuscript of the "Ashby Entertainment"—it was not published for centuries— as can be seen from their appropriation of some of its phrases for use in *The Maid's Tragedy*.[102] Finally, as I shall show, at this early point in his career Beaumont's work is strongly influenced by Marston.

Regardless of how Marston obtained this commission it is a sign of

[100] For Hall and Ashby see Cross, *Puritan Earl*, pp. 122–23. For the Hall-Marston battle see Arnold Davenport, *Poems of John Marston* (Liverpool, 1961).

[101] See Davenport, *Poems of Marston*, p. 376. Probably through his involvement in the "Entertainment" Marston became friendly with some members of the Huntingdons' Leicestershire circle. See "JM to Sir Gervase Clifton," *HMC Report on Various Collections* 7 (1914): 389.

[102] The passage of Marston's "Entertainment" that Beaumont and Fletcher used is ll. 195–210 in Davenport's *Poems of Marston*. Marston opens the masque portion of his "entertainment" (p. 198) with Cynthia remarking on a brightness exceeding her own that emanates from the audience. Beaumont and Fletcher employed this idea as well as some of Marston's imagery for similar praise of the audience by Cynthia and Night at the opening of *The Maid's Tragedy* masque. See Robert K. Turner's edition of the play in Bowers, *Dramatic Works*, 2:1.2.112–36. I do not want to claim too much for this point because the manuscript of the "Entertaiment" in the Bridgewater collection, now at the Huntington Library, was not unique, as we learn from a letter by Marston (Davenport, *Poems of Marston*, p. 44). Thus Beaumont and Fletcher would not have had to obtain their copy directly from Marston.

a commitment at Ashby to new and sophisticated art that a figure like Marston, the Angry Young Man of the London theater, would have been selected for this family celebration. It was the same experimental impulse that would later lead the family to employ the young Milton. But there may have been a political as well as an aesthetic motive behind the decision to choose Marston rather than the obvious candidate for such a task, the supreme masque-maker and friend of Beaumont and Fletcher, Ben Jonson. Unlike Jonson with his sycophantic idealization of the corrupt court of James, Marston kept his distance, a stance more in keeping with the attitudes of the Huntingdons. At times the entertainment sounds as if it were precisely tailored to Ashby's "country" Puritan prejudices about court and city:

> Lacivious youth not dare to speake
>   the language of loose Cytty,
> He that Dyanas bondes doth breake,
>   is helde most rudely witty.
>
> . . . .
>
> Disgratious dullnes yett much marrs
>   the shape of courtly talking
> He that can scilent touch such starrs
>   his soule lyes in his walking.[103]

Marston's entertainment is literally and figuratively a "country" event befitting this audience's preferences. It begins in a park, shifts to a great hall for a masque, then concludes in a park with lines that have become familiar from T. S. Eliot's employment of them in "Burbank with a Baedeker": "So the Countess passed on untill she came through the Little Park where Niobe presented hir with a Cabinet. & so departed" (p. 207). Perhaps what Eliot responded to in this passage was a feeling that a special kind of "magnificence" was being celebrated, but one with a rural cast. Marston gave Lady Alice all the homage he could muster with his limited lyrical gift. But his stress was not so much on her external graces as on what a Spenserian would prefer to have celebrated, her spiritual achievement:

> what may be judg'd Beauty, must have touch
> & proofe from hirs, yet this hir leaste of grace
> (which is the moste in moste): hir beautys but the case
> of fayrest minde.
>
> (pp. 199, 222–25)

---

[103]Davenport, *Poems of Marston*, p. 204, ll. 364–72. Subsequent references to this work are cited by page or line numbers in the text.

Most striking about Marston's entertainment is the presentation of Lady Alice as a latter-day Queen Elizabeth, entering a country world presided over by a "high silvan who commaundes thes[e] woodes" (40), the earl of Huntingdon—his position as chief forester is alluded to—along with yet another Elizabeth, his countess, "bright Nymphe fairer then Queen of fludds" (41).[104] At least under the hallucinatory influence of an entertainment far from London, there is a sense that at Ashby—with royal blood and plausible claims to the throne on both sides of the family—no other monarch or court mattered.[105]

One of the contributors to the Beaumont and Fletcher First Folio expresses absolute certainty that in the Civil War the playwrights would have adhered to the "Better side," that is, to the royalists.[106] He may well have been correct, but what many do not realize is that it was possible to hold "country," radical-Protestant, anti-Catholic, anticourt, anti-James sentiments and still refuse to participate in a rebellion. The "country" earl of Clare, who had many and powerful reasons to retreat to the country, made his moral aversion from the Stuart court so clear that the king himself noted him "as a person discontented."[107] His biographer said,

> From theis disobligations and discontentments some have beene of opinion that had he lived to theis unhappy times he would have sided with those that persecuted the King. But I am most confident of the contrary. For he was so true a sonne of the church of England that he would most firmly have asserted the episcopal jurisdiction, and so tender he was of

[104] That the countess of Huntingdon was named after the late queen and otherwise identified with her seems to have been part of the family lore, as one can see from William Sampson's elegy, *Virtus Post Funera Vivit* (London, 1636), p. 15:

> From dead *Eliza* of bless'd memory,
> She did receive her Christianity.
> A happy Mother makes a happy Childe,
> She had her spirit, and her nature milde.

[105] At nearby Coleorton in 1618 Francis Beaumont's cousin Sir Thomas Beaumont (whom Fletcher mentions in the postscript to his letter to the countess) presented a masque to celebrate the marriage of Sir William Seymour to Lady Frances Devereux, sister to the earl of Essex (Rudolf Brotanek, ed., *Die Englischen Maskenspiele* [Vienna and Leipzig, 1902], pp. 328–38). For various reasons too complex to mention here I suspect it may have been composed by Fletcher. As David Norbrook has shown in *Poetry and Politics in the English Renaissance* (London, 1984), pp. 250–51, the Coleorton masque has explicitly Spenserian and un-Jonsonian qualities.

[106] Glover and Waller, *Works of Beaumont and Fletcher*, 1:xxii. The author of this phrase, Sir George Lisle, called himself Beaumont's "kinsman." Since he was knighted by Charles I and shot by Fairfax after the battle at Colchester, he was scarcely objective on this matter.

[107] Gervase Holles, *Memorials of the Holles Family, 1493–1656*, ed. A. C. Wood (London, 1937), p. 102.

the honour of the House of Peeres (in which he had still beene a principall leader) that he would never have endured to see them so basely prostitute themselves (as they did) to the House of Commons.[108]

But adherence to "country" views might lead to the sort of action and inaction taken by the Hastings and Stanley families. As Lawrence Stone describes their response to the Civil War, they were among the "neutrals and tepid nominal adherents of the King . . . torn between political loyalty to the Crown on the one hand and on the other a desire for religious reform and a suspicion and hatred of the swarms of Catholics who were rallying so enthusiastically round the King. In many cases the result was a paralysis of the will."[109]

The point of this lengthy excursus on Fletcher's patrons should now be clear. The earl of Huntingdon and his family would not have assisted in the growth of Fletcher's "Reputation and credit" (in Massinger's words to the earl of Pembroke) had he differed radically from them on matters that the earl and his family cared about so deeply. In fact, as this study tries to demonstrate, no playwrights of the time were more sympathetic and comprehending than Beaumont and Fletcher of the complex of circumstances that produced the "paralysis of the will" by which so many noble spirits of the time were afflicted.

BEAUMONT: PROFESSIONAL OR AMATEUR WRITER?

Judge Beaumont's will of 1598 does not mention any of his sons, hence it is to be presumed that his whole estate except some small sums specifically mentioned went to his oldest son, Henry. The heir survived his father by only eight years, and in his will of 1606 Henry left Francis a lump sum of money, precisely how much is unclear.[110] To have had any personal resources would have made Beaumont more affluent than almost every one of his fellow dramatists.[111] But it seems to me unwarranted to conclude as Gayley and others have that Beaumont's "dramatic activity" after he received his bequest was undertaken "for sheer love of the art."[112] There is no reason to believe that in those days of strict adherence to the custom of primo-

---

[108] Ibid., pp. 107–8.

[109] *Crisis of the Aristocracy*, p. 743.

[110] See Dyce, *Works of Beaumont and Fletcher*, 1:xxviii and n. k.

[111] The financial details about the Beaumonts' penalty for recusancy suggest that even with all allowances for inflation their estate was not a very large one. Sell, *Shorter Poems of Beaumont*, p. 9, says that "two thirds of sixteen of . . . [Sir John Beaumont's] properties—Grace Dieu, messuages, houses, rectories, granges, and hundreds of acres of farmland in several Leicestershire parishes [yielded a] total annual income of £56."

[112] *Beaumont, the Dramatist*, p. 45.

geniture Beaumont received more than the usual pittance—"that which the cat left on the malt heap"[113]—left to any younger son. John F. Danby is closer to the available facts in viewing Fletcher and Beaumont respectively as "the *declassé* son of the Bishop and the younger son of the Judge."[114] The available evidence suggests that Beaumont acted like most other younger sons, finding some way to eke out a living after a childhood of privilege and a superior education. This would seem to be borne out by the fact that in the very year he received his lump sum inheritance, 1606, he seems to have inaugurated his career as a professional dramatist. 1606 also happens to be precisely the year (or as precisely as such things can be measured) that Beaumont became twenty-one years old.[115] Having attained his majority, he would have been essentially on his own.[116]

The next known scrap of biography confirms the view that not only Fletcher, about whose precarious financial situation there is no doubt, but also Beaumont was a dedicated professional who situated himself as close to his place of employment as possible. According to Aubrey, Beaumont and Fletcher "lived together on the Banke side, not far from the Play-house, both batchelors; lay together; had one wench in the house between them, which they did so admire; the same cloathes and cloake, &c., betweene them."[117] There are no external reasons for supposing that this efficient arrangement describes, as some would have it, a momentary excursion by two rich boys into *la vie Boheme.* What is known is that they wrote an astounding number of plays during their brief period of collaboration—as many as thirteen together and separately between 1606 and 1612. Such productivity suggests financial necessity, not the casual practice of a hobby by affluent amateurs.[118]

[113] Thomas Wilson's often-cited descriptive image for the inheritances of younger sons in *The State of England, 1600,* quoted by Joan Thirsk, "Younger Sons in the Seventeenth Century," *History* 54 (1969): 358–77.

[114] *Poets on Fortune's Hill* (London, 1952), p. 157. As my argument proceeds, it will be obvious that I find a different significance in what this status implies.

[115] Note that I am accepting Sell's new date of ca. 1585 for Beaumont's birth rather than the usual 1584 (*Shorter Poems of Beaumont,* pp. 4–5).

[116] This view of Beaumont's entry into playwriting as a means of earning a living leaves me in slight disagreement with G. E. Bentley in *The Profession of Dramatist in Shakespeare's Time* (Princeton, N.J., 1971), pp. 34–35. He sees Beaumont as becoming a "professional" only after he began to write for the King's Men in 1608. Possibly this is merely a disagreement over terms, but my view is that Beaumont wrote plays to earn money regardless of whether it was for the children's companies or the adults.

[117] Powell, *Brief Lives,* p. 54.

[118] As late as 1612 Beaumont seems to be writing a poem, "Ad Comitissam Rutlandiae," to Sir Philip Sidney's daughter Lady Rutland under conditions that suggest a financial motivation. Just before she died, Beaumont addressed a verse epistle to her that makes it clear that he does not consider himself her social equal, leaving the ob-

Another piece of information sheds further light on the level of Beaumont's dedication to the vocation of writer. In about 1613 Beaumont married an heiress from Kent named Ursula Isley. This was precisely the period when he wrote his marriage masque for the wedding of Princess Elizabeth that concludes with a wish:

> *I would this Paire, when they are laid,*
> *And not a creature nie them,*
> *Could catch [Time's] . . . scythe, as he doth passe,*
> *And cut his wings, and breake his glasse,*
> *And keepe him ever by them.*[119]

These lines gain in poignancy when one considers what happened very soon after Beaumont wrote them. In keeping with the view of Beaumont as an aristocratic amateur, it has been customary to conclude that since none of his writing can be dated later than 1613, he readily abandoned his career after his marriage and retired to gentlemanly inactivity in the country. However, a document long available[120] but inexplicably ignored reveals a very different, sadder last chapter to Beaumont's brief life. I refer to a revelation in a poem by the Leicestershire clergyman and poet Thomas Pestell, "An Elegie I made on Mr. Francis Beaumont, dying 1615–16 at Westminster," about Beaumont's last days. Pestell was in a position to know Beaumont well, having served as curate to the Coleorton Beaumonts; there is no reason to doubt the reliability of his information. In these lines the poet is speaking to Death:

> thou were faine
> To hire an apoplexe, to shend his [Beaumont's] braine,
> Till thou couldst come thyselfe, and hinder so
> That sprightly nectar which from it did flow;
> And yet his puissant witt was nere so drie,
> But even in midst of most infirmitie
> It crown'd his last worke with so faire an end,
> 'Twould puzzle the best witts alive to mend.

(115–22)[121]

---

vious inference that his desire to praise her had the same roots as Jonson's in writing his *Epigram* to Lady Rutland. The same motivation was probably behind Beaumont's elegy on Lady Rutland, mentioned earlier.

[119] In Bowers, *Dramatic Works*, 1:137–38, ll. 326–30.

[120] Pestell's poem on Beaumont was published by Nichols around 1800 and is mentioned in the *DNB* entry on Pestell.

[121] *Poems of Pestell*, ed. Buchan, pp. 71–74. For the complete text of this poem, see appendix B.

The context makes it clear that the last work to which Pestell is referring is an elegy Beaumont wrote about Lady Penelope Clifton, who
died on October 26, 1613. This would date Beaumont's apoplectic
attack sometime between February, the date of his Inner Temple
marriage masque, and October 1613.[122] The stroke (as we would call
it) must not have caused total paralysis, since Beaumont was able not
only to complete the elegy but to father a daughter, born after his
death. (An earlier child was also a girl.) But it did inspire Beaumont
to express, according to Pestell, "frequent wishes" (56) for death;
when it came, he gave it "embraces" (57). Pestell's poem clearly indicates that Beaumont, professional that he was, did not stop writing of
his own volition.

But perhaps the strongest evidence for the depth of Beaumont's
commitment to the vocation of writer appears in his best-known
poem, the verse epistle to Ben Jonson about the Mermaid Tavern.[123]
It expresses Beaumont's complex attitude toward the several worlds
he inhabited: the Mermaid and Temple, the Bankside (in the person
of Jonson), and Leicestershire. At first (and as traditionally understood) the poem seems to be an exile's genial lament for the lost pleasures of the city, for the joys of sophisticated society with its wit com-
bats and mental stimulation. He misses that circle of poets, lawyers,
and minor court officials—many of them also versifiers—whom I. A.
Shapiro has identified as the group that congregated at the Mermaid
and the Mitre.[124] Unlike the "full Mermaide wine" (6),[125] the sort of
liquor he must drink in the country, "water mixt with Claret Lees"
(7), could inspire only the worst writers. For fifteen lines (7–21) in a
paradoxical display of wittiness he proceeds to expatiate on the dull-
ing effects of such thin fare on country wits, including his own:

> It is a Potion sent us downe to drinke
> By speciall Providence, keeps us from fights . . . ;

[122] I assume he did not write the marriage masque after the stroke because his prefatory letter to the printed text of the masque sounds so sprightly.

[123] I. A. Shapiro, "The 'Mermaid Club,' " *Modern Language Review* 45 (1950): 14, has
argued that the grounds for attributing it to Beaumont are somewhat shaky. Shapiro's
doubts about the authenticity of the lengthy title and of the last two lines ("Ben, when
these scenes are perfect," etc.) in the folio edition are certainly valid. But there are
numerous manuscript ascriptions, and external evidence of Beaumont's authorship
has long been clear from Buchan's edition, *Poems of Pestell*. As Buchan shows, pp. liii–
liv, Pestell knew Beaumont well and made use of the "Mermaid Tavern" poem in ways
that show that he knew it to be Beaumont's.

[124] Shapiro, "The 'Mermaid Club,' " showed that, except for Jonson and Beaumont,
it did not contain professional writers.

[125] Line numbers refer to Herford, Simpson, and Simpson's *Ben Jonson*, 11:374–77,
which is the most satisfactory text.

. . . .
 A Med'cine to obey our Magistrates.

(22–26)

Country drink may dull the wits and make country people supine,
but in a sudden shift in identification he claims that "we" country folk
live in a morally superior atmosphere:

> for wee doe live more free, then you; noe
>   hate,
> Noe envie of anothers happie state
>
> . . . .
>   . . . wee want subtilty to doe
> the Cittie tricks, Lye, Hate, and fflatter too:
>
> . . . .
> Only some fellowe with the subtlest pate
> Amongst us, may perchance Equivocate
> At selling of a horse, and that's the most.

(27–41)

This fifteen-line contrast between the simple, even stupid, but good
country gentry and the city's skillful "operators" provides a qualifying
transition to the famous passage on the Mermaid Tavern. From his
country perspective the Mermaid seems like a gymnasium for keeping one's wits in good working order:

> Mee thinkes the litle witt I had is lost
> Since I saw you; for witt is like a Rest
> Held upp at Tennis, which men doe the best
> With the best Gamsters.

(42–45)

At these rallies, he implies (surprisingly, in light of our impression of
Jonson as an earlier version of Dr. Johnson) that he and Ben acted as
spectators at tours de force of wit that involved the participants in
prodigious, sometimes irrecoverable, expenditures of mental energy,
even to the point of risking the loss of their wits:

> What things have wee seene
> Done at the Mermaide? heard words that have beene
> soe nimble, and soe full of subtill flame
> as if that every one from whom they came
> had meant to putt his whole witt in a Jeast
> and had resolv'd to live a foole the rest
> of his dull life.

(45–51)

What he and Ben had "seene / Done"[126] was joyous but strenuous exercise, but his praise is so ambiguous that it is unclear whether the wit was so brilliant that the city needs no more for awhile or so silly that it warrants similar talk by others.

The poet's thoughts then return to the gradual degeneration of his own wit in the simpler country air (59–67).[127] But in the middle of a verse a recollection of what Ben is really like makes him once more refuse to idealize the quality of youthful city wit:

> but one thought of thee
> makes mee remember all these things to bee
> the witt of our young men, fellowes that shewe
> noe part of good, yet utter all they knowe.
> who like trees of the Guard, have growing soules
> Only.
>
> (67–72)

As he laments his degeneration, he thinks of Ben Jonson and perhaps of his "warning" uttered "To the Reader" of *The Alchemist*: "that there is a great difference between those, that (to gain the opinion of Copie) utter all they can, how ever unfitly; and those that use election, and a meane."[128] He perceives "all these things" he has been discussing from a new, distanced point of view. Both the simple witticisms of the country and the flaming subtleties of the city are the wit of men whose rational souls have not yet matured.[129] True wit is based upon maturity and an awareness of the "good."

It is notable that after this discovery Beaumont does not express

---

[126] The implications of this phrase have been lost to many readers because a comma crept between the two words, apparently inserted by the compiler or printer of the 1679 folio. Unfortunately, the 1679 text seems to be the basis of a surprising number of modern versions of this poem, including, the *Oxford Book of Seventeenth-Century Verse* edited by Grierson and Bullough.

[127] Naturally, Beaumont exaggerates the cultural naiveté of his country circle. In addition to the sorts of people he knew at Ashby, there is the example of his nearby cousin at Coleorton, also named Francis Beaumont. Not only did he have something to do with Speght's edition of Chaucer, but he alludes easily to the music of Orlando di Lassus and quotes readily from Spenser. See *Gossip from a Muniment Room . . . , 1574 to 1618*, trans. and ed. Lady Newdigate-Newdigate (London, 1897), pp. 94–134.

[128] Herford, Simpson, and Simpson, *Ben Jonson*, 5:291.

[129] In his commendatory verses for *Cataline*, Beaumont praises the maturity of Jonson's wit (ibid., 11:325):

> And (I dare say) in it, there lies much Wit
> Lost, till thy Readers can grow up to it.
> Which they can nere outgrow, to find it ill,
> But must fall backe againe, or like it still.
>
> (7–10)

the hope that he would like to return to the Mermaid. Neither does he describe Jonson at any point as a wit, nor does he attempt to define Jonson's virtues through a string of witty comparisons as was his wont in other poems. Instead he concludes with a direct statement, verbally acting out, as it were, his withdrawal from wittiness as an end in itself:

> Strong Destiny, which all Controules
> I hope hath lefte a better fate in store
> for mee thy friend, then to live evermore
> Bannisht unto this home; twill once againe
> Bring mee to thee, who wilt make smooth, and plaine
> The way of knowledge for mee, and then I
> who'have noe good in mee, but simplicitye,
> Knowe that it will my greatest comfort bee
> T'acknowledge all the rest to Come from thee.
>
> (72–80)

From subtlety to simplicity, and from simplicity to wisdom: this is the course Beaumont will follow. He will travel a "smooth" path to a state of "comfort" (not the indolent "comfort" of line 1, but the wise "comfort" of line 79). He will reach this state not through the kind of "Rest / Held upp at Tennis" (43–44), the vigorous wit-combats of youthful tavern companions, but through drinking of the restful "rest" (80) of Ben Jonson's wisdom. The oscillating movement in the poem from country friends to city wits to Jonson reflects in miniature the essential shape of Beaumont's tragically brief career: back and forth between town and country, the two worlds enriching each other.

There were, in fact, two Beaumonts. Along with the outrageous wit seeking to outdo Donne, the mellower voice of the "Mermaid Tavern" poem appears in two verse epistles that deserve to be better known. They are similar in structure, tone, diction, and versification because they share a common purpose. In one of them Beaumont says that he "write[s] of nothing;"[130] in another he says that he is "seeking a subject, yet finds none."[131] This is true; the manner of expression is the real subject. In the case of the second epistle he aptly describes the "stile" as that "which men / send Cheese to towne with, and thankes downe agen" (14–15).[132] With a controlled casualness he

---

[130] "To Mr. B. J." in E. K. Chambers, *William Shakespeare* (Oxford, 1930), 2:224, l. 22. Subsequent quotations are from this edition.

[131] "Ad Comitissam Rutlandiae" in *Certain Elegies Done by Sundry Excellent Wits* (London, 1620), sig. A2ʳ, l. 62.

[132] Chambers, *Shakespeare*, 2:223–24, dates the poem "ca. 1615," but for reasons discussed in the next chapter I would suggest a date between June 1608 and late 1609.

runs on from line to line in a series of disclaimers and counterasser-
tions to give the impression that he is merely scribbling:

> Neither to follow fashion nor to showe
> my witt against the State, nor that I knowe
> any thing now, with which I am with childe
> till I have tould, nor hopeinge to bee stilde
> a good Epist'ler through the towne, with
>   which
> I might bee famous, nor with any ytch
> like these, wrote I this Letter, but to showe
> the Love I carrie and mee thinkes do owe
> to you above the number, which can best
> in something which I use not, be exprest.
>
> (1–10)

In this obtrusively understated antistyle, he professes to aspire to the
kind of intuitive natural expression he sees in Shakespeare's best
work:

> heere I would let slippe
> (If I had any in mee) schollershippe,
> And from all Learninge keepe these lines as cleere
> as Shakespeares best are, which our heires shall heare
> Preachers apte to their auditors to showe
> how farr sometimes a mortall man may goe
> by the dimme light of Nature, tis to mee
> an helpe to write of nothing; and as free
> As hee, whose text was, god made all that is,
> I meane to speake.
>
> (15–24)

As well as being evidence of the profoundest importance in the Strat-
fordian argument, the passage shows how much Beaumont had assimilated from Jonson and anticipated of Dryden, a style fit for discourse, near to prose, yet crafted to take advantage of the form of
the line ("our heires shall heare / Preachers," "as free / As hee").
Technically, the tension between the seeming freedom and formal
control is masterful. Through it Beaumont conveys another kind of
wit that appears in the best of his dramatic poetry. It displays no rhetorical gaudiness or the yoking of the heterogeneous by violence, but
cultivated, knowing discourse, the language of gentlemen expressed
in an artless art. The difference from the Donnean Beaumont is so
striking that one must assume that awareness of Jonson as his reader
disciplined him, at least temporarily, to write in a manner his mentor

would admire. Certainly Jonson's answer to one of his epistles is the ultimate praise a student could hope to receive from a teacher: "even there, where most thou praysest mee, / For writing better, I must envie thee."[133]

BEAUMONT AND FLETCHER'S VARIOUS LONDON CIRCLES

Much glib criticism builds on the fact that Beaumont's father was a judge and Fletcher's a bishop. John F. Danby in his brilliant book *Poets on Fortune's Hill* tried to take such criticism one stage deeper by describing Beaumont as disadvantaged by being a younger son and Fletcher as "declassed" by his father's disgrace and consequent indigence. With this more precise social placement Danby constructs an ingenious theory that accounts for the two young collaborators' motives in writing plays and for the particular form they took:

> It was the urge of the younger son to exploit the India of the stage, the desire of the *declassé* to rehabilitate himself in court circles (the memory and the ambition of the Great House still working in each of them) which drove Beaumont and Fletcher to descend on the popular theatre and wrest it from its popular way to something they could approve of and make their social equals applaud. . . . On the one hand they will capture the popular playhouse, on the other they will gate-crash court society.[134]

The self-assurance of Danby's rhetoric has convinced many that he has plucked out the heart of these marginal gentlemen's mystery, but the surviving facts suggest a much different picture. It is true that Fletcher entered the London theatrical world penniless and that Beaumont did not have the resources (even after the recusant penalties) of his older brother. But aside from the three dedicatory poems to *The Faithful Shepherdess*—none of them to courtiers—and the special case of the earl of Huntingdon, no evidence exists that either Beaumont or Fletcher had any personal ties of dependency or *even of friendship* with the great Jacobean courtiers and patrons. I use italics because it cannot be stressed too vigorously that neither Beaumont nor Fletcher can be found in the glamorous circle of London courtiers and aristocrats that Charles Mills Gayley, Beaumont's most thorough biographer, constructed for the two men in *Beaumont, the*

---

[133] Epigram 55, in *Ben Jonson*, ed. Herford, Simpson, and Simpson, 8:44, ll. 9–10.
[134] *Poets on Fortune's Hill*, pp. 160–61.

Dramatist. Gayley's picture has no basis in fact and is constructed out of a tissue of unsubstantiated assumptions.[135]

Instead, insofar as they can be tracked in London, Beaumont and Fletcher are found where one would expect all serious writers to be: not with the wealthy and the aristocratic but with fellow writers and the sorts of urban intellectuals who congregated at the Inns of Court and the Mermaid Tavern. It is probably no coincidence that one early and permanent cluster of friends shared that set of aesthetic and political tastes and convictions that are called "Spenserian": pastoral, anticourt, Protestant, anti-Spanish. There was, first, Michael Drayton, "our still reviving Spencer."[136] Late in his life he testified that he had been a "bosom" companion of the "two Beaumonts," John and Francis. They "freely told to me their hearts, / As I have mine to them."[137] Early in James's reign (1604) Drayton wrote the anticourt satiric poem *The Owl* (it was revised in 1619 with additional signs of oppositionist feelings); it became an important document for various similarly alienated literary figures.[138] Through Drayton and the Inner Temple, Beaumont was also connected to two other Spenserians, William Browne and William Basse.[139] I would also place another alienated writer, John Marston, among Beaumont and Fletcher's friends on the basis of evidence cited elsewhere.

This is not to claim that all of their literary friends were dissident or alienated. Aubrey tells of the acquaintance of the literary and courtly bishop John Earl with Beaumont as well as with Fletcher. There is also Beaumont's profound regard for the court poet Jonson, which Ben returned in public although in private he snarled to Drummond that "Beaumont loved too much himself and his own verses": a judgment that was probably true of both of them.

Although it is unclear precisely who constituted the circle of writers

---

[135] The only possible exception is Gayley's claim of a friendship between Beaumont and the third earl of Dorset (*Beaumont, the Dramatist*, p. 191). Vita Sackville-West, *Knole and the Sackvilles* (New York, 1922), p. 59, probably influenced by Gayley, makes the same claim. It is not impossible since Dorset did patronize many writers, and it is true that a portrait of Beaumont has somehow become a part of the collection at Knole. But no evidence has survived that he knew Beaumont or Fletcher. As for the portrait, Lord Herbert's *Autobiography* records that Dorset collected portraits of those he admired, sometimes (as in the case of Herbert) having secretly commissioned them.

[136] Unidentified contemporary quoted by Norbrook, *Poetry and Politics*, p. 207.

[137] "To Henry Reynolds" in *The Works of Michael Drayton*, ed. J. William Hebel (Oxford, 1932), 3:230, ll. 180–81.

[138] See Norbrook, *Poetry and Politics*, p. 213. *The Owl* is referred to by Beaumont and Fletcher in *The Scornful Lady* in a neutral context. For Drayton's political attitudes see Richard F. Hardin, *Michael Drayton* (Lawrence, Kans., 1973), esp. ch. 4.

[139] See Gayley, *Beaumont, the Dramatist*, pp. 131ff. and 134.

and wits at the Mermaid Tavern,[140] and although the legendary meetings did not take place until the last years of Beaumont's London residence, this surely constitutes another set of friends and acquaintances. Since I. A. Shapiro has peeled away all the pleasant fabrications (e.g., about Shakespeare's presence), there remains a circle of lawyers, minor courtiers and place seekers, M.P.s, and literate gentry. Here again there is no evidence of any noblemen in the group.[141] Beaumont and Fletcher's situation as money-earning playwrights was strikingly different from that of a desperate figure like Donne, whose precarious situation forced him to become a flatterer for hire to many of the foul profligates in James's court as well as to many literary countesses. The young playwrights did not have housefuls of children to feed.

I have reserved for separate discussion Fletcher's friendship with Charles Cotton (known as "the elder" to distinguish him from his son, the poet and translator of Montaigne).[142] This friendship is known from accounts by Cotton's cousin Sir Aston Cockayne, who describes Fletcher to Cotton as "your friend and old companion."[143] Cockayne elsewhere seems to refer to Cotton as "Fletcher's chief bosome-friend."[144] Richard Brome's dedication of the 1639 quarto of Fletcher's *Monsieur Thomas* also implies Cotton's personal tie to Fletcher. It is easy enough to work out the probable origins of this friendship, since Cotton was connected to many London literary figures, among whom Jonson was closest to Fletcher. He also was closely related to the Stanhopes, who were related by marriage to Fletcher's patron Huntingdon. Like many of Fletcher's nonprofessional connections Cotton was an accomplished man of letters. Herrick testified to his great acuity in judging verses, and Walton claimed that he ranked with Sir Philip Sidney in his ability at description. There is no reason to believe that patronage had any significant part in the friendship of Cotton and Fletcher since they could only have become acquainted after Fletcher had made his mark. However, I strongly doubt that Cotton was, as Gayley asserts, Fletcher's "closest friend, if we except Beaumont,"[145] since Fletcher was much older. While his year of birth

[140] See Shapiro, "The 'Mermaid Club.' "

[141] One possible actor friend of Beaumont's was William Ostler, who named a child "Beaumont" in 1612. We know he played in several of Beaumont and Fletcher's plays. See Chambers, *Shakespeare*, 2:331.

[142] For the little known of Cotton, Sr., see Charles J. Sembower, *The Life of Charles Cotton* (New York, 1911), pp. 4–12. For Cotton's economic position at the time of his marriage, see p. 11.

[143] Gayley, *Beaumont, the Dramatist*, p. 227.

[144] Ibid., p. 168.

[145] Ibid.

is not known, Cotton did not matriculate at Cambridge until 1618.[146] This suggests about a twenty-five-year age difference. Moreover, this "bosom" friendship (if indeed it is Cotton to whom Cockayne is referring) is described by a cousin who is trying to appropriate to himself and his family as many famous names as possible. Nonetheless, if one is to trust Brome's dedication, Cotton became something of a champion of Fletcher's work after his death. Some initially unsuccessful plays, Brome says to Cotton, "have since by your candid self and others, been clearly vindicated."[147]

As with Beaumont, Fletcher's clearest connections were with writers. They would begin with another pair of Spenserians, his cousins Phineas and Giles.[148] In addition to Beaumont and Jonson, the list would certainly include his fellow playwrights Nathan Field, George Chapman, Richard Brome, William Shakespeare, and Philip Massinger.[149] Surely, Massinger, not Cotton, would have been Fletcher's closest friend after Beaumont. Fletcher and Massinger collaborated on plays for a dozen years, and their close friendship is attested to by Sir Aston Cockayne. In fact, if one is to believe him, they are still together:

> In the same grave *Fletcher* was buried here
> Lies the Stage-Poet *Philip Massinger*:
> Playes they did write together, were great friends,
> And now one Grave includes them at their ends:
> So whom on earth nothing did part, beneath
> Here (in their Fames) they lie, in spight of death.[150]

BEAUMONT AND FLETCHER'S AUDIENCE

The frequent charge that Beaumont and Fletcher were simply brilliant (or amoral) caterers (or panders) to a primarily courtly audience

[146] Venn and Venn, *Alumni Cantabrigienses*, 1:402. He died in 1658.

[147] "To the NOBLE HONOURER of the Dead Author's Works and Memory, Master CHARLES COTTON," in Glover and Waller, *Works of Beaumont and Fletcher*, 4:174.

[148] It is not clear how friendly they remained. Giles, Jr., spoke very disparagingly about the stage in his prose work *The Reward of the Faithful* (1623).

[149] Field and Chapman contributed prefatory poems to *The Faithful Shepherdess*. Brome mentions his personal acquaintanceship with Fletcher in his First folio prefatory poem. Shakespeare and Massinger collaborated with Fletcher on plays.

[150] Quoted in Gerald E. Bentley, *The Jacobean and Caroline Stage* (Oxford, 1941–68), 4:753. It may tell something about Fletcher that his collaborator and close friend wrote plays in which critics and historians, starting with the great Samuel R. Gardiner, have detected hostility to the Stuarts. See "The Political Element in Massinger," *Contemporary Review* 28 (1876): 495–507. While I basically agree, this is too large a tangle to untie here.

requires detailed attention. There is no question about the court's frequent viewing of their work. According to G. E. Bentley, "of the performances at court [by the King's Men between 1616 and 1642] of plays listed by name, 42 performances (including repetitions) are of plays from the Beaumont and Fletcher folios, compared to 18 performances of plays written by Shakespeare, and 7 performances of plays written by Jonson."[151] It is also true that many lurid accounts of James's court have survived, enough to have earned it the title of "decadent." Not all of them are equally trustworthy, however; sources of many include disappointed place-seekers, Puritans, bishops, politicians like Clarendon with axes to grind, and Victorian moralists. While much is doubtless true, much is exaggerated; much is true of any court, and much was unchanged from Elizabeth's time. The crucial point in any case is that no evidence suggests that this "decadent" court had anything to do with the way Beaumont and Fletcher wrote their plays. Charles the First illustrated what a court could do to the drama if it really tried. After his accession in 1625 he and his queen Henrietta Maria involved themselves in the commissioning and production of plays that conformed to their personal taste. Nothing similar is apparent in James's court, either from the king or from any of his courtiers. Alfred Harbage concluded that "King James had a relish for plays more demonstrated than Elizabeth's, but he too was content to let them spawn naturally among his subjects, and after a few early generosities to the players, his routine payments of ten pounds per court performance became his only effective liaison with the stage."[152] The number of court performances did increase greatly under James, but the frequency and the size of the payments for them were not nearly high enough to support the repertory of a company like the King's Men. Throughout James's reign most of the company's income was derived from the combined receipts of the "private" Blackfriars theater and the "public" Globe. The Globe, it must be stressed, remained vital to the King's Men even after they began their successful operation at Blackfriars. Otherwise they would not have rebuilt it immediately after the fire of 1613. One is always pleased to receive "overtime" pay, as the stipends for court performances would have been considered. But if Beaumont and Fletcher were "catering" to any audience, it would have been the same one Shakespeare strove to please every day—the customers at the two theaters owned by the King's Men.

[151] *The Profession of Dramatist in Shakespeare's Time* (Princeton, N.J., 1971), p. 210.
[152] *The Cavalier Drama* (New York, 1936), p. 8.

Harbage's considered opinion was that "Fletcher wrote for no courtly coterie absorbed in their genteel fads,"[153] but in fact there is no evidence during the Jacobean period of a unity of taste among the courtiers or of any "courtly coterie." An audience at a court performance included a wide variety of personalities, viewpoints, and tastes: king, queen, prince, favorite, courtiers from old and wealthy families, nouveau riche nobles, Scottish camp followers, court chaplains, and representatives of every degree of power, privilege, and purity. Just as there were political and religious differences—pro- and anti-Puritan, pro- and anti-Spanish—there were aesthetic differences. Some peers, like the great art collector the earl of Arundel, felt that England was culturally provincial and ought to recognize and imitate the great achievements in painting, architecture, and literature of the Continent. Many peers were unadventurous in their aesthetic tastes, while most were utterly indifferent to art of any kind.

There is no evidence that at James's court a coterie of afficionados chose dramatic entertainment for the sovereign or dictated its shape. Nor has evidence survived of any enthusiastic patron bringing his client's works to the attention of his courtly peers. Apparently when the sovereign wished to see a play, he trusted the Master of the Revels to select something. He, in turn, would view the latest offerings and would naturally look with special favor on those of the premier acting company, the king's own men. They had in their repertory a large number of plays written by the indefatigable Fletcher and his many helpers, plays that had been highly successful at the Globe and Blackfriars. It is natural to ask next whether the court created fashions in drama by dominating the audience at Blackfriars. Again, no evidence has survived to suggest that courtiers composed a very large element of the audience. As for high-ranked courtiers, Harbage stresses that the "milieu of the private playhouses was not 'lordly.' Lords are no more apt to appear in the orbit of the boys than in that of the men."[154]

For whom, then, did Beaumont and Fletcher write? If one is to believe them, it was not for the average patron, either at the Blackfriars or the Globe. Of course, the audience at the Blackfriars would have included more of the educated and wealthy. But Beaumont's remarks in a prefatory poem for *The Faithful Shepherdess* suggest that from his point of view there was little difference between the two audiences; for both one had to expose oneself in public to a large

---

[153] Ibid., p. 41.
[154] *Shakespeare and the Rival Traditions* (New York, 1952), p. 55.

number of unqualified judges. The audience he describes so disparagingly here is a "private" one:

> Why should the man, whose wit nere had a staine,
> Upon the publike stage present his vaine,
> And make a thousand men in judgement sit,
> To call in question his undoubted wit,
> Scarce two of which can understand the lawes
> Which they should judge by, nor the parties cause,
> Among the rout there is not one that hath
> In his owne censure an explicite faith.[155]

Jonson's description of the audience at the Blackfriars suggests that
to him it was hardly a college of critics:

> Gamester, Captaine, Knight, Knight's man,
> Lady, or Pusil, that weares maske, or fan,
> Velvet, or Taffata cap, rank'd in the darke
>   With the ships Foreman, or some such brave sparke,
> That may judge for his six-pence.[156]

It may be objected that in these poems Beaumont and Jonson were
merely trying to raise Fletcher's spirits after the galling failure of his
play at the private theater, but in a prefatory poem to *Volpone* (1606)
Beaumont speaks with similar scorn, not of the groundlings but of
the "gallants" in the audience. More important, in the commendatory
poem prefixed to Jonson's *Cataline*, written in the year of his greatest
success (1611), Beaumont speaks with disapproval of anyone who
"itch'd after the wild applause / Of common people." He views Jonson as a model because he wrote what he knew to be "good" even
though it meant that his work is "three ages yet from understood."[157]
There is no reason to believe that Beaumont and Fletcher wrote with
less dedication or lower principles. The evidence about their lives and

---

[155] Prefatory poem to *The Faithful Shepherdess*, ed. Hoy, in Bowers, *Dramatic Works*,
3:490, ll. 11–18.

[156] Ibid., p. 492, ll. 3–7. Even allowing for Harbage's visceral distaste for the audience at the private theaters, his material shows persuasively that the general level of
learning and theatrical sophistication there was not particularly high. See *Shakespeare
and the Rival Traditions*, pp. 29–57. The important study by William Armstrong, "The
Audience of the Elizabethan Private Theaters," *Review of English Studies*, n.s., 10 (1959):
234–39, also deglamorizes the audience. Clifford Leech's "The Caroline Audience,"
Modern Language Review 36 (1941): 304–19, shows that the big change in the audience
occurs after 1625 and that there was much similarity between the earlier Jacobean
audience and that which Beaumont and Fletcher encountered.

[157] "To My Friend, Master Ben Jonson upon His Catiline" in Herford, Simpson, and
Simpson, *Ben Jonson*, 11:325.

social circle tends to corroborate the claim that when they conceived a play, they had in mind the saving remnant in the audience, the same knowledgeable and sophisticated friends for whom Jonson wrote: those who circulated Donne's poems in manuscript and wrote the witty nonsense on Coryat, who comprised the literate and far-from-servile parliaments that caused James so much annoyance, who studied or practiced law and reveled at the Inns of Court, in short, the very audience for whom Shakespeare wrote *The Winter's Tale* and *The Tempest*.[158] At the same time, to repeat, there is simply no evidence that Beaumont and Fletcher "catered" to one particular section of the public such as the gentry or the court. It was unnecessary. Like Shakespeare they had the good fortune to write as they pleased while giving pleasure, doubtless in different ways, to all ranks of society.[159]

BEAUMONT AND FLETCHER'S PLACEMENT

The incapacitated Beaumont finally died in Westminster about a month before Shakespeare on March 6, 1616. He was buried in Westminster Abbey near Chaucer and Spenser in the area that has come to be known as the "Poet's Corner." That this was in recognition of his achievement as a writer seems to be the implication of Jonson's First Folio tribute to Shakespeare:

> *My* Shakespeare, *rise; I will not lodge thee by*
> Chaucer, *or* Spenser, *or bid* Beaumont *lye*
> *A little further to make thee room.*[160]

A lesser-known elegy (ca. 1616–23) on Shakespeare by Beaumont's acquaintance William Basse also suggests that Beaumont's place of burial reflects an estimate of him as a writer:

> Renowned Spencer, lye a thought more nye
> To learned Chaucer, and rare Beaumont lye
> A little neerer Spenser to make roome
> For Shakespeare in your threefold fowerfold Tombe.[161]

---

[158] The argument of Ann Jennalie Cook, *The Privileged Playgoers of Shakespeare's London, 1576–1642* (Princeton, N.J., 1981) is not really relevant here since the issue is not the affluence of the audience but the quality of their responses to plays.

[159] See my "The Role of the Court in the Development of Jacobean Drama," *Criticism* 24 (1982): 138–58, for an expanded version of the argument I have presented here.

[160] Quoted by Chambers, *Shakespeare*, 2:208. We know that the placement of the older authors was a form of recognition, since they were so positioned through the personal efforts and financial outlay of Lady Ann Clifford, as described by George C. Williamson in *Lady Anne Clifford, Countess of Dorset, Pembroke, and Montgomery* (Kendal, Eng., 1922).

[161] Chambers, *Shakespeare*, 2:226, ll. 1–4.

To place Beaumont with Chaucer and Spenser is an astonishing tribute that, for whatever reason, was denied to Fletcher. Considering his high reputation throughout the seventeenth century, very little is known about him. There is no solid evidence of Fletcher's marrying or indeed of anything else about his life except the dates of his plays, the identity of some of his friends and social connections, the record of his death in the plague of 1625, and his interment at the church nearest to the Globe, St. Mary Overy's (now Southwark Cathedral).[162] On the Bankside near to the Globe and next to his second collaborator, Philip Massinger, was the proper resting place for this "stage-poet."

The information assembled in this chapter suggests that the general view of the character, aims, and social status of Beaumont and Fletcher is not accurate. Nothing known about their lives ties them to the king and his court. The "facts," such as they are suggest a pattern of alienation, possibly influenced by family traditions and experiences, if not opposition to the centers of power. It is true that Fletcher as well as Beaumont had claims to higher social status than most Jacobean dramatists. But as far as we can see—admittedly, not very far—both conducted themselves primarily as professional dramatists whose loyalties and commitments were to their art, to their fellow artists, and to sympathetic friends in both city and country.

[162] Aubrey's story (*Brief Lives*, ed. Powell, p. 54) that Fletcher caught the plague in 1625 because he delayed a trip to the country in order to have a new suit of clothes made has the ring of authenticity about it. He heard it from the tailor of the suit, who in his old age served as a clerk at St. Mary Overy's—doubtless there grilled by Aubrey in pursuit of records about Fletcher.

Chapter Two

BEAUMONT AND FLETCHER'S EARLIEST WORK

OVIDIAN POLITICS: *SALMACIS AND HERMAPHRODITUS*

At the precocious age of seventeen Beaumont published his first poem, the Ovidian epyllion *Salmacis and Hermaphroditus*.[1] Despite its obvious dependence on *Venus and Adonis* and especially *Hero and Leander*, this tenfold expansion of Ovid's hundred lines displays astonishing sophistication and technical proficiency. It deserves scrutiny in its own right, as several recent studies have demonstrated,[2] but here I want to show how it foreshadows Beaumont's earliest play and his subsequent writing.

What one notices first about *Salmacis* is the high velocity of the narrative. It is the poet's prayer that "one line may draw the tother, / And every word skip nimbly o're another" (11–12).[3] "Nimble skipping" describes well the rapid jumps from episode to episode, from one piece of mythological embroidery to the next. The breezy, casual manner of the narrator is that of an observant reporter telling what he has heard. At the start of the poem he offers a highly decorated portrait of Hermaphroditus followed by one of Salmacis. Just when it seems that Beaumont is simply retelling Ovid's slight tale, the description of Salmacis's beauty leads to four hundred lines of apparently irrelevant digression about intricate relationships among the gods. He tells of their sexual frustration, jealousy, pettiness, their use of love as a tool for power. Only in passing does one note that Beaumont is employing a very limited cast with as rich and complex a history as that in a Congreve play. Phoebus has had a penchant for both Salmacis and Hermaphroditus, Hermes has cuckolded Vulcan who,

---

[1] Published anonymously in 1602; attributed to Beaumont in the unreliable 1640 edition of his poems and in manuscripts. See my note in *Notes and Queries* 16 (1969): 367–68 for corroboration on the basis of precise verbal similarities between *Salmacis* and his brother John Beaumont's *The Metamorphosis of Tobacco* and between *Salmacis* and *The Woman Hater*. In addition, there is Nichols's report that the eighteenth-century scholar Peter Whalley possessed a manuscript of a poem by Fletcher commending Beaumont's "Ovidian" poem, as I mentioned in the previous chapter.

[2] Hallett Smith, *Elizabethan Poetry* (Cambridge, Mass., 1952), pp. 70–74; William Keach, *Elizabethan Erotic Narratives* (New Brunswick, N.J., 1977), pp. 190–218; Ann Thompson, "Death by Water: the Originality of *Salmacis and Hermaphrodite*," *Modern Language Quarterly* 40 (1979): 99–114.

[3] *Elizabethan Minor Epics*, ed. Elizabeth Story Donno (New York, 1963). Line numbers in the text refer to this edition.

in behalf of Aphrodite, frustrates Jove's desires with Salmacis; Vulcan
also comes to Phoebus's aid after Hermes has revenged himself on
Phoebus for the sake of Bacchus. Everyone is jealous and lustful,
and—most important—everyone's desire is frustrated. Jove, Bacchus,
Cupid, Apollo, even the chaste Diana, are in one way or another deprived of sexual gratification.

Thus the wooing of Hermaphroditus by Salmacis in the last four
hundred lines occurs in a world where even the gods are unable to
fulfill their desires. Nor does any love exist in this world. Everyone is
selfish and preoccupied with his own affairs, and the two title figures
are no different. Salmacis is a lazy nymph who sits churlishly by her
fountain—significantly, it is the very one where Narcissus drowned
(399–402)—combing her tresses:

> Oft in the water did she looke her face,
> And oft she us'd to practise what quaint grace
> Might well become her, and comely feature
> Might be best fitting to so divine a creature.

(383–86)

When she sees the incomparably beautiful Hermaphroditus, she instantly courts him with lascivious importunity. His indifference to her
charms springs from his preference for an even more beautiful
"nymph" whom he views in Salmacis's eyes:

> How should I love thee, when I do espie
> A farre more beauteous Nymph hid in thy eye?
> When thou doost love, let not that Nymph be nie thee;
> Nor when thou woo'st, let that same Nymph be by
>   thee.

(691–94)

Salmacis "perceiv'd he did espie / None but himself reflected in her
eye" (697–98) and blocks his view by closing her eyes—a clear enough
image of the blindness of her desire.

It is not merely the narcissism of the characters that interests Beaumont but the inverted nature of the sexual role playing. As in *Hero
and Leander* ambivalent sexuality appears in some of the gods' preferences, but the matter is made explicit when Salmacis like Shakespeare's Venus acts as if she were a man wooing a woman:

> Beleeve me, boy, thy blood is very stayd,
> That art so loth to kisse a youthfull mayd.
> Wert thou a mayd, and I a man, Ile show thee,
> With what manly boldnesse I would woo thee.

(713–16)

Like Adonis the "bashfull boy" responds to the "lovely lasse" by blushing and running off. Finally she seizes him and nearly rapes him, at which point the metamorphosis occurs:

> in one body they began to grow.
> She felt his youthfull bloud in every vaine;
> And he felt hers warme his cold brest againe.
> And ever since was womens love so blest,
> That it will draw bloud from the strongest brest.
> Nor man nor mayd now could they be esteem'd:
> Neither, and either, might they well be deem'd.
>
> (902–8)

The satiric barb against "womens love" (905) recalls the fragment of Ennius that Beaumont quotes on the title page: "Salmacida spolia sine sanguine et sudore" (spoils of Salmacis [gained] without blood or sweat). Hermaphroditus's fate thus becomes the vehicle of an anti-feminine joke against the insatiable and irresistible lust of Woman.

But the poem cuts deeper. In the opening lines the narrator promises that he will speak "of amorous love / Such as would bow the hearts of gods above" (1–2). The destructive nature not of love but of self-love when unleashed on others is Beaumont's theme, as may be seen by considering more closely the two lines describing the metamorphosis:

> Nor man nor mayd now could they be esteem'd:
> Neither, and either, might they well be deem'd.
>
> (907–8)

Doubtless the last line is Beaumont's version of Ovid's "Neutrumque et utrumque videntur," but it bears a suggestive similarity to Shakespeare's lines in "The Phoenix and the Turtle": "To themselves, yet either neither." The tale of Salmacis and Hermaphroditus, of two lovers turning into one creature, might have provided a vehicle for a love poem similar to Shakespeare's or to such poems as Donne's "Canonization," where "to one neutral thing both sexes fit," or to Beaumont's acquaintance William Browne's more traditional use of Ovid in *Britannia's Pastorals*:

> Sweet death they needs must have, who so unite
> That two distincts make one Hermaphrodite.[4]

[4] *Poems of William Browne of Tavistock*, ed. Gordan Goodwin (London, n.d.), 1:93, ll. 298–99.

Such had been the normal application of the Ovidian tale in the Renaissance, as an emblem of ideal marital union.[5] Instead, this poem ends with the mean but characteristic request by Beaumont's Hermaphroditus that whoever swims in his fountain "may nevermore a manly shape retain, / But halfe a vergine may returne againe" (917–18). Unlike Shakespeare's birds, Beaumont's lovers remain "two distincts" in divided union. With all its good humor and Ovidian, mythological trappings, *Salmacis* remains a coolly realistic, unromantic description of a universe (since the gods too are a prominent element) composed of self-centered narcissists incapable of love. Unlike most Elizabethan Ovidian poems, it does not exult the power of passion; here passion burns, melts, divides, and finally dehumanizes.

Much that is most characteristic of Beaumont and of the plays he wrote with Fletcher may be found in embryo in this surprising and unique treatment of Ovid's story: a cool, ironic presentation of a dizzying succession of events; a complex, carefully intertwining plot; clear, precise language; and self-centered characters. Even Beaumont's critical treatment of courts and princes, a rather unlikely topic in this setting, somehow makes its appearance when Jove visits the palace of Astraea. When he tries to enter,

> there was such a busie rout before;
> Some serving men, and some promooters bee,
> That he could passe no foote without a fee:
> But as he goes, he reaches out his hands,
> And payes each one in order as he stands;
> And still, as he was paying those before,
> Some slipt againe betwixt him and the dore.
> At length (with much adoo) he past them all,
> And entred straight into a spacious hall,
> Full of darke angles and of hidden wayes,
> Crooked Macanders, infinite delayes;
> All which delayes and entries he must passe,
> Ere he could come where just Astraea was.
>
> (168–80)

A porter at Astraea's door utters the warning, "None must see Justice but with emptie purse" (186), and only after paying out the last of his "*douceurs*" (like Bishop Fletcher) is Jove permitted to "see divine Astraeas face" (192). The circumstantial detail of the court and its entourage sounds like an extract from a Tudor satire. But as Douglas

---

[5] See Donald Cheyney, "Spenser's Hermaphrodite and the 1590 *Faerie Queene*," *PMLA* 87 (1972): 192–200.

Bush first pointed out, to a literate contemporary the mention of "Astraea" in this context in 1602 would inevitably evoke the court of Queen Elizabeth, then in the tired last year of her reign.[6]

Finally the goddess inquires of Jove "what lucklesse cause / What great contempt of state, what breach of lawes" (223–24) could bring the "King of gods" to her court. With much evasive detail Jove describes how he happened to be visiting the Earth and fell asleep:

> But a faire Nymph was bathing when he wak'd,
> (Here sigh'd great Jove, and after brought forth) nak'd.
>
> (245–46)

The comical delay of the revealing rhyme word—Jove wants Astraea's assistance in a plan to gain Salmacis—is typical of Beaumont's irreverent treatment of princes who neglect or misuse their office. Even in his earliest work and in an unlikely kind of poem, Beaumont felt impelled to include some political satire. When some four years later Beaumont tried to write a play, he reached back to *Salmacis* and the impulses behind it—including the political—to get himself started.

PRIVATE THEATERS AND POLITICS

The early stages of Beaumont and Fletcher's dramatic careers have been obscured by an oft-cited passage in Dryden's *Essays of Dramatic Poesy* of 1668: "The first play that brought Fletcher and . . . [Beaumont] in esteem was their *Philaster*: for before that, they had written two or three very unsuccessfully."[7] For a statement made sixty years after the fact, it was reasonably accurate. It is certain that *The Knight of the Burning Pestle* (1607) and *The Faithful Shepherdess* (1608–9) failed initially, and that *Philaster* (1608–10) was very successful. But between their earliest work, *The Woman Hater* (1606), and *Philaster* there are about four years to account for. Some or all of as many as eight plays written together or separately may be assigned to this interval. In this group with varying degrees of certainty may be placed (in addition to those previously mentioned) *Cupid's Revenge* (1607–8), *The Scornful Lady* (1608–10), and *The Captain* (1609–12). There are reasons for believing that a first version of *Love's Cure* was written during this period, and that if Beaumont wrote *Madon*, a lost play attributed to him, it would have been composed then.[8] Nor were all these plays

---

[6] See *Mythology and the Renaissance Tradition*, 2d ed. (New York, [1932] 1963), p. 185. Keach, *Elizabethan Erotic Narratives*, p. 204, rightly calls this episode "the most conspicuously topical of any of the satirical episodes in the Elizabethan epyllion."

[7] *Essays of John Dryden*, ed. W. P. Ker (Oxford, 1900), 1:81.

[8] For the *Love's Cure* problem see George Walton Williams's introduction to his edi-

failures; on the evidence of the ten quartos published in the seventeenth century, perhaps the most objective measure of such matters, *The Scornful Lady* was the most successful play in the canon.

As a result of Dryden's statement most commentators treat *Philaster* as the start rather than what it was, the climax of a series of dramatic efforts. Furthermore, Dryden obscures the fact that although this most famous of collaborations achieved its greatest success with Shakespeare's "public" acting company, the King's Men, it grew to maturity among the child actors. Whether or not this is a fact of much significance has been a topic of scholarly controversy. No one would deny the large difference between the private and public plays of the sixteenth century, between the excessively witty, highly stylized court allegories of Lyly and the "rattling thunderclaps" of Marlowe and Kyd. In about 1590 the private theaters were closed by the government, apparently for their involvement in the "Martin Marprelate" controversy. When they reopened in about 1600, theatrical conditions had changed in several important respects. The playwrights recruited for the new theaters—Chapman, Jonson, Middleton, Marston—had all, if only briefly, served apprenticeships in the far-from-courtly stable of Henslowe's hacks. Jonson, in fact, continued to write for both kinds of theaters without discernible differences among his plays. Marston's *Malcontent*, written originally for boys, was staged by the King's Men with only minor alterations, and Dekker's *Satiromastix*, originally a public play, had private performances. Such interchangeability is unthinkable for the plays of Lyly and Kyd.

As important as the public theater experience for the new generation of private theater playwrights was a subtle change in the makeup of their audience. In Alfred Harbage's words, the majority of the public audience were "plain people" while the private audience "was a sector of the London playgoing public, which isolated itself on particular occasions and required plays calculated to its particular meridian."[9] Harbage's description of the character of this second-generation private theater audience is the most satisfactory anyone has managed to construct:

> So far as the majority of its members can be placed in any familiar structure of society, they were the precariously well-to-do. Only a tiny minority of them, even in Lyly's time, could have been officially courtiers, but their eyes turned toward Whitehall. They enjoyed gossip about the court and satire upon its members, particularized if possible but generalized if

tion of the play for Fredson Bowers, gen. ed., *The Dramatic Works in the Beaumont and Fletcher Canon* (Cambridge, Eng., 1966–), 3:3–7; for *Madon*, see E. K. Chambers, *The Elizabethan Stage* (Oxford, 1923), 3:233.

[9] *Shakespeare and the Rival Traditions* (New York, 1952), p. 56.

not. . . . The coterie audience was an amalgam of fashionable and academic elements, socially and intellectually self-conscious. Of the "pub-
lics" available in England at the time, it was the most *avant-garde*, the
most sophisticated, the most interested in art as art. One can picture the
young Elizabethan intellectuals fingering the newer things in the book-
stalls before dropping into the nearby theatre: many of them must have
come from the direction of Gray's Inn, Lincoln's Inn, the Middle and
Inner Temples, and the lodging houses in Westminster, or along Fleet
Street and the Strand.[10]

Harbage quietly corrects certain widespread misconceptions about
this audience. First, it is not accurate to say that the private theaters
had a primarily courtly ambiance in the London of 1600. In the period since there had last been private theaters, the percentage of
courtiers would have been diminished by the influx of affluent and
educated people flocking to the nation's center of fashion, opportunity, and vitality. This audience was much concerned with the court,
but only as interested, sometimes critical, outsiders. Second, at the
private theaters there existed the sort of artistic "sophistication" often
ascribed to the court. A few courtiers like Fulke Greville and the earl
of Arundel were genuinely knowledgeable, but for the majority artistic matters were of secondary importance. Then as now "aesthetes"
came from an unconventional segment of the bourgeoisie.

Clearly the audiences of the two theaters differed. What of the
plays they were offered? The most extensive attempt to prove that
they were radically different remains Harbage's *Shakespeare and the
Rival Traditions* of 1952. In Harbage's view, the private playwrights
waged a remarkably unified and effective war on the traditional English attitudes portrayed at the public theaters, most notably by
Shakespeare. He argues this in successive chapters titled "The Divine
Plan," "The Dignity of Man," "Sexual Behavior," "Wedded Love," and
"The Commonweal." Probably no one was better qualified than Alfred Harbage to write the definitive study on this subject, but what
he produced is a puzzlingly shrill and unremitting attack on the private theater plays and playwrights, on literary coteries, on avant-
garde modern literature (even including a barely disguised parodic
description of Joyce's *Ulysses*). Much of Harbage's argument is unper-
suasive because, as he himself acknowledges, "the scope of the present study has prevented the pursuit of ramifications and the preser-
vation of nice distinctions."[11] He insists on scoring points through
rhetoric rather than argumentation and by a persistent wrenching of

[10] Ibid.
[11] Ibid., p. 301.

passages from context, often exaggerating alleged indecencies and unorthodoxies in "coterie" writers and exonerating the same sort of thing in Shakespeare.

It is unfortunate that Harbage chose to present his case in such a polemical manner because, if scaled down with a multitude of qualifications, the fact remains that there were many clear differences between the two kinds of theaters. As Marco Mincoff points out:

> [The private theaters had] the most advanced and fashionable writers of the day. . . . It was here that the most biting satire and the crassest realism were served to an audience from which the groundlings were certainly eliminated and . . . the lower class of citizen too. . . . Yet there is no hint of the court about these plays, nothing of the pastoral that Lyly had once fostered at Paul's, or of Sidney's *Arcadia*. The life depicted centres in the city, and the aristocracy is quite as much an object of satire as the citizens.[12]

This much may be admitted, but Mincoff goes on to claim that the private theaters represented "a movement of bourgeois intellectuals distinctly reminiscent of Bloomsbury during the nineteen twenties." They perceived the Crown "with its monopolies and prerogatives" as their antagonist. He believes that the court noticed this animosity and the concomitant adherence of the public theater companies to more conservative values and attitudes. He cites as evidence the fact that from 1601 to 1610, when the children's theaters were at their height, "the King's Men appeared at Court nearly twice as often as all the remaining companies together" with 103 performances; the Prince's Men, next favorite, had 33 appearances, and the Queen's Men had 15. During the same period, according to Mincoff's calculations, the Revels Children and Paul's Boys between them were invited to perform only 23 plays at court (pp. 5–6).

Mincoff's claim that the private theaters were the mouthpiece of some kind of "oppositionist" movement against the Crown is too extreme. But a scaled-down version of it is echoed by many contemporary statements and records. For example, the playwright Thomas Heywood in 1607 describes the private theaters as

> inveighing against the state, the court, the law, the citty and their governements, with the particularizing of private men's humors (yet alive) noble-men, and others: . . . committing their bitternesse, and liberall in-

---

[12] "The Social Background of Beaumont and Fletcher," in *English Miscellany: A Symposium of History, Literature, and the Arts* 1 (1950): 3. Page numbers of subsequent references to this article are noted parenthetically in the text.

vectives against all estates, to the mouthes of children, supposing their
juniority to be a priviledge for any rayling, be it never so violent.[13]

Heywood is writing to make it clear that the men's companies do not
indulge in this kind of disorderly activity. As another public play
stresses, not from the men but from the boys did one hear "dark sen-
tences, / Pleasing to factious brains; / And every other where place
me a jest, / Whose high abuse shall more torment than blows."[14] During the years when Beaumont and Fletcher were serving their dramatic apprenticeship at the private theaters, overwhelming evidence
suggests that factious, dissident, pungent criticism of various aspects
of the established order was the stock in trade of the private theaters.
Sometimes the criticisms were very small: jokes against knights,
Scotchmen, monopolies, and the like. Sometimes it was the sort of
traditional anticourt material that had been in circulation since the
Middle Ages. Sometimes it reflected new currents in continental political thinking about the role of princes and the legitimacy of tyrannicide.

In a few cases the private companies produced *drames à clef* that
endangered not only their acting companies but their own lives.
About John Day's *The Ile of Gulls* of 1606 one M.P. wrote, "At this
time [ca. February 1606] was much speech [in the House of Com-
mons] of a play in the Black Friars, where, in the 'Isle of Gulls,' from
the highest to the lowest, all men's parts were acted of two diverse
nations."[15] The degree of offensiveness of the play is not completely
clear from the printed text. Perhaps it was the children's additions in
performance that caused "sundry [to be] . . . committed to Bride-
well."[16] Even in the printed text, however, it does not take much
imagination to find passages that touch on the king's dishonest favorites, on the Scots, on homosexuality at court, and on a very foolish
sovereign. Day also inserts an extended, completely undramatic list
of specific "grievances," all on contemporary problems, that are described as contrary to "the byas of true and pristine government":

> Marchandise . . . through the avarice of purchasing Officers, is rackt
> with such unmercifull Impost that the very name of Traffique growes
> odious even to the professor. . . . Townes so opprest for want of wonted
> and naturall libertie, as that the native Inhabitants seeme Slaves & the

---

[13] *Apology for Actors*, quoted by Chambers, *Elizabethan Stage*, 4:253–54. Chambers
shows that it was probably written in 1607 and later touched up.

[14] Epilogue to *Mucedorus* (1610), *Drama of the English Renaissance*, ed. Russell Fraser
and Norman Rabkin (New York, 1976), 1:480, ll. 40–43.

[15] Chambers, *Elizabethan Stage*, 3:286.

[16] Ibid.

Forrayners free Denizens. . . . Offices so bought and sould that, before the purchaser can be sayd to be placed in his Office, he is againe by his covetous Patrone displac't. . . . Common Riots, Rapes and wilfull Homicide in great mens followers not onely not punished, but in a manner countenaunced and aplauded.[17]

This is primitive political propaganda, almost like a WPA play of the 1930s and born out of a similar sense of the uses of art.

But Day's play was tame compared with two productions by the children at Blackfriars in 1608. Chapman's direct rendition of recent French history in his *The Tragedy of Biron* offended the French ambassador, causing the imprisonment of authors and players and the closing of all the theaters. Another play by the same company is lost, all evidence of it apparently destroyed for reasons that the account by the French ambassador de la Boderie makes obvious:

ilz [the children] avoient dépêché leur Roi, sa mine d'Escosse, et tous ses favorits d'une estrange sorte; car apres luy avoir fait dépiter le ciel sur le vol d'un oyseau, et faict battre un gentilhomme pour avoir rompu ses chiens, ils le dépeignoient ivre pour le moins une fois le jour.[18]

A child playing the king himself, cursing, striking a gentleman, drunken: as many in a Blackfriars audience would know, none of these antics was invented. It is not surprising that when the play was brought to the attention of James, he "vowed" (in the words of a contemporary) that the children of Blackfriars "should never play more, but should first begg their bred and he wold have his vow performed." The company was dissolved and the "maker" was punished.[19]

Throughout their brief and disorderly history the private theaters entertained their customers with bird bolts and an occasional cannon bullet, "carping both at Court, Cittie, and countrie," as someone said about the most consistently troublesome of the private theater playwrights, John Marston.[20] It is difficult to estimate how much these theater companies were motivated by the various political ideologies—"civic humanism," "classical republicanism," "Neo-Stoicism,"

[17] *The Works of John Day*, ed. A. H. Bullen (London, 1881), p. 60.

[18] Quoted in Chambers, *Elizabethan Stage*, 2:53. "They [the children's acting company] jested at their king, at his Scottish face, and at all his uncouth favorites; for after having made him curse the heavens just because of the flight of a bird, and after having him beat a gentleman for injuring his dogs, they represented him as drunk at least once a day." Chambers misunderstood "sa mine d'Escosse," believing it referred to James's ill-fated effort to mine silver in Scotland.

[19] Ibid., 53–54.

[20] Anthony Nixon, *The Blacke Yeare* (London, 1606), sig. B2^r.

"anti-Divine Right Common Law Parliamentarianism" (to invent a new term), and so forth—that were being discussed by the learned and thoughtful. It is difficult to know how many of them considered themselves to be or were influenced by people who might be labeled recusants or Puritans or "Younger Sons" or "Alienated Intellectuals" or "Country House Radicals" or "Mere Gentleman" or any of the various groups and subgroups whose alienation from the Stuarts contributed to the Great Rebellion. Something serious must have motivated the playwrights and backers of the private theaters to speak out with a clear knowledge of what breaking the libel laws might cost them: the loss of their ears and the slitting of their noses.

Marston as Private Theater Playwright

To pursue further the question of what might impel someone to be a private theater playwright, it is useful to consider the writer most deeply implicated in the movement, John Marston. When the theater at St. Paul's was reopened in about 1600, the choirmaster Thomas Gyles was the ostensible head of the operation. He had held the managing position when the Paul's Boys last performed in the 1580s—when almost every play produced was written by John Lyly, whom Gabriel Harvey described as "the Vicemaster of Poules, and the Foolemaster of the Theater."[21] These punning insults suggest that Lyly was the professional theatrical man on whom the musician Gyles depended to compose and produce the plays for his choirboys.

When Paul's was reopened, Gyles would once again have required a "vicemaster" to serve as his theatrical advisor. The evidence suggests to me that this role (unofficial, I stress) was initially filled by John Marston. At first the Paul's company seems to have been virtually a private preserve for Marston's plays. His *Jack Drum's Entertainment, Antonio and Mellida, Antonio's Revenge*, and possibly also *What You Will* and *Satiromastix* (with Dekker) were performed there in the first few years of the decade. No other playwright can definitely be connected with Paul's at that time. In his prologues and in the plays themselves, Marston expresses a degree of involvement in the fortunes of the theater company that extends beyond mere concern for the acceptance of his own work. He praises inordinately the new audience composed of "Select, and most respected Auditours,"[22] promises them a new kind of antiromantic drama free from the "mouldy

[21] Quoted by Michael Shapiro, *Children of the Revels: the Boy Companies of Shakespeare's Time and Their Plays* (New York, 1977), p. 17.

[22] *Antonio and Mellida* in *The Plays of John Marston*, ed. H. Harvey Wood (Edinburgh, 1934–39), 1:11.

fopperies of stale Poetry, / Unpossible drie mustie Fictions,"[23] ap-
plauds the acting of the children, and gives assurances that "the Children of *Powles* . . . in time will do it hansomely."[24] In his hope that
"the Boyes / Will come one day into the Court of requests" (that is,
give performances at court),[25] he reveals personal concern for the
economic success of the enterprise. Marston's later history strength-
ens the possibility that his connection with Paul's went beyond playwriting. For whatever reason, he left Paul's and by investing one hundred pounds became a one-sixth shareholder in the Queen's Revels
Company at Blackfriars, for which he also wrote his subsequent plays.
Uniquely, Marston was a Jacobean playwright possessed of capital,
and he was willing to invest it in a theatrical enterprise. Chambers
attributes the daring political satire for which the Queen's Revels became notorious to Marston's new, influential position.[26] The adver-
sarial policies of the children's theaters make no sense, in my opinion,
if (as Harbage felt) they were organizations solely devoted to money-
making. Economically, they were always unprofitable, and the course
they persisted in following was a hazardous one. Is it not plausible to
assume for these theaters and for Marston himself the same mixture
of motives that is involved in most new artistic ventures—that along
with economic there were aesthetic, ideological, perhaps even idealistic motives?

Granting that, it must be admitted that it is not clear what precisely
drove Marston. One of the few indications appears in the preface to
The Malcontent, where he says that his "free understanding" leads him
to cast "disgrace . . . on those, whose unquiet studies labor innovation,
contempt of holy policie, reverent comely superioritie, and establisht
unity."[27] This, I take it, is his way of expressing concern at Jacobean
assaults on traditional English customs and institutions. Like Beaumont's, Marston's father was an important and wealthy Inns of Court
lawyer, and Marston himself spent some years at the Middle Temple.
Perhaps this background led him to respect the common law and
those in Parliament who were using it as a tool against innovation.
What is certain is that Marston was endowed with a singular pugnac-
ity. As early as 1599 in his verse satire *The Scourge of Villainy* he proclaimed that he would denounce vice wherever he saw it, come what
may. His "satyrick vaine," he said, will not be "muzled": "No gloomy

[23] *Jack Drum's Entertainment*, ibid., 3:179.
[24] Ibid., 234.
[25] Ibid.
[26] *Elizabethan Stage*, 2:51.
[27] *Plays of Marston*, ed. Wood, 1:139.

Juvenall, / Though to thy fortunes I disastrous fall."[28] This bit of
youthful bravado proved prophetic. Throughout his career Marston
was unremittingly obstreperous: two volumes of his satires were publicly burned, and he was imprisoned twice for plays he had written.
Eventually, it appears, he was evicted from the theater for offenses
against the king himself, since he seems to have been the author of
the satiric play about James that has survived only in the description
by the French ambassador quoted earlier.[29] Whatever his motives,
Marston devoted his career as a writer to speaking freely about what
he apparently perceived to be a "world . . . turnde upside downe."[30]

When Marston broke his father's heart by refusing to study the law
and becoming a dramatist in 1598, his social position and economic
independence set him apart from the other professional playwrights.
His willingness to enter the theater legitimatized a much-reviled profession and created a precedent for men of comparable position, notably Beaumont and Fletcher. To the young writers as they were
about to launch their careers at the private theaters, this somewhat
older man, with whom they shared so much in background, beliefs,
and values, must have seemed an attractive model, to be imitated
warily.[31]

[28] *The Poems of John Marston,* ed. Arnold Davenport (Liverpool, 1961), p. 117, ll. 193–
96.
[29] See my *John Marston of the Middle Temple* (Cambridge, Mass., 1969), pp. 256–57,
for the details of Marston's apparently enforced conversion from playwright to cleric.
[30] *The Malcontent,* in Wood, *Plays of Marston,* 1:177.
[31] In his second verse letter to Jonson (discussed in chapter 1), Beaumont seems to
be alluding to the last act in Marston's playwriting career. In presenting his text of the
poem, E. K. Chambers, *William Shakespeare* (Oxford, 1930), 2:223, proposed the date
"ca. 1615," but because of Beaumont's stroke and Pestell's assertions discussed in chapter 1, no date of composition after Beaumont's poem to Clifton in 1613 is possible. I
would tentatively suggest a date between June 1608 and late 1609 based on what I
believe to be a reference by Beaumont in the following lines to the climactic event in
Marston's artistic career:

> hath not his state almost as wretched beene
> as his, that is ordainde to write the geinne
> after the fawne, and fleere shall bee? as sure
> some one there is allotted to endure that Cross.
>
> (ibid., ll. 29–33)

I have restored the original final word in line 30 because Chambers' emendation of
"grinne" is unnecessary. "Geinne," meaning "fetter" or "rack," fits the interpretation I
suggest, but even if "grinne" is insisted on, something like the same meaning results
since "grinne" can mean "snare" or "halter." (There is no recorded use of "grin" as a
substantive before 1635.) Marston's *Fawn* and Sharpham's *Fleire* (alluded to by Beaumont in lines 30 and 31) cannot be dated later than 1606, already suggesting a date

The Inefficiency and Unpredictability of Jacobean Theatrical Censorship

Most scholars of Jacobean censorship and theatrical regulation do not believe political dissidence was a significant aspect of the Jacobean stage. They tend to agree that "the control of the drama by James, his family, and his immediate Court advisers" was nearly absolute.[32] I do not dispute this general conclusion, but the orthodox view of the system, at least during the Jacobean period, as a smooth-running, terrifying instrument of conformity oversimplifies a complicated and often confusing situation. In fact, serious violations of the standards and regulations of the Master of the Revels and the Privy Council for drama occurred intermittently throughout the Jacobean period and went unpunished. The Venetian ambassador went so far as to say, "In this country . . . the comedians have absolute liberty to say whatever they wish against anyone soever."[33] The censors' regulations were enforced inconsistently or could be bypassed, there is evidence of divided authority and disorganized administration, and sometimes the censors' superiors (for example, the Lord Chamberlain, the earl

---

nearer to the time when such allusions would be timely. In June 1608 a John Marston was committed to Newgate. Chambers (*Elizabethan Stage*, 3:428) plausibly conjectures that this was the playwright and that he was punished for the satiric play at Blackfriars that depicts King James in very unflattering situations. At the opening of the verse letter under discussion Beaumont announces that he is not writing it "to showe / my witt against the State" (1–2), perhaps suggesting that this is a perilous activity as recently proved. Marston was frequently outspoken, and it would appear that he eventually suffered for it; it is probable that behind his decision to enter the church was some sort of official ultimatum. In September 1609—surprisingly, in light of his former activities and attitudes—he was ordained a deacon, and in December he became a priest. In the lines quoted above Beaumont, I suggest, is speaking to Jonson in guarded language about the wretched future life of a mutual friend. He had written *The Fawn* (a political play, as I have argued elsewhere), a fellow Middle Templar Sharpham had written another, *The Fleire*, and now that Marston is ordained, he can write about the rack (which can refer both to the torture instrument and to his involuntary servitude in the church). It is a recent calamity that this man must learn to bear. As for Beaumont's certainty that someone is "allotted to endure / that Cross," John Davies in his epigram on Marston in *The Scourge of Folly* (1610) uses the same language when he describes Marston's enforced change of muses as a blessed cross. Chambers finds a reference in ll. 24–27 to installations in the Order of the Garter in 1613 or 1615, but an installation occurred in May 1608, a date that fits well with my June 1608 terminus a quo.

[32] Glynn Wickham, *Early English Stages 1300–1600* (London, 1959–), vol. 2, part 1, p. 94. See also Gerald E. Bentley, *The Profession of Dramatist in Shakespeare's Time* (Princeton, N.J., 1971); Fredrick S. Siebert, *Freedom of the Press in England, 1476–1776* (Urbana, Ill., 1952); Russell Fraser, *The War against Poetry* (Princeton, N.J., 1970).

[33] *Calendar of State Papers and Manuscripts Relating to English Affairs Existing in the Archives and Collection of Venice*, ed. Allen B. Hinds, vol. 16 (London, 1910), p. 111.

of Pembroke, in *The Game of Chess* episode) exploited the gaps in the
system for their own political purposes. Thus it is unjustifiable to dis-
pose a priori of a political interpretation of a Jacobean play. It is hard
to deny that Victorian scholars overdid matters, seeing an earl of Essex or a Mary, Queen of Scots, behind every arras, but it needs to be
stressed that particularly during the 1600s when the children's companies were thriving, the censors' rules could be and were violated
with some impunity.[34]

Sex and Food at Court: *The Woman Hater*

It was thus within the private theater tradition and perhaps partially
inspired by it that Beaumont and Fletcher began their dramatic careers with a court satire. In a manner prefigured by *Salmacis*, satire
of "great men" occurs in the opening moment of the earliest surviving play in the Beaumont and Fletcher canon, *The Woman Hater* of
1606.[35] A duke asks two courtiers why they think that he would be
awake at four in the morning. After several guesses that assume that
dukes would be concerned with urgent public matters, the ruler reveals that his reason is

> Waightier farre:
> You are my friendes, and you shall have the cause;
> I breake my sleepes thus soone to see a wench.
>
> (1.1.27–29)[36]

The suspense before coming out with "wench" is reminiscent of Jupiter's delaying the admission that Salmacis was "nak'd." It seems that
Beaumont, hesitant in his first moment as a playwright, reached for
his old poem to get him started. When the duke is told that it is four
in the morning, he responds:

> Is it so much, and yet the morne not up?
> See yonder where the shamfac'd maiden comes

---

[34] See my " 'The Comedians' Liberty:' Censorship of the Jacobean Stage Reconsidered," *English Literary Renaissance*, 16 (1986): 123–38, for an extended defense of these
assertions.

[35] The Stationers Register entry of 1606 says it was "lately acted by the Children of
Powles." It was first published anonymously in 1607, and its prologue refers to one
author. The second quarto of 1648 assigns the play to Fletcher; a reissue of this quarto
in 1649 gives it to Beaumont and Fletcher. Cyrus Hoy, *Studies in Bibliography* 11 (1958):
98–99, sees it as substantially by Beaumont with revisions by Fletcher in five scenes;
George Walton Williams in his edition for Bowers, *Dramatic Works*, assigns important
additional scenes to Fletcher (1:151). I am treating the play as a collaboration.

[36] Quotations in the text are from the edition by George Walton Williams, cited
above.

Into our sight, how gently doeth shee slide,
Hiding her chaste cheekes, like a modest Bride,
With a red vaile of blushes; as is shee,
Even such all modest vertuous women be.

(1.1.3–8)

In this speech are a number of precise verbal echoes of lines 597–602 of *Salmacis*, and the duke's speech ending the first scene is constructed from other passages in the poem (1–12, 576). There is no justification for the duke's lyrical language, and very soon Beaumont feels at ease with a plainer blank verse. It is revealing of the way Beaumont's mind worked that in his earliest moment as a dramatist he used Jupiter as a model for the duke: both are philandering "great men" and objects of satire.

But Beaumont needed more than an old poem to launch him into the alien territory of the theater. In the title figure Gondarino and the gourmet Lazarello, his counterpart in the subplot, *The Woman Hater* displays an obvious debt to Ben Jonson's humors characterizations. The indebtedness to John Marston, still a member of the Middle Temple and an active dramatist when Beaumont was beginning, is so pervasive that it would be more accurate to call *The Woman Hater* "Jonsonian" as filtered through and modified by Marston. There are echoes of at least six of Marston's works, particularly *The Dutch Courtesan*.[37] From this play the authors borrowed the name of the prostitute (Francischina), the pursuit of a succulent fish, and the manner in which the double plot is linked (in each part a character is led to believe he is going to be executed). The model for the heroine Oriana, in part at least, was Marston's virtuous but "liberated" Crispinella, an outspoken advocate of frank speech: "lets neere be ashamed to speake what we be not ashamd to thinke, I dare as boldly speake venery as think venery."[38] These and similar sentiments, sometimes adopted verbatim from Montaigne's "Upon Some Verses of Virgil" in Florio's translation, helped to shape characters in several of Marston's plays: Dulcimel in *The Fawn*, the title figure of the tragedy *Sophonisba*, as well as Crispinella. Oriana clearly echoes the substance of Crispinella's sentiments on frank speech, as do two of Fletcher's later heroines. She is thus the first in a long line of bold, open, unconstrained Beaumont and Fletcher heroines who bear the mark of Montaigne and Crispinella, even when not using their words.[39]

---

[37] I also detect touches from *Pigmalion's Image*, *Sophonisba*, *The Scourge of Villainy*, *The Fawn*, and *The Malcontent*.

[38] *The Dutch Courtesan*, in Wood, *Plays of Marston*, 2:98.

[39] Among the most prominent are Maria in *The Woman's Prize*, Lillia Bianca in *The*

But perhaps the most important similarity in *The Woman Hater* to Marston's work is the pervasive political satire. The prologue assures that there will be no "fit matter to feed his————mallice on" (the dash presumably standing for some such word as "Majesty's") and that the play does not contain the sort of satire that will cause the author "the dear losse of his eares." Then comes the sort of negative-enwrapped double entendre that couldn't quite cost the authors their ears:

> But you shall not find in it [this play] the ordinarie and over-worne trade
> of jeasting at Lordes and
> > Courtiers, and Citizens, without taxation of any particular or
> > new vice by them found out, but at the persons of them:
> > such, he that made this, thinkes vile; and for his
> > owne part vowes, That hee did never thinke, but
> > that a Lord borne might bee a wise man,
> > and a Courtier an
> > honest man.[40]

Beginning as the conventional disavowal by satirists of ad hominem intent, the patent irony of "never" in the fourth-from-last line and perhaps some sort of wry tonal diminuendo suggested by the arrangement of the words on the page cast doubt on the possibility of discovering a wise lord or an honest courtier.

From its earliest moment *The Woman Hater* shows no wise lords or honest courtiers—quite the contrary. The duke, who describes himself as "a patterne for all Princes [and] a loving Prince," admits he is not awake at four in the morning vigilantly investigating "some waightie State plot" or trying "to cure / Some strange corruptions in the common wealth" (1.1.16, 9, 11–12). He is doing something "Waightier farre": pursuing "a wench" (1.1.27–29). The duke is equally amoral and candid about his policy on awards and preferment, and the authors are careful to frame him as a general representative of his breed:

> We Princes do use, to prefer many for nothing, and to take particular
> and free knowledge, almost in the nature of acquaintance of many;
> whome we do use only for our pleasures, and do give largely to num-

---

Wild Goose Chase, Evanthe in *A Wife for a Month*, and Celia in *The Humorous Lieutenant*. These female heroines had something to do with Fletcher's success, if one is to believe the prologue to the second issue (1649) of the second quarto of *The Woman Hater*, addressed to women, which says that Fletcher "to the Stars, your Sex did raise; / For which, full Twenty yeares, he wore the Bayes" (1:236, ll. 23–24).

[40] P. 157, ll. 18–26. Williams's edition is the first modern version that retains the visual arrangement (reproduced above) of the last seven lines of the prologue of the first quarto of 1607.

beres; more out of pollicy, to be thought liberall, and by that meanes to make the people strive to deserve our love; then to reward any particular desert of theirs, to whom we give. (1.1.63–68)

In the same shameless vein he admits that he enjoys the flattery a prince receives (1.1.77–82). Later one learns that in this court a man may be selected as the favorite "for beeing an excellent Farrier, for playing well at Span-counter, or sticking knives in walles, for being impudent, or for nothing"—or for having "the face to bee a favorite on the suddaine" (1.3.147–49). Lacking these attributes, he can, of course, purchase a knighthood if he has enough money (2.1.158–65). It is true that almost all the topics in *The Woman Hater* can be found in Tudor satire from at least the time of Skelton. But the mixture and emphasis of the elements in *The Woman Hater* have a special Jacobean flavor. At a time when the reigning monarch was notorious for his susceptibility to flattery, his reckless and irresponsible awarding of titles, land, and money, and his taste for handsome faces "on the suddaine," Beaumont and Fletcher began their dramatic career with their eyes on a particular court while keeping the language general enough to avoid "his———mallice."

The two courtiers whom the duke addresses at the play's opening have been special beneficiaries of his frivolous policies. One was "made a Lord at the request of some of his friendes for his wives sake" (2.1.144–45); the other was awarded a knighthood "for wearing of red breeches" (2.1.153–54). Later the dangerous consequences of the duke's games are made plain. The idiotic, would-be politic statesman Lord Lucio, whose wife obtained his lordship, believes without question the accusations of some Tacitean-Jacobean "intelligencers" against a complete innocent. In this comedy the charges are easily dismissed, but the accompanying lecture by the virtuous Count Valore against the employment of such tactics has an unmistakable authorial ring to it: "our healthfull state needes no such Leeches to suck out her bl9ud" (5.2.102–3).

It is difficult to isolate particular criticisms of the court from the flow of the action. Whatever the apparent topic—whether it involves the hater of women of the main plot or the lover of food of the subplot—the authors manage to connect it to some aspect of courtly depravity. When the gourmet-courtier lists the various kinds of "hands" that have *not* touched the succulent fishhead he is avidly pursuing, he lists as a matter of course the "Court hand, / Whom his owne naturall filth, or change of aire, / Hath bedeckt with scabs" (1.3.224–26). Again, in the vein of Beaumont's elegy on Lady Markham, no lady in the court has "so full an eie, so sweet a breath, / So softe and white a flesh" as his fishhead (3.2.66–67). One courtier fears damage to his reputation if he is discovered in a brothel, but his servant urges him to "enter, for ye can know nothing here, that the Court is ignorant of, onely the more eyes shall looke upon yee, for there [the court] they winck one at anothers faults" (4.2.107–9). Another courtier has gained a reputation for "wit in the Court" by making "fine jests upon country people in progresse time" (3.2.56–58). By sheer accumulation the court becomes the muckhill on which all men's vices are cast.

Through synecdoche the court takes on the appearance of a Mandevillian land of unnatural monsters. Among the "fine sights" one may see at court are

> many faces of mans making, for you shall find very fewe as God left them: and you shall see many legges too; amongst the rest you shall behould one payre, the feete of which, were in times past sockelesse, but are now through the change of time (that alters all thinges) very strangely become the legges of a Knight and a Courtier: another payre you shall see, that were heire apparant legges to a Glover, these legges hope shortly to be honourable; when they passe by they will bowe, and the mouth to these legges, will seeme to offer you some Courtship. (1.3.12–21)

This passage has the ring of specific, personal satire. Although too early to be alluding to the future duke of Buckingham, legs could take one very far at James's court, as William Larkin's portrait of Villiers at the National Portrait Gallery emphasizes.

But according to the authors it is the stomach that has highest importance for the courtier himself. Such is the implication of the subplot about Lazarello. He is described as "the hungry courtier" in the subtitle to the 1649 quarto, but the dramatis personae of that edition characterizes him more accurately as a "Voluptuous Smell-feast" (p. 237), for he is "a gentleman, well seene, deeply read, and throughly grounded in the hidden knowledge of all sallets and pothearbs whatsoever" (2.1.252–54). When he learns that the duke has received as a present the head of an umbrano, a fish of legendary delicacy, he dedicates his life to obtaining a taste of it. He pursues it from house to house as it is sent first to the General Gondarino, the "woman hater" of the title, then to Gondarino's mercer, then to the mercer's bride-to-be, who resides at a brothel. Finally Lazarello marries one of the prostitutes there in order to achieve his goal.

Lazarello's position as a courtier is stressed from the first mention of his name:

Duke. Lazarello? what is he?
Arrigo. A Courtier my Lord, and one that I wonder your grace knowes

not: for he hath followed your Court, and your last predecessors, from
place to place, any time this seaven yeare.

(1.1.48–51)

Throughout the play Lazarello refers to the court as his home, cour-
tiership as his vocation, and courtiers as his colleagues. I stress this
because to some degree one is made to feel that his actions and passions are representative of his class. When he invokes the assistance
of the "Goddesse of plentie," he promises that he will give an annual
feast

> And to it shall be bidden for thy sake,
> Even al the valiant stomacks in the Court:
> All short-cloak'd Knights, and al crosse-garter'd
>   gentlemen:
> All pumpe and pantofle, foot-cloth riders;
> With all the swarming generation
> Of long stocks, short pain'd hose, and huge stuff'd
>   dublets.

(1.2.22–27)

In his mock-heroic farewell to the court after he believes that he has
failed in his quest for the elusive fishhead, he again suggests that eating is a prime courtly activity:

> Farewell *Millaine*, fare well noble Duke,
> Farewell my fellow Courtiers all, with whome
> I have of yore made many a scrambling meale
> In corners, behind Arasses, on staires,
> And in the action often times have spoild
> Our Dublets and our hose, with liquid stuffe:
> Farewell you lustie archers of the Guard.

(3.3.85–91)[41]

If Lazarello is representative of the court, what of Gondarino, the
virulent, inveterate "woman hater" of the main plot? In a satiric play
by a children's company set at a court where "faces" and "legs" are

---

[41] James D. Knowles finds "parallels between Lazarello's pursuit of the umbrano and
the attempts to reform the royal household by reducing the number of diets" (*Times
Literary Supplement*, Aug. 26, 1988, p. 935). He makes the interesting suggestion that
the play emanates from some kind of "fluid, reformist political climate after 1603,"
about which we have been enlightened by the Jacobean revisionist historians. Beaumont and Fletcher, by this account, would then presumably be supporters or spokes-
men of government policy in this play. But this ignores the relationship between Laz-
arillo and the larger areas of anticourt satire in the play: the duke's irresponsibility and
womanizing, his arbitrary preferment of favorites, the employment of intelligencers.

profitable, Gondarino's unremitting hatred of women might well be touching on the homosexuality and attendant misogyny that had become an important aspect of Jacobean court life. But even the daring childrens' companies ventured into this dangerous area very rarely,[42] and in this play I see only one possible innuendo on that topic:

> *Count.* . . . hee doth hate women for the same cause that I love them.
> *Lazarello.* Whats that?
> *Count.* For that which Apes want: you perceive me Sir?
>
> (2.1.178–80)[43]

I take the count to be saying that his apish, libidinous drives are radically different from the general's. Perhaps "you perceive me Sir" was accompanied by a gesture to clarify these admittedly cryptic words.

But the satire in *The Woman Hater* is not exclusively about the court. Somebody remarks of Lazarello, "How like an ignorant Poet he talkes" (2.1.266). In his ardent expressions of love for his fishhead, of stoic resignation when he thinks it lost, of philosophical generalizations on human miseries, Lazarello is as much a vehicle for literary as political satire. Obviously his language is overwrought, but the authors see more than pretentious artifice in Lazarello's poetical outbursts. The habitual use of such self-intoxicating language, the play shows, leads to a kind of madness. When Lazarello realizes that the fish has been delivered to the brothel, he inspires himself to action with rhetoric worthy of Aeneas or Hotspur:

> Bee'st thou in hell, rap't by *Proserpina*,
> To be a Rivall in blacke *Plutoes* love:
> Or moves thou in the heavens, a forme divine:
> Lashing the lazie Spheres:
> Or if thou beest return'd to thy first being,
> Thy mother Sea, there will I seeke thee forth,
> Earth, Ayre, nor Fire,
> Nor the blacke shades belowe, shall barre my sight,
> So daring is my powerfull appetite.
>
> (4.2.136–44)

Such uncontrolled ranting is one of the hallmarks of the plays written by Beaumont and Fletcher, both separately and in collaboration. So

---

[42] See Harbage, *Shakespeare and the Rival Traditions*, pp. 211–14. *The Ile of Gulls* (1606, hence precisely contemporary with *The Woman Hater*), by the Children of the Queen's Revels, seems to me to come the closest of any Jacobean play to raising the issue of homosexuality in James's court.

[43] Gondarino did have a wife who had been "slaine" for some "offence" (2.1.118). Although she was dead he still "hated" (2.1.17) her—one assumes from his obsessions that it was for committing adultery.

also are critical comments on its excess offered by pastoral figures whose "honest plaine sence" (2.1.238) has not been corrupted. Here it is Lazarello's servant who responds to his master's travel plans by reminding him, reasonably enough, where he is: "Sir, you may save this long voyage, and take a shorter cut; you have forgot your self, the fish head's here, your owne imaginations have made you mad" (4.2.145–47). His diagnosis is confirmed by what immediately ensues:

> *Lazarello.* Tearme it a jealous furie good my boy.
> *Boy.* Faith Sir tearme it what you will, you must use other tearmes ere you can get it.
>
> (4.2.148–50)

Now the enraptured Lazarello shifts to the heavier beat of tetrameter couplets:

> The lookes of my sweet love are
> faire,
> Fresh and feeding as the Ayre.
>
> (4.2.151–52)

The boy continues to try to bring Lazarello to his senses but cannot stop his verbal autointoxication. Finally Lazarello agrees to marry the whore in order to obtain the fish, his furor poeticus still clearly in control:

> *Lazarello.* . . . I am here
> The happiest wight, that ever set his tooth
> To a deare noveltie: approch my love,
> Come let's goe to knit the true loves knot,
> That never can be broken.
> *Boy.* [*aside*] That is to marry a whore.
> *Lazarello.* When that is done, then will we taste the gift,
> Which Fates have sent, my fortunes up to lift.
> *Boy.* When that is done, you'l begin to repent, upon a full stomacke; but I see, 'tis but a form in destiny, not to be alter'd.
>
> (5.3.73–82)

As is frequently the case in Beaumont and Fletcher's work, one looks to the prose for sense and sanity.

Lazarello is an amusing fool, but in some ways, improbable as it may sound, he is a precursor of a long succession of (so-called) tragi-comic heroes like the title figure of *Philaster* and the ranting King Arbaces of *A King and No King*. His undeviating pursuit of an idée fixe, his passionate, impetuous nature, and his mock-heroic poetry sound like a brilliant parody of these heroes. But if the parody *pre-*

cedes what is parodied, if Lazarello and his near-kin Antonio of the
early collaborative play *The Coxcomb* foreshadow Philaster, may this
not suggest that the creative impulse for that famous hero and some
of his successors had roots in comedy? This is a subject on which I
shall elaborate later.

Returning to the woman hater Gondarino, one first sees him indulging his apparently harmless humor in the privacy of his own
home. The heroine Oriana, forced by a storm to seek refuge there,
soon discerns his bias. She is amused by his absurd excesses, but she
also feels that she must "torment him to madnes . . . [for] his passions
against kind" (2.1.397–98) and thus cure him. Certain that her beauty
is irresistible, her plan is to attract him and then scorn his advances.
Gondarino does not come close to succumbing. Her seemingly lascivious actions confirm his prejudice and inspire a succession of violent
invectives against Oriana's and womankind's lustfulness. In the un-
swerving certainty that Oriana and all women are whores, his
speeches are as out of contact with reality as Lazarello's. But in Gondarino's misogyny there is very little of the witty inventiveness and
variety that Beaumont and Fletcher give their "Voluptuous Smell-
feast." Perhaps in a seventeenth-century audience his scenes would
have mined the same vein of harsh laughter that was stimulated by
visits to the madhouse. In any case, about halfway through the play
the authors radically shift the focus of the plot by transforming Gondarino into a slanderous villain who claims to the duke and Oriana's
brother that she has been his mistress. To substantiate his lie, he
tricks Oriana into residing in a brothel, where she is put to the traditional test: death or dishonor. Naturally she shows herself to be as
pure and brave as she has previously been witty and free; the two
kinds of traits are by implication linked. As a reward for passing the
test, Oriana is given to the duke in marriage (an ambiguous gift from
what we have seen of him), and as punishment for his vile slanders
the heroine is given the opportunity to torture Gondarino one last
time. She unleashes a group of women who kiss him and otherwise
inflame him into another round of antifeminine ranting. Finally, he
is sentenced to exile from womankind, a punishment, as Gondarino
justly observes, "that I would have sworne and doe [swear to]"
(5.4.214) even before Oriana's appearance. His humor is not ex-
pelled. Like Lazarello and most of Beaumont and Fletcher's comic
figures—and unlike Jonson's and Marston's—Gondarino remains un-
touched by the lessons of a would-be tutor.

For a first play *The Woman Hater* is remarkably accomplished. Only
an undeveloped third plot betrays the authors' inexperience in the
form. In it a precursor of Jonson's Subtle, a pandar, convinces a cred-

ulous mercer that by magical powers gained through "learning" he
may marry an heiress. After bilking him of some of his wares, the
pandar marries the mercer to one of the whores from the same
brothel Lazarello obtained his wife.[44] Perhaps the point was to be that
most wives come from the brothel. Hence the woman hater is not
altogether mad: he has simply not left room for the existence of the
exceptional heroic woman like Oriana. But the plot is too slightly developed for such an idea to be felt.

Nonetheless, from the first moments of the prologue one hears a
jointly devised, supremely self-confident voice that knows its audience intimately. It realizes that its members have no patience for anything but "the latest." This audience may not be artistically cultivated,
but it is insistently au courant: "Gentlemen, Inductions are out of
date, and a Prologue in Verse is as stale, as a blacke Velvet Cloake,
and a Bay Garland" (p. 157, ll. 1–2). What did these bright young
collaborators concoct to attract such a jaded, fashion-conscious audi-
tory? It is remarkable how fully they arrived at their general solution
in their first joint effort. Apparently they determined that a kind of
sensational, plot-centered drama that anticipates in many ways what
has come to be called melodrama would be the vehicle that would
enable them to teach and delight. Halfway through this apparently
light humors play nothing seems less probable than its resolution in
the sort of "death or dishonor" scene they constructed for Oriana. It
is even less predictable that Lazarello's "heroic" talk about his beloved
fishhead could be distorted by the "Intelligencers" so that he too
would be threatened with death. In fact, nearly every play in the
Beaumont and Fletcher collaboration—even some comedies (even,
most improbably, *The Knight of the Burning Pestle*)—has similar moments.[45]

On the flexible framework of their protomelodrama Beaumont
and Fletcher were able to hang almost everything they required.
First, their ingenious plotting captivated their audience by the supris-
ing, involving twists and turns of its action. As William Cartwright
aptly described it,

> all stand wondering how
> The thing will be untill it is; which thence
> With fresh delight still cheats, still takes the sence;

---

[44] After he has cheated the mercer, the pandar says, "What you have lost in this, you
may get againe in Alcumie" (5.3.7). Was this small plot the germ of *The Alchemist*
(1610)?

[45] The reader will note that I am not employing the term "tragicomedy." My reasons
for this I defer to a later point.

The whole designe, the shadowes, the lights such
That none can say he shewes or hides too much:
Businesse growes up, ripened by just encrease,
And by as just degrees againe doth cease,
The heats and minutes of affaires are watcht,
And the nice points of time are met, and snatcht:
Nought later then it should, nought comes before,
Chymists, and Calculators doe erre more.[46]

Second, with the audience firmly in their hands, Beaumont and Fletcher were able to attach a metadramatic dimension. In this play, especially, the artifice is emphasized by a pattern of sophisticated allusions to other contemporary plays. The consequent distancing effect made possible criticism of linguistic excess and emotional overreaction. People ought not to act and sound like actors in a play, as Lazarello's "boy" reiterates. Third, the surreal distortion of external reality inherent in melodrama made it, in their version, a powerful moral vehicle. In a dissolute court inhabited by walking stomachs and seductive legs and irresponsible rulers, the only way to retain one's integrity is to accept death as an alternative to dishonor. Almost no one will risk this except, in Beaumont and Fletcher's reiterated view, an occasional resolute woman. The moral and political implications of this extreme vision—that almost everybody associated with a court is corrupt or corrupting—aligned Beaumont and Fletcher with the more radical of the private theater dramatists. We find no good kings, no virtuous courts in their work. Few have been willing to acknowledge a serious basis for these plays, only their capacity to fascinate and thrill. They remain synonymous with vacuous entertainment, "playful" theatricality—in Cartwright's terms, a two hour "delight" but something of a cheat.

[46] Arnold Glover and A. R. Waller, eds., *The Works of Francis Beaumont and John Fletcher* (Cambridge, 1905–12), 1:xxxvii–xxxviii. For another, similar description of Beaumont and Fletcher's plotting, see H. Harington's poem prefatory to *The Wild Goose Chase*, ibid., 4:410.

Chapter Three

FORM AND POLITICS IN *THE KNIGHT OF THE BURNING PESTLE*

INITIAL FAILURE AND PRIVATE THEATER "SOPHISTICATION"

The Beaumont seen so far is in nearly every way a prime example of a cultivated Oxford and Inns of Court litterateur. But through *The Knight of the Burning Pestle* (1607)[1] one glimpses a kind of artist-intellectual more prevalent in contemporary New York than Jacobean London. He reveals himself to be steeped in the "pop" art of ballads, the "schlock" art of bourgeois success plays, and the "junk" art of chivalric romances. He also displays a nearly Shakespearean awareness of the habits of mind and the speech patterns of London burghers. Beyond all this is a formal innovativeness that shapes these disparate materials into a pattern as pleasurable and original as it is profoundly significant. If it was written in eight days (as the publisher's prefatory dedication claims) and by a twenty-two-year-old, *The Knight* has miraculous dimensions as well.

There had been nothing quite like this play, not Peele's *The Old Wive's Tale*, or Jonson's "commentator" plays, or the inductions by Marston or Day. The text makes it clear that *The Knight* was designed for a children's company, hence for an audience often described as "sophisticated." One must picture the audience in 1607 alerted, perhaps, by the title to receive a standard private theater comedy in the best modern manner. The play opens as expected with a prologue formulaically disclaiming any satiric intention. Suddenly a member of the audience, a "citizen," climbs onto the stage and is followed closely by his wife. As everyone knows, the couple interrupts the action, in-

---

[1] E. K. Chambers, *The Elizabethan Stage* (Oxford, 1923), 3:220–21, shows that the play must first have been produced by the Queen's Revels boys' company. The first quarto of 1613 was published anonymously. The second quarto of 1635 attributes it to Beaumont and Fletcher. Most (but not all) scholars give the play to Beaumont alone. Cyrus Hoy, "The Shares of Fletcher and his Collaborators in the Beaumont and Fletcher Canon," *Studies in Bibliography* 11 (1958): 91–92, considers the play the unaided work of Beaumont. I am persuaded of the 1607 date by the intricate network of considerations summarized by Andrew Gurr's edition for Fountainwell Drama Texts (Berkeley, Calif., 1968), pp. 1–3, as well as by those of Brian Gibbons in his preface to the Scolar Press facsimile (1973) of the play; also by Sheldon P. Zitner, ed., *The Knight of the Burning Pestle*, The Revels Plays (Manchester, 1984), pp. 10–12.

sists on producing an absurd, primitive play with their own apprentice in the starring role, and nearly wrecks the "intended" play with
their witless running commentary.

The epigraph from Horace on the title page of the first quarto of
The Knight suggests that the young, inexperienced Beaumont had assumed that he was writing for an audience capable of responding to
something new, but that he found them unable to meet his challenge:

> Quod si
> Iudicium subtile, videndis artibus illud
> Ad libros et ad haec Musarum dona vocares:
> Boeotum in crasso iurares aere natos.[2]

The poet is describing Alexander the Great as someone with "deli-
cate" taste in the visual arts, "but if you'd see how he responded to
books and the Muses' gifts, you'd swear he was born in the thick air
of Boeotia." In allusion to the reception of *The Knight*, "natum" was
changed to "natos," suggesting that the whole audience responded
like insensitive Philistines. The publisher's dedication elaborated on
the epigraph. On first production *The Knight* experienced the fate of
every genuinely avant-garde work: "the wide world . . . for want of
judgement, or not understanding the privy marke of *Ironie* about it
utterly rejected it."[3] Such a result is not surprising, but it is worth
emphasizing because scholars constantly refer to the private theater
audiences as "sophisticated." The nearly simultaneous initial failure
of Fletcher's *The Faithful Shepherdess* indicates that even the best Jacobean audience, like every other one in the history of drama, con-
tained only a small number who could accept and comprehend the
truly new.[4] By the 1630s, presumably, word had circulated about

[2] *The Knight of the Burning Pestle* (London, 1613), sig. A1r. Although Hoy mentions
the epigraph in his edition (cited below), unaccountably he does not print it. The quarto's dedication by Burre to Robert Keysar mentions the play's "father," but nothing
indicates whether Beaumont was involved in the publication of the quarto and hence
in the selection and alteration of the passage from Horace. In favor of Beaumont's
personal responsibility is the fact that the quarto of *Salmacis* also had a Latin epigraph
that was closely tied to the poem.

[3] From the dedication to Robert Keysar by Walter Burre in the edition by Cyrus Hoy
included in *The Dramatic Works in the Beaumont and Fletcher Canon*, Fredson Bowers,
gen. ed. (Cambridge, 1966–), 1:7, l. 6. Subsequent references in the text are to this
edition. Zitner in his edition of *The Knight*, p. 38, also accepts Burre's explanation for
the failure as the most likely. However, in his subsequent remarks he tends to discuss
the citizens as though they were representative members of the audience. My view is
that the failure of *The Knight* derived from Beaumont's having pushed a receptive and
educated audience beyond its aesthetic capacities.

[4] A prologue was inserted in the quarto of 1635 that was appropriated nearly verbatim from Lyly's *Sapho and Phao* (1584) with a significant phrase added. It expresses

what the play was doing, and it achieved some popularity. Since then it has had a steady, if intermittent and largely academic, stage life; in the twentieth century *The Knight of the Burning Pestle* is the only play in the Beaumont and Fletcher canon that is widely admired.[5]

THE "PLAYERS' PLAY"

As with *Don Quixote*, almost every scholarly discussion of *The Knight of the Burning Pestle* begins—and often ends—with the citation of countless sources and analogues to demonstrate that the play is primarily a literary satire.[6] But one's first impression is of an *un*literary rather than a "literary" work—a paradoxical mixture of musical gaiety and angry contentiousness, of naive fancifulness and crass materialism, of an unadorned, bare stage and stage-struck, illusion-filled characters. The essential action is, literally, a continual battle between the players and the "citizens" for possession of the stage. The child players, old professionals that they are, eventually manage to present the play they have promised their audience but only after enduring blatant interruptions from bullying, uncomprehending, vulgar, impolite intruders who, in their turn, get their money's worth by interpolating a running commentary on whatever strikes their fancy and by forcing onto the stage a play of their own "impromptu" devising. One feels in the presence of "reality" rather than of "literature" as one watches the very process of creation—or destruction—of a work of art.

To see what Beaumont's seemingly chaotic form accomplishes, one must try to separate its intertwined components. There is, first, the players' play, "The London Merchant" (as they had planned to call it). It is usually described as a parody of the prodigal son plays that had been having a certain vogue in the Jacobean public theaters.[7] In accordance with the formula, *The Knight of the Burning Pestle* depicts the efforts of the apprentice Jasper to marry Luce, daughter of his master Venturewell. Predictably, this "London Merchant" prefers the suit of a wealthy older man, a buffoon named Humphrey, who makes love to Luce in ludicrous, doggerel couplets. Jasper eventually wins

---

the hope that readers will be "free from unkinde reports, or *mistaking the Authors intention, (who never aymed at any one particular in this Play)*" (ed. Hoy, p. 9). The added words (italicized by me) were probably pro forma, but they suggest unease that the play could still be misconstrued.

[5] See Zitner, ed., *The Knight*, pp. 42–46.

[6] See especially the edition by Herbert S. Murch (New York, 1908).

[7] Beaumont seems even to have borrowed the name of his heroine, "Luce," from a recent example, *The London Prodigal* of 1605.

Venturewell's approval, not by an act that demonstrates his heroism or moral probity but by his wit. He disguises himself as a ghost and terrorizes his master Venturewell into consent.

In the most original and pleasant part of this "main" plot, Beaumont shows that Jasper has acquired his devil-may-care ways from a father similarly contemptuous of bourgeois manners and values. As Jasper's mother says,

> th'art thy fathers owne sonne, of the right bloud of the *Merri-thoughts*, I may curse the time that er'e I knew thy father, he hath spent all his owne, and mine too, and when I tell him of it, he laughes and dances, and sings, and cryes, *A merry heart lives long-a*. And thou art a wast-thrift, and art run away from thy maister. (1.298–303)

Merrythought spends his days joyously singing old ballads while the last of his inherited fortune melts away. His songs make an attractive case for the sort of life he leads:

> 'Tis mirth that fils the veines with bloud,
> More then wine, or sleepe, or food.
> Let each man keepe his heart at ease,
> No man dies of that disease.
> He . . . .
> . . . who ever laughes and sings,
> . . . .
> . . . contented lives for aye,
> The more he laughes, the more he may.
>
> (2.444–57)

Merrythought has boundless faith that the universe will take care of him:

> Not a *Denier* left, and yet my heart leapes; I do wonder yet, as old as I am, that any man will follow a Trade, or serve, that may sing and laugh, and walke the streetes: my wife and both my sonnes are I know not where, I have nothing left, nor know I how to come by meate to supper, yet am I merry still; for I know I shall finde it upon the Table at sixe a clocke, therefore hang Thought. (4.316–21)

Flouting tradition, Beaumont gives the victory to the grasshoppers rather than the ants. Not only does Jasper win Luce, but Merrythought triumphs over his conventional wife and the capitalist Venturewell, both of whom must sing ballads to signify their acquiescence to his way of life.

But the distinction between the two sides in the players' play is not as simple as I have made it. The most extreme instance of how Beaumont complicated matters occurs when Luce manages to escape to Jasper in the forest. Suddenly one perceives a very different landscape; it is the menacing forest where Fletcher set his nearly contemporaneous *The Faithful Shepherdess*. The first hint of a change is the ardent language of the lovers at their reunion, without a trace of Humphrey's burlesque lovemaking. After Luce falls asleep, Beaumont creates a soliloquy for Jasper that almost seems to have been written for another play. The apprentice imagines his beloved dreaming of her imminent sexual fulfillment: "chast delights, imbraces, wishes, / And such new pleasures, as the ravisht soule / Gives to the sences" (3.49–51). As he dwells obsessively on her unique perfections, his orgasmic rapture overwhelms him, leaving him physically depleted:

> Oh my joyes!
> Whither will you transport me? let not
>   fulnesse
> Of my poore buried hopes, come up together,
> And over-charge my spirits: I am weake.
>
>   (3.55–58)

In his impotent condition he succumbs to a mood of insecurity about her love. To test her constancy he draws his sword, awakens Luce, and threatens to kill her. At this point a search party headed by Luce's father overpowers and wounds the "weake" Jasper, takes Luce home, and leaves her lover bereft and humiliated.

Jasper's "test" is a surprising, even outrageous insertion in a burlesque comedy, but no responsible director can dodge its seriousness. The soliloquy that precedes it is too prolonged and the language too resistant to the imposition of comic tones—although, of course, any passage is now fair game for directors searching for novelty.[8] This is not to say that the speech lacks "the privy marke of Ironie"; its pretensions, confusions, and dishonesty mark it as a totally ironic self-indictment:

> Some say (how ever ill) the sea and women
> Are govern'd by the Moone, both ebbe and flow,
> Both full of changes: yet to them that know,

---

[8] One of my few major disagreements with David A. Samuelson's excellent essay, "The Order in Beaumont's *Knight of the Burning Pestle*," *English Literary Renaissance* 9 (1979): 302–18, is with his claim that Jasper's test "introduces a burlesque of the precious lovers. . . . This brief vignette anticipates by a year or so Beaumont and Fletcher's tongue-in-cheek scene between Philaster and Arethusa when 'love lies a-bleeding' " (p. 308). I wish I could detect some burlesque here, and "tongue-in-cheek" does not do justice to the kind of satiric comedy I perceive when Philaster wounds Arethusa.

> And truly judge, these but opinions are,
> And heresies to bring on pleasing warre
> Betweene our tempers, that without these were
> Both void of after-love, and present feare,
> Which are the best of *Cupid*. Oh thou child
> Bred from dispaire, I dare not entertaine thee,
> Having a love without the faults of women,
> And greater in her perfect goods then men:
> Which to make good, and please my selfe the stronger,
> Though certainely I am certaine of her love,
> Il'e try her, that the world and memory
> May sing to after times, her constancie.
>
>   (3.59–73)[9]

Jasper rejects as heresy the view that women are innately changeable, but even the most judicious experts he has read on the subject are willing to concede, he claims, that "pleasing warres" between the sexes on such topics as female inconstancy lead to the pleasures of reconciliation ("after-love") and an apparently vitalizing insecurity ("present feare"). These, in his curious view, are the "best" moments of love. He himself, he asserts, need never entertain the kinds of doubts other men have because his beloved is perfect. But a not-very-privy mark to Jasper's insecure frame of mind appears in his nervous reiterations: earlier he said Luce was "onely faire . . . onely kinde / . . . onely to thee *Jasper*" (54–55). Now to validate ("make good") what he already knows to be true about her perfection ("goods"), to make good her "goods" about which "certainly" he is "certain," he will—thanks to the force of his doubletalk logic—wage a "pleasing warre," testing Luce's fidelity by threatening to murder her! He awakens Luce with sword in hand, and when she realizes what he is planning to do, she reacts with as much love as heroism:

> If thou wilt kill me, smile and do it quickly,
> And let not many deaths appeare before me.
> I am a woman made of feare and love,
> A weake, weake woman, kill not with thy eyes,
> They shoot me through and through. Strike I am ready,
> And dying stil I love thee.
>
>   (3.99–104)

[9] I agree with the elimination by Dyce and later editors (not Hoy) of the exclamation mark after "child" in l. 66. The result is in keeping with the ambiguity of Jasper's attitudes throughout the passage.

The interaction between a cowardly, sadistic, weak man with a sword and a "weake, weake" woman with a heroic spirit momentarily derails this hilarious comedy from its apparent destination.

In case there is any doubt about how one should view Jasper, Beaumont makes him test Luce again by feigning his death and eavesdropping on her reaction while in his coffin. The scene becomes as serious, as out of key with most of the play, as Jasper's forest soliloquy. Without the least mark of irony Luce grieves at length and movingly: "Hast thou deceiv'd me thus, and got before me? / I shall not long bee after" (4.238–39). She concludes with a lovely dirge, if less than wholly true, "*For him that was of men most true*" (4.268). Only then does Jasper climb out of his coffin, his thirst for "positive reinforcement" temporarily satisfied.

It ought to be clear that this action puts Jasper into a different category from that of such perfect and exemplary apprentices as Golding in another sophisticated play on the prodigal son theme, *Eastward Ho!* by Chapman, Jonson, and Marston. Jasper must be placed among the strange "heroes" of Beaumont and Fletcher's most famous romances, where the pulling out of a sword and sometimes its use against a helpless and usually a loving woman is a frequent gesture. Some version of it occurs in *The Faithful Shepherdess*, *Philaster*, *A King and No King*, and *The Maid's Tragedy*, to cite only the most famous instances;[10] the remarkable fact is that such an episode occurs in a play like *The Knight*. At some unconscious level it would seem that Beaumont suspected heroic, widely admired figures of possessing uncontrollable, perverse impulses. With the infinitely open form of *The Knight* Beaumont could pack such feelings into an unlikely receptacle like Jasper without its seeming too implausible.

After his perverse, contorted testing, it is difficult to admire Jasper without strong reservations, even if Luce continues to, and one comes to entertain similar doubts regarding the other protagonist, his father Merrythought. Certainly, his unending mirth is attractive, his songs are one of the pleasantest features of the play, and his responses to adversity are amusing and admirable, but as one watches his automatic, unvarying joviality under all conditions, one comes to realize that Beaumont conceived him as a Jonsonian humors character, afflicted with an overabundance of the sanguine humor. To sing indif-

---

[10] Three other early plays have similar episodes. In *The Woman Hater* Arrigo tests the virtuous Oriana by threatening to rape her at knifepoint (5.4.38). In *Cupid's Revenge* the innocent and loving Urania saves the life of the passive hero Leucippus by receiving the fatal knife stab intended for him. In *The Coxcomb* the pure and loving Viola is nearly raped by her drunken lover and is constantly tested by him.

ferently at the news of his penury or even at the announcement of his shrewish wife's departure from his home is one thing, but one may even feel some sympathy for the contemptible Venturewell when his inquiry about his lost daughter excites nothing but bored impatience from Merrythought: "Il'e heare no more a your daughter, it spoyles my mirth" (2.502–3). And his cool, unruffled response to the announcement of his son's death seems to be carrying a good thing too far.

These qualified responses to the two heroes suggest that nothing in *The Knight* is quite as simple as it is usually described, not even the opposition between the two sets of values that "The London Merchant" dramatizes. As we have seen, in reversing the normal outcome of such plays, the players' play exposes the banality of bourgeois pieties and makes a moral point. Instead of the repentance of the prodigal—actually two, Mr. Merrythought and Jasper—the dutiful, bourgeois characters are converted to a carefree, casual, mirth-filled attitude toward life. Singing triumphs over money-grubbing, the old-fashioned merry-thinking of Mr. Merrythought proves more effective than the careful capitalistic ventures of Venturewell, the London merchant of the original title. But it is characteristic of Beaumont's way that one may also feel when looking at Merrythought that turning all the year into playing holidays may produce a tedious old fool and that Jasper, cunning and resourceful as he shows himself to be, may (like his counterpart Rafe) have read more books—I refer to the "learning" that inspires his test of Luce—than are good for his mental health.

THE INTRUDERS' PLAY AND THE CHIVALRIC REVIVAL

The play the citizens manage to force onto the Blackfriars stage is a gross, absurd, disjunct set of scenes, featuring the immortal grocer's apprentice Rafe. Its title, "The Knight of the Burning Pestle," is suggested by the players and indicates their disdain for its obsolete, inflated heroics.[11] It is in apparent deference to the citizens' tastes and preferences that the obedient apprentice acts out a succession of hilarious knightly adventures: first, a botched attempt to help Mrs. Merrythought, because of which she loses a casket of jewels and money (found by the careless Jasper after he has thrown away his own few pieces of money); next, a "knightly" duel but a realistic one,

[11] It has often been suggested that "pestle" also contains an obscene pun that was made possible by its Elizabethan pronunciation (something in the neighborhood of "pizzle"). Such a joke would fit with the many sexual innuendoes and double entendres scattered through the play.

since the actor playing Jasper administers a sound thrashing to Rafe; then, a heroic battle in which Rafe "rescues prisoners" (in fact, venereal disease patients) from the giant Barbarossa (in fact, a barber-surgeon); and finally, a brief sojourn in Moldavia with the Princess Pompiona whom Rafe leaves lovelorn and desolate but with three-pence in pin money for the trouble he has caused. In all these scenes of slapstick and burlesque, one may note that Beaumont never makes Rafe a simple *miles gloriosus* like such cowardly braggarts as Jonson's Captain Bobadill. Rafe always conducts himself with dignity and tries to live up to the highest ideals of knighthood. Thus it is not accurate to view him simply as the embodiment of the citizens' foolish fantasies. His ingenuous efforts to be a perfect knight make him a rebuke to the foul-mouthed, extravagant, often immoral men who swaggered around Jacobean London with their newly gained titles of "knight" purchased for forty pounds. Rafe, reading his romances, laments that "there are no such courteous and faire well spoken Knights in this age, they will call one the sonne of a whore, that *Palmerin* of England, would have called faire sir; and one that *Rosicler* would have cal'd right beauteous Damsell, they will call dam'd bitch" (1.235–38). Nell expresses the same sentiment: "our Knights neglect their possessions well enough, but they do not the rest" [i.e., "relieve poore Ladies"] (1.233–34, 231).

The treatment of contemporary "knights" suggests a dimension to the citizens' play that has barely been noticed. It is usually taken for granted that in portraying Rafe and Nell as avid readers of chivalric romances Beaumont is satirizing "pop" culture and the reading taste of the petty bourgeoisie. It is true, as Edwin H. Miller has pointed out, that there was "an endless torrent of abuse" from humanists on the harmful moral influence of such literature on the "vulgar" and "unlearned." But Miller demonstrates that many of the powerful, learned, and sophisticated men of the sixteenth and seventeenth century also were avid readers of chivalric romances—among them Burghley, the earl of Pembroke, Sir Robert Sidney, and Drummond of Hawthornden. The very cultivated Edward de Vere, earl of Oxford, "quixotically thought himself 'descended of the doughty Knight of the Swan.' "[12] The most obvious example of a literary intellectual with such tastes was, obviously, Beaumont himself. Perhaps, as in our time, some educated people read such romances in their youth. Others, Zitner suggests, may have regarded it as "a half-secret intellectual indulgence—like television."[13] Perhaps there was nothing at all fur-

---

[12] *The Professional Writer in Elizabethan England* (Cambridge, Mass., 1959), pp. 79–81.
[13] Preface to *The Knight*, p. 30.

tive about an attachment to such literature in the days before there was an invidious distinction between highbrow and lowbrow art.

To many upper-class Jacobeans it was not altogether clear that the Age of Chivalry was dead, or perhaps it is more accurate to say that they liked to pretend that it was not. Thanks to the work of Frances Yates, Roy Strong, and Mark Girouard, among others, modern readers can understand much about the courtiers' desire to don armor and engage in tournaments to fight for the honor of the Virgin Queen. But it is not easy to determine what kind of reality the participants ascribed to themselves. George Clifford, earl of Cumberland, who fought under the Arthurian title of "Knight of Pendragon Castle" when he served as Queen Elizabeth's champion at the annual Accession Day tournament is a good example. His title was not a fiction since he owned a castle named Pendragon. Cumberland spent much of his life resembling a knight-errant, having expended vast sums of money on a private navy he had assembled for his own profit and the queen's glory. In his youth he acted like a northern medieval lord: for whatever reason he decided in 1572 to arm Skipton Castle with fourteen cannons.[14] The days of such freewheeling aristocrats came to an end under Burghley and Elizabeth. By the turn of the century Cumberland was domesticated into a militarily impotent tilting champion. Dissolute, at least thirty-five thousand pounds in debt, in his later years he lived off the proceeds of a license to export cloth, a prime example of J. H. Hexter's connection between the weakening of the aristocracy's military power and the decline of its status in society.

Among many of the younger, more sophisticated courtiers of the late sixteenth century the "medieval" was all the rage in clothing, architecture, painting, and such high literature as *The Fairy Queen*. One may recall Huizinga's injunction that "play does not exclude seriousness" in noting Sir Henry Lee's and (following him) the earl of Cumberland's annual assumption of the role of queen's champion; the mock-siege of the queen's Fortress of Perfect Beauty in 1581 by a group collectively known as the Four Foster Children of Desire, which included Sir Philip Sidney and Fulke Greville; and the masquerading as Knights of the Round Table of the earl of Pembroke and his friends at Ludlow Castle in 1594.[15]

On the accession of James there was no sudden shift in cultural style. Almost precisely when *The Knight of the Burning Pestle* was being

[14] Helen Maud Cam, "The Decline and Fall of English Feudalism," *History* 25 (1940): 225–33.

[15] See Mark Girouard, *Robert Smythson and the Elizabethan Country House* (New Haven, Conn., 1983), p. 212.

composed, 1606, the third earl of Pembroke, his brother Philip, the earl of Southampton, and the duke of Lennox called themselves "The Knights Errant" and with "sound of trumpet before the Palace-gate of Greenwich" issued a challenge "to all honourable Men of Arms and Knights Adventurers of hereditary note and exemplary nobleness, that for most maintainable actions do weild their swords or lances in the quest for glory."[16] These courtiers were encouraged in their seemingly archaic frivolities by the precocious Prince Henry, who enjoyed being compared to King Arthur. The speeches composed by Ben Jonson for "Prince Henry's Barriers" of 1610 show that the prince wanted to raise chivalry from its present decayed state, ultimately aiming to establish England as the military leader of Europe. Even the scholarly King James was not immune to the neochivalric vogue. When Prince Charles and Buckingham went on their silly trip to Spain to further the Spanish match in 1623, the king described them as "dear adventurous knights worthy to be put in a new romanso."[17]

At slightly lower levels of society one can detect further similarities to Rafe. Sir Edmund Verney reports on a skirmish in Ireland and gallantly adds, "after[wards] we put some four score men to the sword, but like valiant knights errant, gave quarter and liberty to all the women."[18] Surely no one since Sir Gawain took the vows of knighthood as seriously as Edward Herbert (later Lord Herbert of Cherbury) when he was inducted into the Knights of Bath in 1603. He noted particularly that they pledged "never to sit in place where injustice should be done, but they shall right to the uttermost of their power; and particularly ladies and gentlewomen that shall be wronged in their honour, if they demand assistance, . . . not unlike the romances of knight errantry."[19] Herbert's autobiography devotes more time to establishing his status as a man of honor than it does to his considerable achievements as a poet and philosopher.

The same, seemingly anachronistic commitment to knight-errantry characterizes Herbert's younger contemporary, Sir Kenelm Digby. Described by Aubrey as "the most accomplished cavalier of his time" and by an Oxford don as the "Mirandola of his age,"[20] Digby's slightly fictionalized memoirs reveal him to be an altogether more complicated figure than Sidney. Everyone has heard of his love for the beautiful, highborn, sexually loose Venetia Stanley. After a long

[16] John Nichols, *Progresses of King James I* (London, 1828), 1:49.
[17] Quoted by G. M. Trevelyan, *England under the Stuarts* (New York, 1922), p. 129.
[18] *Memoirs of the Verney Family* (London, 1892–99), 2:135.
[19] *Autobiography of Edward, Lord Cherbury*, ed. Sidney Lee (London, 1886), p. 45.
[20] *Brief Lives*, ed. Anthony Powell (New York, 1949), p. 43.

courtship whose complexities resemble a "love and honor" romance, Digby and Venetia married, but in the process his reputation had suffered. He felt that he had to defend himself against the charge that love had reduced him to an effeminate slackness: "it was necessary for him to employ himself in some generous action that would give testimony to the world how his affections had nothing impaired the nobleness of his mind, nor abated the edge of his active and vigorous spirits." Thus he left the beautiful Venetia for an implausible privateering expedition in the Mediterranean. A "glorious" victory in the Venetian harbor of Scanderoon reassured the world—or so Sir Kenelm claims—that his "nobleness . . . was nothing impaired."[21]

In much the same manner, the knight-errant Rafe, having completed one adventure, searches for new ways to keep his honor bright:

> *Rafe.* But yet before I go, speake worthy Knight,
>   If ought you do of sad adventures know,
>   Where errant Knight may through his prowesse winne,
>   Eternall fame and free some gentle soules,
>   From endlesse bonds of steele and lingring paine.
>
>   . . . .
>
> *Host.* Sir Knight, this wilderness affoordeth none
>   But the great venter, where full many a Knight
>   Hath tride his prowesse and come off with shame,
>   And where I would not have you loose your life,
>   Against no man, but furious fiend of hell.
> *Rafe.* Speake on sir Knight, tell what he is, and where,
>   For heere I vow upon my blazing badge,
>   Never to blaze a day in quietnesse;
>   But bread and water will I onely eate,
>   And the greene hearbe and rocke shall be my couch,
>   Till I have queld that man, or beast, or fiend,
>   That workes such damage to all Errant Knights.

> (3.208–27)

With these ringing words the apprentice Hotspur fearlessly commits himself to the "Great Venture," the confrontation of the giant Barbarossa in his lair, where he will gain a victory scarcely less meaningful than Digby's at Scanderoon. From the reckless Hotspur to the calculating Hal to the ruthless Prince John to the pestle-packing Rafe one can locate some of the major milestones on the road from Camelot to Disneyland. Perhaps more clearly than anyone in England

---

[21] *Private Memoirs of Sir Kenelm Digby* (London, 1827), p. 301.

Beaumont and Fletcher saw the inauguration of the postheroic age. When they started writing, Sidney was dead, the raid at Cadiz (manned by an abundance of upper-class Rafes) had been a fiasco, Essex's inept expedition to Ireland led eventually to his shame and execution, Raleigh, the last Elizabethan hero, was moldering in the Tower, and James's foreign policy was felt to be an ignominious "peace at any price." It is not clear that Beaumont had in mind the application of *The Knight* to the upper portions of Jacobean society when he wrote it in 1606, but it became the point of departure for his later work. Almost immediately after *The Knight* the heroes of the more important collaborative plays seem to be upper-class descendants of the two apprentices of *The Knight*—as attractive and inept as Rafe, as obscurely driven and perverse as Jasper, their dedication to the "great venter" as quixotic—foolish but nonetheless admirable.

As his treatment of George the Grocer suggests, Beaumont saw that life in a postheroic age might have its attractions. By act 4 George seems sated by Rafe's knightly adventures and returns to his original notion: "I'le have something done in honor of the Citty, besides, he hath bene long enough upon Adventures" (p. 75, ll. 14–16). Thus, in the remaining scenes Rafe is no longer the "Knight of the Burning Pestle"; henceforth he enacts the more modest dreams of a London grocer. As May Lord he gives a speech from a London conduit about the joys of springtime. He also acts as a very exacting leader of a London trainband. Finally he dies the serene death of a London citizen, and his soul flies to its resting place in Grocer's Hall. For the citizen, London is the real world to conquer, the center of his most ardent dreams of success, and the urbane Beaumont does not condescend to these: a secure life in a grocer's shop, the love of a maid on Milk Street, camaraderie among one's fellows in the trainband, the beauties of a London May Day. George's rejected suggestion for the title of the play is ultimately the proper one, for the citizens' collaborative play is at once a critique and a description of a "Grocer's Honor." *The Knight of the Burning Pestle* suggests that the Age of Chivalry was dead and that in 1607 England was already becoming a nation of shopkeepers.

BEAUMONT'S DISENGAGED IMAGINATION

Thus far I have discussed separately the various components of *The Knight of the Burning Pestle*'s intricate form. Within the separate parts a dialectic process occurs so that one is made to feel both something attractive and something repellent about Jasper and Merrythought, about carefreeness and carefulness, about naivete and worldly cunning. Since the three separate components—the players' play, Rafe's play, and the citizens' commentary—interrupt and interpenetrate each other, the total effect is even more complicated than I have indicated. For example, after Merrythought tells his wife that all his life he has had meat on the table and that if it won't appear, he can always laugh himself to death, Nell cannot restrain herself from commenting to George:

> *Wife.* It's a foolish old man this: is not he *George*?
> *Citizen.* Yes Cunny.
> *Wife.* Give me a peny i'th purse while I live *George*.
> *Citizen.* I by Ladie cunnie, hold thee there.
>
> (1.358–61)

Merrythought's faith that without any effort something will always turn up does indeed sound foolish, but when one hears George and Nell's easy, smug adherence to mammon, made the more unattractive by their familiar name-calling, one is almost driven to march with Merrythought to certain starvation. Beaumont stands outside this classic confrontation, content to record the tones with absolute precision and use his novel form to light up every corner of this issue.

A richer exploitation of the potentialities of the form occurs when the separate plot strands literally join. In the second act Rafe, instead of staying rigidly within the little episodes designed for him by the citizens, blunders into the players' play. The location is the forest just after Jasper has beaten off Luce's rich, foolish suitor Humphrey and just before he initiates his ill-advised "test" of her constancy. Naturally, the citizens agree with Venturewell that Humphrey is preferable as a husband to the penurious Jasper. They order Rafe to fight Jasper and reclaim Luce for Humphrey, much to the annoyance of the player-director who wants his play to follow its scenario:

> *Citizen.* . . . . I'le ha *Raph* fight with him, and swing him up welfavourdlie, sirrah boie come hither, let *Raph* come in and fight with *Jasper*.
> *Wife.* I, and beate him well, he's an unhappy boy.
> *Boy.* Sir you must pardon us, the plot of our Plaie lies contrarie, and 'twill hazard the spoiling of our Plaie.
> *Citizen.* Plot mee no plots, I'le ha *Raph* come out, I'le make your house too hot for you else.
> *Boy.* Why sir he shall, but if anie thing fall out of order, the Gentlemen must pardon us.
>
> (2.254–63)

The boy-director is helpless before the powerful George, but the actor playing Jasper is not. In a most complex moment the multilayered figure labeled "Jasper" (here an actor annoyed by the interruption of his professional activity) "defeats" Rafe while mockingly narrating his actions in the language of the apprentice's chivalric romances:

Wife. Breake's pate *Raph*, breake's pate *Raph*, soundly.
Jasper. Come Knight, I am ready for you, now your Pestel.

> *Snatches away his Pestle.*

    Shall try what temper, sir, your Morters off:
    [*Recites*] With that he stood upright in his stirrops, and gave the
        Knight of the Calve-skinne such a knocke,

> [*Knocks* Raph *Down.*]

that he forsooke his horse and downe he fell, and then he leaped upon him and
    plucking of his Helmet—
Humphrey. Nay, and my noble Knight be downe so soone,
    Though I can scarcely go I needs must runne.

> *Exeunt* Humphery *and* Raph.

Wife. Runne *Raph*, runne *Raph*, runne for thy life boy, *Jasper* comes, *Jasper* comes.

> (2.296–306)[22]

Much Renaissance drama calls attention to its artificiality, but in such scenes none anatomizes more remorselessly than *The Knight of the Burning Pestle* the flimsy materials out of which the dramatic experience is built.[23] The dramatic emperor is shown to be walking around shamelessly unclothed. The actors are not only acting, they are showing us that they are acting. By refusing to be passive and by revealing that they do not comprehend dramatic conventions, the citizens' responses suggest how fragile and liable to destruction a theatrical performance is. As described in chapter 1, Beaumont believed that in an audience of a thousand "scarce two . . . can understand the lawes / Which they should judge by."[24] George and Nell fully confirm the

[22] I have adopted Zitner's rearrangement of the quarto text, p. 95. It clarifies that Jasper shifts from verse to mimic a chivalric romance.

[23] This aspect of *The Knight*—what is now modishly called its "metadramatic" dimension—has been the subject of a series of excellent critical studies over the past twenty-five years: Inge Leimberg, "Das Spiel mit der dramatischen Illusion in Beaumonts *The Knight of the Burning Pestle*," *Anglia* 81 (1963): 142–74; Ronald F. Miller, "Dramatic Form and Dramatic Imagination in Beaumont's *The Knight of the Burning Pestle*," *English Literary Renaissance* 8 (1978): 67–84; Samuelson, "Order in Beaumont's *Knight of the Burning Pestle*"; Lee Bliss, " 'Plot mee no plots': The Life of Drama and the Drama of Life in *The Knight of the Burning Pestle*," *Modern Language Quarterly* 45 (1984): 3–21; and Sheldon P. Zitner in the introduction to his Revels edition of *The Knight*.

[24] "To my friend Maister *John Fletcher* upon his Faithful Shepheardesse," prefatory poem to *The Faithful Shepherdess*, Cyrus Hoy, ed., in Bowers, gen. ed., *Dramatic Works*, 3:490, ll. 15–16.

validity of his complaint. But as the wife warns Rafe to run away from
the pursuing Jasper, one notices that the citizens do not need to suspend their disbelief at the theater because they have no disbelief to
suspend:

> *Wife. George*, what wilt thou laye with mee now, that Maister *Humphrey*
>   has not Mistress *Luce* yet, speake *George*, what wilt thou laie with me?
> *Citizen.* No *Nel*, I warrant thee *Jasper* is at *Puckeridge* with her, by this.
> *Wife.* Nay *George*, you must consider Mistress *Lucies* feete are tender,
>   and, besides, 'tis darke, and I promise you truely, I doe not see how
>   hee should get out of *Waltham* forrest with her yet.
> *Citizen.* Nay Cunny, what wilt thou laie with me that *Raph* has her not
>   yet.

> (2.409–18)

One is doubtless to laugh at the fact that while the citizens know they
are sitting on the floor boards of a stage, they believe they are looking
into a dark forest where Luce may injure her tender feet. At first this
inability to distinguish one kind of phenomenon from another seems
like a fatal incapacity for a theatergoer, but in the way value judgments are modified in the course of this play, the distinction between
the imaginative and the unimaginative grows hazy and seems unim-
portant. George may not be having an "aesthetic" experience, but his
hope that Rafe win Luce is one of the happiest and, in human terms,
truest comic inventions in the play. The magic power of the stage has
unleashed this hard-headed man's capacity to dream, to fantasize that
this extension of himself, his own Rafe, may get the heroine.

Nothing Beaumont had written previously could have prepared us
for the innovativeness of the complex form of this play; equally surprising is the unstrained, authoritative correctness of the portraits
and the sound of the voices of the citizens. Beaumont knows things
about them that an upper-middle-class young man from Leicestershire gentry has no right to know: that Nell carries in her purse lico-
rice to keep "open . . . [the] pipes" in her throat (1.71) and "greene
ginger" to cure bruises (2.250–51); that she has not one, but two ways
to cure chilblains: "with a mouse skinne," or at bedtime by rolling the
feet in "warme embers" (3.190, 192); that to get rid of worms she
would recommend "*Carduus Bendedictus* and Mares milke" (3.304–5).
He knows how George lights up when he thinks of his days in a London trainband. He knows how the couple sounds when they encour-
age each other and when they daydream. He also knows their dark
underside. It is difficult to understand why these brutal characters
are almost always described as "amiable": "Sirrah, you scurvie boy,
bid the plaiers send *Rafe*, or by Gods—and they do not, I'le teare

some of their periwigs beside their heads: this is all Riffe Raffe" (1.interlude.9–11). George's threats are the kind a burly bully would use on a helpless child. If matters in "The London Merchant" are not progressing to his satisfaction, he always has in reserve a "hardhat's" solution: "Il'e bring halfe a dozen good fellows my selfe, and in the shutting of an evening knock't up, and ther's an end" (2.13–14). Nell, in particular, seems to enjoy physical violence: "call *Rafe* againe, I pre'thee sweet heart let him come fight before me, and let's ha some drums, and some trumpets, and let him kill all that comes neere him, and thou lov'st me *George*" (2.128–31). George responds with the same delicious mixture of the uxorious and the violent: "Peace a little, bird, hee shall kill them all and they were twentie more on 'em then there are" (2.132–33). His plan for punishing Merrythought for an insult to Nell shows him to be sneaky as well as vindictive: "I have a tricke in my head shall lodge him in the Arches for one yeare, and make him sing *Peccavi*, e're I leave him, and yet hee shall never know who hurt him neither." Always a supportive wife, Nell encourages his "good" action: "Do my good *George*, do" (4.21–24).

Joyce's ominous citizen in the "Cyclops" episode of *Ulysses* is merely an extension of some of the citizens' latent tendencies. Why, then, the invariable tones of affection and admiration when describing them? I would suggest that these sentiments are really a response to the immediacy, the extraordinarily vivid existence that results from the mating of precise naturalistic detail and a special advantage inherent in *The Knight*'s form. The publisher's preface to the 1613 quarto speaks of *The Knight* as being "of the race of *Don Quixote*."[25] There is no question of the priority of the first part of the *Quixote*, but Beaumont seems independently to have hit on an idea that contributes much to the special power of the second part of Cervantes' work. Early in the sequel (published after *The Knight* in 1615), the Don learns that part 1 has been published and that his exploits are widely known. When he arrives at a castle in chapter 31 and receives an enthusiastic, if mock-serious, reception from a duke and duchess who have read part 1, the character of Don Quixote is thereby translated to a different, more "real" level of existence; he has broken out of his fictional frame and lives in the world of history and fact. By having characters enter the stage from the audience, Beaumont gives them something of the same "reality." They are not from backstage where

[25] P. 7, l. 22. For a thorough discussion of the various ways the first part of *Don Quixote* could have been known in England in 1607, see Lee Bliss, "*Don Quixote* in England: the Case for *The Knight of the Burning Pestle*," *Viator* 18 (1987): 361–80. There is, of course, no validity to the publisher's claim that Rafe was a year older than Cervantes's hero. The novel was published in 1605 but written even earlier.

fictional "characters" live. The citizens exist totally outside the palace
of art. They may offer a recipe or sympathy to a "character" or entertain themselves by assigning some activity to Rafe. But the "characters" do not respond to their advances. Unless as actors they are
unusually provoked,[26] the "characters" remain mute, waiting patiently for any interference to cease, then resume their appointed
tasks. They seem like different kinds of beings. Usually the "characters" speak a "literary" poetry. The citizens' prose is a precise rendition of the colloquialisms and special locutions of contemporary London, and of their own free associations and speech mannerisms; its
apparently random wanderings light up every crevice in their narrow
mercantile souls. One may not want to invite them to dinner, but one
is certain that they are alive.

In the preface to his edition of *The Knight*, Sheldon Zitner describes
well how Beaumont's satire of the citizens' ignorance on aesthetic
matters is counterbalanced by his appreciation of their vitality. This
leads him to add,

> But Beaumont's sympathy has a character and limitations. It results
> from an attraction to energetic and amusing activity rather than . . .
> from benevolent concern. The Citizens are likeable because of, not in
> spite of, their faults, and their faults are of their station—an arrange-
> ment which, among other social arrangements, Beaumont accepts as a
> given, beyond satire's reform or populism's moral earnestness. His sym-
> pathies are nonchalant and distant, depending perhaps on a misplaced
> conviction of the security of his own class. It was in the nature of such a
> view to find congenial the grossness that makes Citizen Nell vivid, and to
> allow the small cruelties that make Merrythought interesting. (P. 39)

Like almost all criticism of Beaumont (and of Fletcher) this thoughtful and subtle comment ultimately depends on a view of Beaumont's
background and social status that my first chapter attempts to challenge. The "class" to which I have consigned Beaumont—some Jacobean version of the declassé intelligentsia—was hardly a secure one,
and the plays as I see them are the product of a different kind of
disengagement than the rest of Zitner's remarks would suggest:

> In addition, its disengagement encouraged the easy and spectacular
> transformations in the later acts [of this play]. . . . Beaumont never quite
> returns to the vein [of *The Knight*]. But can we not already see the
> grounds in outlook and temperament for the *coup de theatre* and the

[26] The prime example is Merrythought's obscene taunt to Nell (3.541–44)—presumably a gesture of impatience by an actor similar to that in the duel between Jasper and
Rafe.

empty loyalties of the later plays, for Evadne's horrid disclosure and Amintor's ideological nullity? (P. 39)

This is the orthodox view of Beaumont that this book hopes to dispel—one of an amused, comfortably poised, irresponsible, aristocratic sensationalist, the producer of "good theater" that is (to quote T. S. Eliot again) "superficial with a vacuum behind it."[27]

I concur with Professor Zitner in finding the author of *The Knight* "disengaged." For him the epithet suggests a bemused aristocratic aesthete, uncommitted to any cause or belief but delighted to sacrifice anything for the "big scene." For me the term describes the habit of mind that enabled Beaumont to see the other side of every issue or character or attitude he created. In his later plays it leads him to the sceptical questioning of all absolutes, whether of court or country, lover or rhetorician. Here its centripetal power produced an intricate, beautifully shaped work constructed out of diverse materials, expressing various points of view.

In contemplating Beaumont's achievement in *The Knight*, it is necessary to consider the significance of the failure at the box office of this radical experiment. There is often something healthy and right about an audience's instincts in such matters. No one regrets the verdict on Henry James's plays or would want more work by Fletcher in the vein of *The Faithful Shepherdess*. But the public's rejection of *The Knight* may have been the costliest mistake in the history of English drama. What may have been lost is a great genre artist capable of plays like *Bartholomew Fair* and a remarkably prescient commentator on the state of England. Through *The Knight* one can view the citizens moving into the battle that eventually closed the theaters. Whether or not they were meant to be viewed as Puritans—their social class as well as one speech suggest that they were[28]—the polarization of attitudes toward the theater is already visible to Beaumont. From the opening words there is an atmosphere of hostility as the citizen complains that for "this seven yeares" the private theaters have been flinging "girds at citizens" (induction, p. 11, ll. 6, 8). This is amply justified by the players' play, which expresses a radical disagreement with the citizens about what matters most in art and life. Beaumont even made an uncanny guess about the kind of drama the Puritans would be willing to tolerate, for Rafe's scenes can be viewed as simplified versions of the so-called drolls that attracted large audiences

---

[27] *Selected Essays* (New York, 1932), p. 135.

[28] Nell uses recognizably Puritan terms in a plea to Merrythought: "your wife is your owne flesh, the staffe of your age, your yoke-fellow, with whose helpe you draw through the mire of this transitory world: Nay, she's your owne ribbe" (3.537–40).

at the old public theaters during the Interregnum. At the beginning of his dramatic career, Beaumont saw the perilous future with startling clarity. Meanwhile, the interim was to be his and Fletcher's after they licked their wounds and decided how to repair the damage of their two abortive forays into the avante-garde. Perhaps out of economic necessity they, like Shakespeare, decided to write work that was less aggressively original. They left it to Jonson to posture against "that strumpet, the stage" and to "sing high and aloof, / Safe from the wolf's black jaw, and the dull ass's hoof."[29] After Beaumont had felt his way into the skins of the various figures who inhabit *The Knight of the Burning Pestle*, elitist condescension was no longer viable.

---

[29] "Ode to Himself" in C. H. Herford, Percy Simpson, and Evelyn Simpson, eds., *Ben Jonson* (Oxford, 1925–52), 8:175, ll. 34, 35–36.

Chapter Four

THE FAITHFUL SHEPHERDESS: THE POLITICS OF CHASTITY

THE DEFINITION OF PASTORAL TRAGICOMEDY

At about the time that *The Knight of the Burning Pestle* was being "utterly rejected" by a private theater audience, John Fletcher's *The Faithful Shepherdess* (1608–9) was "before / They saw it halfe, damd" by essentially the same audience.[1] Beaumont's play required a "sophisticated" audience to react to innovations of form and subtleties of tone and attitude. Fletcher's required, or at least would have profited from, the kind of "sophistication" that knows what is most in vogue in "advanced" circles. In neither sense did the private theater audiences pass the test. It is not surprising that *The Knight* was rejected. To an unprepared group its novelties might well have seemed simply chaotic and silly. But if there had existed at the private theaters the kind of "sophisticated" audience now found in New York and London, one that will bear stoically any kind of assault and endure any amount of tedium when assured of a play's avante-garde status, *The Faithful Shepherdess* would have been accepted with respect if not enthusiasm. It represented Fletcher's effort to present an English version of the pastoral dramas of Tasso and Guarini, the very latest in Italian sophistication. Such plays were designed for court audiences with a taste for slow movement, rhetorical display, and the kind of scenery and spectacle usually reserved for the masque in England.

On the face of things, *The Faithful Shepherdess* was a curious project for Fletcher to undertake. If one may trust the chronology, before it

---

[1] There is no reason to doubt that this is unaided work by Fletcher. There are many reasons for rejecting E. K. Chambers's view (*The Elizabethan Stage* [Oxford, 1923], 3:222) that another solo Fletcher play, *The Woman's Prize*, came earlier. Chambers's evidence for production at a private theater, while internal, is conclusive: "The presence of Field, Chapman, and Jonson amongst the verse-writers [of the prefatory poems] and the mentions in Beaumont's verses of 'the waxlights' and of a boy dancing between the acts point to the Queen's Revels as the producers" (ibid.). The verse quoted is from Ben Jonson's "To the Worthy Author M. *John Fletcher*" in Cyrus Hoy's edition of *The Faithful Shepherdess* in Fredson Bowers, gen. ed., *The Dramatic Works in the Beaumont and Fletcher Canon* (Cambridge, 1966–), 3:492, ll. 7–8. Citations in the text refer to this edition.

he may have had some share in Beaumont's court- and city-centered *Woman Hater*; after it his plays with and without Beaumont are notable for fast-paced plots evocative of the here and now, however remote or exotic their ostensible settings. Why then did the most audience-sensitive of Jacobean dramatists make young boys playing characters with names like "Amoret" spout closet drama poetry of this sort:

> O *Perigot*:
> Thou that wast yesterday without a blott,
> Thou that wast every good, and every thinge,
> That men called blessed: thou that wast. . . .
>
> (4.4.89–92)

In fact, as remote as this may appear from his later work, an experiment of this sort is altogether plausible if one considers the taste of influential figures surrounding Fletcher at this time. There were, first, his cousins Giles and Phineas Fletcher. As described earlier, after his father's death in 1596 and for some years John Fletcher lived in his uncle Giles's house along with these two poets, whose lifelong devotion to Spenser and the pastoral is their major claim to fame. Next there was Ben Jonson, who was well versed in the sort of Continental poetry and aesthetics that this play exemplifies.[2] His commendatory poem in the quarto and his later praise of *The Faithful Shepherdess* to Drummond as a "tragicomedy well-done" suggests some personal involvement in the project.[3] George Chapman, who describes himself in his prefatory poem to *The Faithful Shepherdess* as a "good friend" of Fletcher, had already written a pastoral tragedy for Henslowe in 1599.[4] Marston, whose importance to Beaumont and Fletcher I have already discussed, may also have alerted Fletcher to a kind of play that one would not associate with either writer. Some years ago G. K. Hunter discovered that a rather surprising source for some parts of *The Malcontent* was the 1602 translation of Guarini's *Il Pastor Fido*.[5] In addition, *The Malcontent*, as far as I can determine, was the first play in English to be explicitly labeled a "tragicomedy."[6]

[2] Through his brother Nathaniel, who was until 1606 chaplain to Sir Henry Wotton in Venice, Fletcher would have had direct access to what was happening in Italy.

[3] *Conversations with Drummond* in *Ben Jonson*, ed. C. H. Herford, Percy Simpson, and Evelyn Simpson (Oxford, 1925–52), 1:138.

[4] Lee Bliss, "Defending Fletcher's Shepherds," *Studies in English Literature* 23 (1983): 297n.

[5] "English Folly and Italian Vice," *Jacobean Theatre* 1 (London, 1960): 100. The anonymous translation was apparently by a relative of the queen's champion, Sir Edward Dymocke.

[6] It was entered in the Stationers' Register as "An Enterlude called the Malcontent,

Clearly there was interest in Fletcher's circle in the nature and possibilities of a "new" genre. After the failure of the play in the theater, Fletcher apparently convinced himself that it might have been averted had he provided a prologue that explained his intentions. It was too late for that, but for his readers he offered a terse, condescending definition of tragicomedy that is more revealing as an index of his frame of mind than enlightening on its subject:

TO THE READER.

If you be not reasonably assurde of your knowledge in this kinde of Poeme, lay downe the booke or read this, which I would wish had bene the prologue. It is a pastorall Tragie-comedie, which the people seeing when it was plaid, having ever had a singuler guift in defining, concluded to be a play of country hired Shepheards, in gray cloakes, with curtaild dogs in strings, sometimes laughing together, and sometimes killing one another. (P. 497, ll. 1–7)

He adds that when he failed to provide a play filled with "Whitsun ales, creame, wassel and morris-dances, [the audience] began to be angry" (8–9).[7] Fletcher then makes a sociological point about the shepherds and shepherdesses in his pastoral tragicomedy: they are "owners of flocks," not mere "hyerlings" (19–20). Perhaps he insists on this distinction to make credible the elaborate and educated speech of the shepherds, but it also serves a socio-political purpose. The characters in the play are "owners"; they resemble those who make England what it is.

Fletcher then proceeds to the meat of his definition:

A tragie-comedie is not so called in respect of mirth and killing, but in respect it wants deaths, which is inough to make it no tragedie, yet brings some neere it, which is inough to make it no comedie: which must be a representation of familiar people, with such kinde of trouble as no life be questiond, so that a God is as lawfull in this as in a tragedie, and meane people as in a comedie. (20–26)

After offering this "correct" definition, Fletcher concludes in the same short-tempered, pedantic tone he started with: "Thus much I hope will serve to justifie my Poeme, and make you understand it, to teach you more for nothing, I do not know that I am in conscience bound" (26–28). In his insistence that tragicomedy is a third, distinct genre, Fletcher (while dependent on Italian theorists) breaks new

Tragicomoedia" (Chambers, *Elizabethan Stage*, 3:431). It is difficult to imagine that anyone but the author would have been responsible for the designation.

[7] Ll. 8–9. Perhaps Fletcher's bitter experience directly influenced Shakespeare to include the sort of material in *The Winter's Tale* that Fletcher had omitted.

ground in English dramatic theory. Yet his definition does not take one very far into the play itself; it merely states that it was critically allowable to produce a mixed kind of play. Many scholars have pointed out that English playwrights had been writing tragicomedies for some years without bothering to label them. Moreover, Fletcher's definition is not sufficiently exclusive. Using a play as remote as Middleton's *A Chaste Maid in Cheapside,* Una Ellis-Fermor demonstrated that it conforms to all the requirements of Fletcher's tragicomic formula.[8] Of course it is unfair to subject a definition designed to satisfy a momentary polemical need—to defend the validity of a work to a group that did not know that such "mixed" fare was now "allowable"—to rigorous critical scrutiny. But we should be warned that the notions of genre developed for *The Faithful Shepherdess* have a limited usefulness for later plays by Beaumont and Fletcher. None of them is a pastoral even if several have pastoral elements in them, and they depict larger worlds in a great variety of tones.

ELIZABETHAN CHASTITY AND JACOBEAN LUST

It is clear from its earliest moments that Fletcher has written a play in which the pastoral and the tragic would play a part. The "faithful shepherdess" of the title is mourning the death of her one true love and consecrating herself to a life that will be free

> from all ensuing heates and fires
> Of love, all sports, delights and games,
> That Shepheards hold full deare.
>
> (1.1.7–9)

As Fletcher had mentioned in the preface, this would be a pastoral without the revelry of "whitsun ales, creame, wassel and morris-dances." The inhabitants of his Thessaly are a variety of lovers ranging from the purely spiritual to the basely sensual. Almost all lead troubled lives. Either they are unloved or their loves pose problems. The grieving faithful shepherdess Clorin has attracted the strange, idealistic love of the shepherd Thenot, who vows that as long as she remains pure and unassailable he will try to win her, all the while hoping he fails. Next, there are the innocent lovers Perigot and Amoret. In a situation reminiscent of the false Una of book 1 and the false Florimell of book 3 of *The Fairy Queen,* Perigot is victimized by the shepherdess Amaryllis and her amoral helper, the Sullen Shepherd. Transforming herself by magic into the shape of his beloved Amoret,

---

[8] *The Jacobean Drama: an Interpretation* (London, 1936), pp. 203–5.

Amaryllis tries to seduce Perigot, causing the confused hero twice to make gestures toward suicide and twice to wound the true, helpless, and ever-loving Amoret. Finally, in a third strand of the plot, Fletcher invents a variant on the Daphnis and Cloe story, employing their very names. Cloe is desperately dissatisfied with her virginal state and eager to take up with anyone who will relieve her of it: "It is Impossible to Ravish mee, / I am soe willing" (3.1.212–13). She finds Daphnis loving but much too virtuous. Another shepherd, Alexas, wants to assist her, but just as she is about to gain her wish, the lustful Sullen Shepherd tries to take Alexas's place and in the confusion poor Cloe is left a reluctant virgin. Eventually all but the Sullen Shepherd (who is exiled) are enabled or persuaded to lead virtuous lives.

In the background, constantly referred to but never seen, is the ruler of the country, the great Pan. He is the spiritual as well as the secular leader, and the central tenet of his religion is chastity, rigorously enforced by his priests. But just after one meets the chaste Clorin in the opening moments of the play, one learns that Pan is engaging in a tryst with "His Paramoure, the *Syrinx* bright" (1.1.56), and later that Pan

> In a corner of the wood,
> Where never mortall foote hath stood,
> Keepes dancing, musicke and a feast
> To intertaine a lovely guest.
> .   .   .   .
> I never saw so great a feast.

(3.1.174–79)

The sex-starved Cloe assumes with good reason that Pan is the proper figure to pray to for the alleviation of her condition: "Now / Great *Pan* for *Sirinx* sake bid speed our plow" (2.4.107–8).

The ambiguities in Pan's role are notable in a play that insistently preaches the overriding importance of chastity. Fletcher's treatment of the Perigot-Amoret-Amaryllis relationship provides a vivid example. Recall that Amaryllis magically transforms herself into Perigot's innocent beloved Amoret and tries to seduce him. Out of a vast disillusionment with his loved one and with womankind, Perigot responds by twice trying to murder the true Amoret and twice trying to commit suicide. When the same kind of trick is played on the Red Cross Knight in book 1 of *The Fairy Queen*, his instant belief in Una's lechery shows that he is spiritually immature, in need of an elaborate course of moral regeneration. In the later Beaumont and Fletcher collaboration *Philaster*, the hero is presented as something of a comic figure for responding to a similar situation by stabbing women and attempting suicide at every turn. In *The Faithful Shepherdess* Perigot's violence is triggered not by any appearance of faithlessness in the figure he believes to be Amoret, but merely by her apparent desire to engage in premarital intercourse with the man she loves. When Perigot eventually realizes how he has been deceived, his violent actions are presented as though they had been amusing mishaps in a pleasant comedy of errors:

> My deare, deare *Amoret*, how happy are
> Those blessed paires, in whom a little jarr
> Hath bred an everlasting love, to strong
> For time or steele, or envy to do wrong!
> How do you feele your hurts? alasse poore heart
> How much I was abusd, give me the smart
> For it is justly mine.
>
> (5.5.109–15)

His "steele" may have done much wrong, but the play exonerates Perigot completely. However misguided, all his actions were dictated by a fanatical devotion to the sacred cause of chastity.

This one deduces from the treatment of chastity in the other strands of the plot. For example, the character of Daphnis appears to be a comic representation of an immature adolescent who preserves his virginity and adheres to conventional morality out of a fear of sex. At the end he is no longer a source of amusement; he is ranked with the heroes because, however contemptible his motives for doing so, he has remained chaste. Cloe, on the other hand, seems throughout to be consumed by lust. She deserves the fate of Spenser's Hellenore, who became mistress to a ménage of satyrs. But somehow under compulsion and with no explanation she becomes a believer in a chaste life: "And I a newe fire feele in mee, / Whose base end is not quencht to be" (5.5.17–18). Treated in a similar manner is the hapless shepherd Alexas, who was wounded just before he was to have sexual contact with Cloe. He learns from the chaste Clorin that she cannot heal his wound

> Till thou hast layed a syde all heates, desiers,
> Provoking thoughts, that stirr upp lusty fiers,
> Commerse with wanton Eyes: strong bloud, and will
> To execute, theise must bee purg'd untill
> The vayne growe Whiter: then Repent and pray
> Great *Pan*, to keepe you from the like decaye,
> And I shall undertake your cure with ease.
>
> (4.2.109–15)

This warning conveys the prevailing attitude of "the establishment" in Thessaly, and Fletcher makes no real attempt to express another point of view, as Milton does in Comus's encomium on nature's bounty. Everywhere the supreme value of chastity is assumed and asserted. When a feeble justification of natural desire is offered to the stern Priest of Pan, it is done, significantly, by the one unreformable character, the Sullen Shepherd:

> Good holynesse declare,
> What had the danger bene if being bare,
> I had imbracd her, tell me by your Art:
> What comming wonders wood that sight impart?
>
> (5.3.139–42)

The priest's response is terse and unmistakable: "Lust, and branded soul" (143). The Sullen Shepherd makes one more brief effort at argument, advancing a primitive version of Comus's justification:

> Yet tell me more,
> Hath not our Mother *Nature* for her store,
> And great increase, sayd it is good and just,
> And willd that every living creature must,
> Beget his like?
>
> (5.3.143–47)

Again the priest, plainly a representative of the prevailing viewpoint, shows no interest in dallying with such specious nonsense:

> Yee are better read then I,
> I must confesse in Blood and Letchery:
> Now to the Bowre and bring this beast along,
> Where he may suffer Pennance for his wrong.
>
> (5.3.147–50)

And so the Sullen Shepherd, remaining forever unenlightened, is exiled from Pan's kingdom.

These harsh simplifications are further underlined at the conclusion of this final scene. It is Clorin with her Prospero-like mastery of the natural power in herbs who restores the lustful to spiritual health. Every character gathered in her virginal grove is subjected to a magical chastity device. All having been "brought againe / To virgin state" (5.5.158–59), they are handed over by Clorin, fully certified as "patients full of health" (5.5.167), to the care and scrutiny of the Priest of Pan. As her valedictory, Clorin gives a thirty-four-line directive on pastoral care to the priest. She urges that he scrutinize, in a manner reminiscent of Calvin's Geneva, the private conduct of his flock:

> Keepe them from after ills, be ever neere
> Unto their actions: teach them how to cleare
> The tedeous way they passe through, from suspect:
> Keepe them from wrong in others, or neglect
> Of duety in them selves, correct the bloud,
> With thrifty bitts and laboure: . . .
>
> . . . .
>   have a care,
> Thou man of holy life, now do not spare
> Their faults through much remissnes.
>
>   (5.5.168-73, 178–80)

She suggests sorting out the good shepherds from the bad, teaching "stricknes" to the young maidens in order that they may fend off sexual temptations, "banish[ing] all complement"—apparently the admiring endearments youths exchange in courtship—"but single truth" (185, 187). Chapman claims in his commendatory poem that Fletcher's play creates a "golden world," but it would be an Arcadia policed by the severe guardians of a "single truth."

The prime exemplar of chastity is the faithful shepherdess herself, Clorin, who asserts:

>   there is a power
> In that great name of virgin, that bindes fast
> All rude uncivill bloods, all appetites
> That breake their confines: then strong chastity,
> Be thou my strongest guarde, for heere Il'e dwell
> In opposition against Fate and Hell.
>
>   (1.1.124–29)

As James J. Yoch points out in a ground-breaking essay on this play, "The civilizing function of Clorin's virtue [resembles] the powers so long proclaimed for the Virgin Queen."[9] Certainly the language in which the virgin is described is reminiscent of the effusions of the cult of Elizabeth:

>   behold a fairer sight,
> By that heavenly forme of thine,
> Brightest faire thou art devine:
> Sprong from great immortall race
> Of the Gods: for in thy face,

---

[9] "The Renaissance Dramatization of Temperance: the Italian Revival of Tragicomedy and *The Faithful Shepherdess*" in *Renaissance Tragicomedy: Explorations in Genre and Politics*, ed. Nancy Klein Maguire (New York, 1987), p. 127.

Shines more awfull majesty,
Then dull weake mortalitie
Dare with misty eies behould.

(1.1.57–64)

This play, featuring a goddesslike but human figure reminiscent of the Virgin Queen, concludes with what Yoch calls

token flattery of King James I in his symbolic role as Pan, whom Natalis Comes observed was the "governor and moderator of all things" in some ancient texts. The final song and dance extend the lessons of the play from herbal formulas and individual relations into political dimensions by celebrating:

> *his honour and his name,*
> *That defendes our flockes from blame.*
> *Hee is great, and he is just*
> *Hee is ever good and must,*
> *Thus be honnerd.*

(5.5.226–30)[10]

Yoch shows that Guarini viewed the tragicomic mode as inherently political, concentrating on the relationship between temperate personal conduct and an orderly commonwealth. In Guarini "characters reveal their strength by patiently adapting to exterior circumstances"; for Fletcher "a heroine and her handyman [the satyr] succeed by actively overcoming lust, healing bodies, and restoring order to the community" (p. 116). Guarini's tragicomedy suggests a more patient and passive response to the blows of fortune than Fletcher's, but in Yoch's view, the intention for both was essentially conservation of the established order.

A more radical interpretation of Fletcher's politics in *The Faithful Shepherdess* seems to me suggested by Yoch's initial illumination. He states that "Clorin illustrates the Elizabethan ideal of chastity in a ruler" (p. 130). But Clorin is not a ruler, merely a shepherdess with maguslike powers similar to Prospero's. The ruler, constantly mentioned, always invisible, is the paradoxical figure Pan, whose rigorous priest enforces a religion of chastity that Pan himself does not observe. If Clorin is evocative of the dead "queen and huntress chaste and fair," it is natural to consider whether Pan can be identified with King James. As Natalis Comes observed, there is ancient precedent for identifying the governor with Pan, and as Yoch points out (p. 137, n. 60), the connection between Pan and James was made by Jonson in his masque *Pan's Anniversary* of 1620. Furthermore, like the Pan of

---

[10] "The Renaissance Dramatization of Temperance," p. 132.

this play, James spent a notable amount of his time secluded from his subjects, hunting and cavorting with his Ganymede of the moment at Theobalds and other country estates. If Clorin's backward glances to a better time when her love was alive and she danced to the "shrill pleasing sound of merry pipes" evoked a departed golden world, the lust in action in Fletcher's Thessaly resembled the situation in contemporary England. Lawrence Stone states that "sexual license at the Jacobean Court . . . may well have rivalled or excelled the more notorious conditions at the Court of Charles II." There were sex scandals under Elizabeth, but "the real breakthrough into promiscuity at Court only occurred under James."[11] Looked at thus, *The Faithful Shepherdess* employed the contemporary Italian conception of pastoral tragicomedy in a plea to the "owners" of flocks—Fletcher's stress on that aspect of his definition now takes on a special meaning—for England's moral regeneration. If, as Pan's priest says sternly to the Sullen Shepherd, his lustfulness is "a canker to the state / Thou livest and brethest in" (5.3.134–35), how much truer is this of Pan himself. Not only is such a reading consistent with what is known of Fletcher's socio-political background, it also reveals that this apparently anomalous work anticipates the central theme, regal intemperance, of the most important plays of the collaboration.

The Cause of the Failure

Yoch concludes his study of the play on a glowing note:

> In his dazzling deconstruction of familiar formulas, Fletcher achieved a freshly post-modern system, continental and English, pagan and Christian, fantastic and homespun, for delivering the invocation to temperance which religion and philosophy prepared Renaissance readers to recognize in tragicomedies. (P. 133)

If the play was so dazzling, one must ask as with *The Knight of the Burning Pestle* why it was such a clearcut and bitter failure. A loyal and angry Beaumont attacked a system in which a man of Fletcher's talents was judged by a thousand ignoramuses. Their "very reading makes verse senceles prose," and they "must spend above an houre, to spell / A challenge on a post, to know it well." In language worthy of Coriolanus Beaumont growls that if Fletcher had not needed help, he would not have "hurld" his lines at "these publicke things" (34–36, 31, 29). Fletcher, one may recall, also put the onus for the failure on the audience's ignorance. Anyone who has perused Fletcher's main model, Guarini's *Pastor Fido*, will easily believe the report that in its

---

[11] *The Crisis of the Aristocracy* (Oxford, 1965), pp. 664–65.

first performance at Mantua in 1598 sixteen hundred lines were omitted without the audience being aware of it.[12] On a smaller scale, the same might happen in a production of Fletcher's play. This is not to say that a very entertaining play could not have been written along the lines Fletcher planned. The material is exciting and serious, as Lee Bliss has shown.[13]

Many of the familiar and popular elements of Beaumont and Fletcher's plays are visible in *The Faithful Shepherdess*. What makes the play excruciatingly boring, if always sophisticated and high-minded, is Fletcher's language and dramaturgy. George Chapman's prefatory poem praises *The Faithful Shepherdess* for being "both a Poeme and a play."[14] It certainly is a poem. Whether it also deserves to be called a play rather than a closet drama is the question, as W. W. Greg implies in asserting that Fletcher "cared for nothing but a scenic framework to be filled in with poetic embroidery." He adds that the poetry is "of marvelous beauty," and he is not alone in praising this aspect of the play.[15] There are, it is true, occasional pretty, decorative passages, as in the octosyllabic couplets of the priest's exhortation:

> Shepheards all, and maidens faire,
> Fold your flockes up, for the Aire
> Ginns to thicken, and the Sunne
> Already his great course hath runne.
> See the dew drops how they kisse
> Every little flower that is,
> Hanging on their velvet heads,
> Like a rope of christal beades.
>
> (2.1.1–8)

An additional twenty-five lines of the same sort make the speech fade into fuzziness. More frequently, the nature passages give a worked-

---

[12] John Shearman, *Mannerism* (London, 1967), p. 92.

[13] "Defending Fletcher's Shepherds," pp. 295–310. My disagreement concerns the difference between what Fletcher actually wrote and what the play can be made to sound like in prose paraphrase. As Bliss describes the play without a detailed look at the language, her high estimate (that it nearly achieves "perfection of an almost unique kind") sounds justified. But she never confronts the literary problems I discuss below: the static pace, lengthy speeches, overwrought rhetoric, and the awkward language Fletcher was forced into by his rhyming.

[14] "To his loving friend M. *Jo. Fletcher* concerning his Pastorall," 3:492.

[15] Preface to his edition of the play in A. H. Bullen, gen. ed., *The Works of Francis Beaumont and John Fletcher* (London, 1904–12), 3:7. See also Charles Lamb, who felt that, were it not for some regrettable lapses in morality, "it had finally been a Poem fit to vie with *Comus* or the *Arcadia*" (*The Works of Charles and Mary Lamb*, ed. E. V. Lucas [New York, 1905], 4:312).

up impression, as of details gleaned from Gerard's *Herball* to authenticate the pastoral setting:

> these for frenzy be
> A speedy and a soveraigne remedie,
> The bitter Wormewood, Sage, and Marigold,
> Such simpathy with mans good they do hold:
> This Tormentil whose vertue is to part
> All deadly killing poison from the heart,
> And heere *Narcissus* roote, for swellings best:
> Yellow *Lecimacus*, to give sweete rest
> To the faint Shepheard.
>
> (2.2.19–27)

Fletcher's dramatic verse is noted for its fluency and ease. No matter how artificial, the situation is anchored and made more convincing by the fast pace and authenticity of the dialogue. In *The Faithful Shepherdess* the effect is of someone straining to present sensational, ingenious, or bizarre situations in insistently beautiful, "golden" poetry. Often the direction of a speech is immediately obvious and the elaboration adds nothing:

> Then heare mee heaven, to whome I call for right,
> And you fayre twinckling starres, that crowne the night,
> And heare mee woods, and silence of this place,
> And ye sad howers, that moove a sullen pace,
> Heare mee ye shadowes, that delight to dwell,
> In horred darknesse, and ye powers of Hell,
> Whilst I breath out my last.
>
> (4.4.128–34)

After the catalog of inanimate objects summoned to hear her defense, Fletcher switches to another repetitive rhetorical device:

> I am that mayde,
> That yet untaynted *Amoret* that played
> The careless Prodigall, and gave awaye
> My soule to this younge man that now dares saye:
> I am a stranger, not the same, more wild,
> And thus with much beleife, I was beguild.
> I am that Mayde.
>
> (4.4.134–40)

Here Perigot wrongly believes that he is being addressed by the false Amaryllis transformed once again into Amoret's shape. But the brilliant, rapid twistings and turnings with which Fletcher developed such situations in his later plays is not possible with such lengthy arias, this one no less than twenty-eight lines. The dramaturgy is better suited to opera. The poetry by itself is usually too prolix, repetitive, and diffuse to arouse interest, at least to Jacobean audiences habituated to a faster pace. Often the rhyme produces grotesqueries of word order that simply cannot work on the stage:

> come, my temples binde
> With these sad hearbs, and when I sleepe you finde
> As you do speake your charme, thrice downe me let,
> And bid the water raise me *Amoret*.

> (2.3.97–100)

Soon Fletcher and his collaborator would become the toast of London for producing such startling lines as Evadne's "A maidenhead *Amintor* / At my yeares?" in the famous wedding night scene of *The Maid's Tragedy* (2.1.193–94). The vast difference between this and Amaryllis's stilted "Still thinkst thou such a thinge as Chastitie, / Is amongst woemen? (3.1.296–97) in *The Faithful Shepherdess* is a measure of how much Fletcher gained from the collaboration.

In her essay on this play, Lee Bliss claims to find that an inclusive openness of attitude is basic to the play: "both principles [abstinence and amorous plenitude] are shown to be divine, attractive, authoritative."[16] The play celebrates "unruly passion tamed to harmony and socially sanctioned fruitfulness, the integration of Pan's rhythms into human institutions."[17] However, she acknowledges difficulties with her argument caused by what she calls Fletcher's "lapses" into a too-rigorous "stress on abstinence": "Such clear moral distinctions and narrow commandments can only suggest both the priest's and the priestess's ignorance of a troubling complexity in the goals they serve and the lives to which they minister. As framing spiritual advisors, they remain oddly estranged from the world Fletcher dramatizes."[18] The problem with this reading is that Fletcher is as estranged as his priest and priestess from the play Bliss would prefer him to have written. By devoting the entire last act to the endorsement of stringent and simplistic attitudes, he makes clear where he stands.

The quarto prefatory poems by Jonson and Nathan Field indicate that the audience also found the play excessively moralistic. Jonson says that the play was disliked "since it had not to do / With vices," and he praises Fletcher for his "innocence."[19] Field takes the same

---

[16] "Defending Fletcher's Shepherds," p. 304.
[17] Ibid., p. 309.
[18] Ibid.
[19] Hoy, ed., in Bowers, gen. ed., *Dramatic Works*, 3:492, ll. 8–10, 11.

line of defense, attacking "our pregnant age, that does despise / All
innocent verse, that lets alone her vice." He also speaks of the "elegant proprietie / Of words, including a morallitie / So sweete and profitable."[20] At that high moment in Jacobean drama, the audience expected more from a play than *The Faithful Shepherdess* offered.
Aesthetically, they required a more mimetic art; and under the influence of the Master of Negative Capability, they required a more "sophisticated" awareness of the complexity of moral choices. In 1633
The Faithful Shepherdess found its proper home in the effete court theater of Queen Henrietta Maria.[21] There it must have seemed like an
astonishing anticipation of the reigning taste for stylish high-mind-
edness. It was considered important enough in the Cavalier literary
world to be translated into Latin in 1638 by Sir Richard Fanshawe.

In any case, for this study the greatest value of *The Faithful Shepherdess* is what it reveals about the young Fletcher before he had become an equal partner with Beaumont. Their political attitudes were
remarkably similar, but at the same time that Beaumont was a cos-
mopolitan Inns of Court wit playing with Ovidianism and indulging
in court satire, deeply immersed in the manners and mores of London, Fletcher appears as a young man brought up in a succession of
bishop's palaces, a fit companion for the Spenser-saturated academic
first cousins with whom he had been living. In this play he sounds
more narrowly "Puritanical" than Milton who, in fact, adapted some
passages from *The Faithful Shepherdess* for *Comus*.[22] Whatever distaste
Milton expressed for Jacobean drama—in some passages quite vehement—his occasional use of John Fletcher's work suggests that he ex-
empted him. As he read this play about people lost in a dark forest,
saved from their worst mistakes and purged of their passions by su-
pernatural forces, *The Faithful Shepherdess* must have looked to him
like a work by one of those Spenserian Fletchers.

---

[20] Ibid., 3:489, ll. 5–6, 11–13.

[21] It is probably no coincidence that in this same year a second quarto was printed of
the 1602 translation of Guarini's *Il Pastor Fido*.

[22] As many editors have noted, there is a clear similarity between Sabrina's healing
powers in ll. 902ff. and Amoret's; and between *Comus*, ll. 78ff., and *The Faithful Shepherdess*, 3.1.180ff.

Chapter Five

THE SCORNFUL LADY AND "CITY COMEDY"

BEAUMONT AND FLETCHER must have been fast learners. Shortly after their disastrous experimental plays, Fletcher with some assistance from Beaumont wrote one of the most popular plays in their canon, *The Scornful Lady* (ca. 1608–10).[1] First produced by the Children of the Queen's Revels and later by the King's Men, the comedy was printed in no fewer than ten quartos in the seventeenth century. To Edmund Waller it was Fletcher's masterpiece in comedy, and Dryden described it (along with *The Merry Wives of Windsor!*) as "almost exactly formed."[2] Today it is not immediately obvious why it was singled out for such praise and popularity. It seems to be a rather gross and implausible portrayal of the battle of the sexes, better done in later plays like *The Wild Goose Chase*. Nonetheless, as a phenomenon—the most popular play by the most popular playwrights of the century—it deserves careful scrutiny.

The popularity of Beaumont and Fletcher's plays, if one is to believe James Shirley's preface to the First Folio of 1647, was not based simply on their recreational value:

[This book contains] *the Authentick witt that made Blackfriers an Academy, where the three howers spectacle while* Beaumont and Fletcher *were presented,*

---

[1] For this date see Baldwin Maxwell's compelling arguments in *Studies in Beaumont, Fletcher, and Massinger* (Chapel Hill, N.C., 1939), pp. 17–28. Chambers's suggestion in *The Elizabethan Stage* (Oxford, 1923), 3:229, of 1613–17, accepted by Harbage and Schoenbaum's *Annals*, cannot be correct because no work by Beaumont can be dated after 1613. The title page of the first quarto of *The Scornful Lady* (1616) ascribes it to both Beaumont and Fletcher, but every scholar who has studied the problem gives Fletcher the much larger share of the writing. Cyrus Hoy, "The Shares of Fletcher and his Collaborators in the Beaumont and Fletcher Canon," *Studies in Bibliography* 11 (1958): 96, sees evidence of Beaumont's hand in only three scenes. I do not question the attributions of specific scenes, but there is internal evidence of collaboration at the planning stage. The treatment of Lady and of Young Loveless differs significantly from that of comparable figures in Fletcher's later unaided work and resembles plays in which Beaumont collaborated or was the sole author. A mixture of traditional anti-feminine material and pure perversity in the character of ladies is a hallmark of his plays. The nearly contemporaneous *Woman's Prize* (1611) written by Fletcher alone employs the same kind of material but handles it with far greater sympathy for women.

[2] "Upon Mr. *John Fletcher's* Playes," Arnold Glover and A. R. Waller, eds., *The Works of Francis Beaumont and John Fletcher* (Cambridge, 1905–12), 1:xxiiii; "Essay of Dramatic Poesy," *Essays of John Dryden*, ed. W. P. Ker (Oxford, 1900), 1:79.

were usually of more advantage to the hopefull young Heire, then a costly, dan-
gerous, forraigne Travell . . . ; And it cannot be denied but that the young spirits
of the Time, whose Birth & Quality made them impatient of the sowrer wayes of
education, have from the attentive hearing these pieces, got ground in point of wit
and carriage of the most severely employed Students, while these Recreations were
digested into Rules, and the very Pleasure did edifie. How many passable dis-
coursing dining witts stand yet in good credit upon the bare stock of two or three
of these single Scenes.[3]

For high-spirited gallants impatient with formal education, concen-
tration in the works of Beaumont and Fletcher at the Blackfriars
Academy socialized and refined them more effectively than a *Wan-
derjahr*, or Oxford and Cambridge, or courtesy books.

As a text for that purpose *The Scornful Lady* must have been particularly effective. While posing as a city comedy, it has the generalized
quality of a didactic morality play. The scornful lady of the title has
no name; this is even pointed out:

> *Elder Loveless.* . . . Pray where and when [have we met]?
> *Welford.* In such a Ladies house Sir:
>   I need not name her.
>
> (5.1.29–31)[4]

Consistent with her namelessness no effort beyond the invocation of
the commonplaces of antifeminine lore is made to account for her
actions. At the climax of the play when she is most disturbed by the
outcome of her own perverse course, she describes herself as Everywoman: "Is it not strange that every womans will / Should tracke out
new waies to disturbe her selfe?" (5.2.1–2). The other women are
equally typical. There is Lady's very shadowy sister with the biblically
appropriate name of Martha. Another woman is known only as
"Widow"—a rich one, of course. A fourth is a comic waiting woman,
ironically named Younglove. She is, perhaps, "Older Everywoman":
ugly, perpetually lustful, and as scornful of her pathetic lover as her
mistress is of hers. Of the men, too, little is known beyond the suggestions of their names and roles. Elder Loveless, in pursuit of Lady,
is an older brother; he is a responsible, sober, persistent lover. Young
Loveless is, inevitably, a spendthrift scapegrace. He maintains a
drunken entourage of characters with names like "Captain," "Poet,"
"Traveller," and "Tobacco-Man." The other male characters are so

---

[3] Glover and Waller, *Works of Beaumont and Fletcher*, 1:xi.
[4] All references in the text are to the edition of Cyrus Hoy in Fredson Bowers, gen.
ed., *The Dramatic Works in the Beaumont and Fletcher Canon* (Cambridge, 1966–), vol. 2.

two-dimensional that it comes as a surprise when one named Welford reveals that he has a first name, Harry.

These characters speak in the witty, colloquial style—much of it prose—one might hear from the mouths of young gentry in a tavern. No play in the canon better illustrates Dryden's famous comparison of Beaumont and Fletcher with Shakespeare: "they understood and imitated the conversation of gentlemen better; whose wild debaucheries, and quickness of wit in repartee, no poet before them could paint as they have done."[5] A passage late in the play provides a good example. Two couples have just emerged from their first sexual encounters, the men in both cases having gained their desire by a certain amount of trickery:

> *Elder Loveless.* [referring to Lady] How like you this dish, *Welford*, I made a supper on't, and fed so heartily, I could not sleepe.
> *Lady.* By this light, had I but sented out your traine, ye had slept with a bare pillow in your armes, and kist that, or else the bedpost, for any wife yee had got this twelve-month yet: I would have vext you more then a tyr'd post-horse: and bin longer bearing, then ever after-game at *Irish* was. Lord, that I were unmaried againe.
> *Elder Loveless.* Lady, I would not undertake yee, were you againe a *Haggard*, for the best cast of sore Ladies i'th Kingdome: you were ever tickle footed, and would not trusse round!
> *Welford.* Is she fast?
> *Elder Loveless.* She was all night lockt here boy.
> *Welford.* Then you may lure her without fear of loosing: take off her Creance. You have a delicate Gentlewoman to your sister [Welford's bedmate, Lady's sister]: Lord what a pretty fury she was in, when she perceived I was a man: but I thanke God I satisfied her scruple, without the Parson o'th towne.
>
> (5.4.76–93)

It would be easy to find wittier repartee in Shakespeare, but nowhere, I think, dialogue so saturated in the manners and morals of the seventeenth-century gallant. The easy allusion to the parlor game of "Irish,"[6] the quick thrust and counterthrust of technical terms from falconry used for sexual double entendres, the unabashedly triumphant tone in which the two gallants celebrate the satisfaction of their appetites—and this without any pretense of conventional morality: all this may not "suit all men's humours" (as Dryden asserts about Beau-

---

[5] "Essay of Dramatic Poesy," *Essays of Dryden*, 1:81.

[6] Alexander Dyce, ed., *The Works of Beaumont and Fletcher* (London, 1843–46), 3:108–9, explains that in the game of "Irish" it takes a great deal of skill to play the "after-game."

mont and Fletcher's comedies), but it certainly suited a Blackfriars audience.

As befits a play for an academy, *The Scornful Lady* opens by posing two problems of the utmost importance:

> *Young Loveless.* [My task is] to make a Userer honest, or to loose my land.
> *Elder Loveless.* And mine is to perswade a passionate woman, or leave the
> Land.
>
> (1.1.8–11)

The two brothers go about their tasks very differently. The older one is an abject Petrarchan lover imperiously ruled by the fair cruel Lady. A proto-Millamant who hates being taken for granted, she has condemned him to a year of travel because he has had the temerity to kiss her in public. In the first lines of poetry in the play, she ringingly asserts,

> Beleeve me; if my wedding smock were on,
> Were the gloves bought and given, the Licence come,
>
> . . . .
>
> Were my feete in the dore, were *I John*, said,
> If *John* should boast a favour done by me,
> I would not wed that yeare.
>
> (1.1.144–45, 150–52)

For four acts the older brother tries to subdue this proud, brilliant adversary by a series of tricks as inept and transparent as those that the appropriately named title figure of Beaumont and Fletcher's precisely contemporaneous *The Coxcomb* (1608–10) employed on his witty wife. First, the Elder Loveless makes an ineffectual play for her sympathy by appearing before her in disguise and announcing that he has been drowned. This pitiful news had inspired barely suppressed pleasure from his younger brother, who as his heir envisaged an end to his financial problems (2.2). Lady does seem genuinely distressed until she sees through his "Players tricks" (3.1.270) and sends him away in humiliation. In the fourth act Elder Loveless again tries to trick her into cancelling his exile, this time by announcing that he no longer cares for her. Again she detects his act and mocks him brutally for his effort.[7]

Before viewing the resolution of this relationship one might now

---

[7] In 5.2.1–21 she acknowledges the self-destructive component of her perverse behavior, but she also expresses the feeling that these impulses spring from the same source as her sense of power and freedom. This fascinating attempt at a psychological explanation of her conduct is not developed. In most of the play one need only read the same literature as the Wife of Bath's scholarly husband to comprehend her.

call sadomasochistic, one must consider the action of the far livelier and more original subplot. It concerns the economic difficulties of the wastrel, Young Loveless, who has squandered his great wealth— no less than ten thousand pounds—and placed himself at the mercy of a flint-hearted usurer. His older brother tries to solve his problems by rational planning, but Young Loveless prefers a wilder course:

> *Young Loveless.* Why ile purse [i.e., steal purses]; if that raise mee not, Ile bet at bowling alleys, or man whores; I would fain live by others: but Ile live whilst I am unhangd, and after the thoughts taken.[8]
>
> *Elder Loveless.* I see you are tide to no particular imployment then.
>
> *Young Loveless.* Faith I may choose my course: they say nature brings foorth none but shee provides for em: Ile trie her liberalitie.
>
> (1.1.182–88)

Elder Loveless saves the "Prodigall" (as the dramatis personae of the second quarto describes him) from this reckless path by placing him in charge of his house while he goes on his supposed travels. Immediately Young Loveless installs a wild rout of bacchanalian revelers there. Not only does he flout the orders of the sober steward Savile, who had been specifically empowered to curb his "wildnesse" (1.2.42); he requires (and obtains) the latter's active participation in his orgies. The unbroken round of drunkenness and wenches is not portrayed as particularly attractive; and the prodigal's lack of sorrow at the supposed death of his brother establishes him as barely pleasant. Beaumont and Fletcher violate the rule that improvident, feckless younger brothers be charming, large-hearted figures whose easily forgivable vices have led to their troubles; instead of his ruin, Young Loveless's unamiable nonchalance gains him economic success. After he believes that he has inherited his brother's estate, he agrees to sell it to the usurer Moorcraft. With the cash thus obtained he purchases a knighthood, woos a wealthy widow whom the usurer is also courting, learns that his brother is still alive, coolly refuses to return the money to the usurer, and, having acquired the knighthood that was a condition for marriage with her, gains the widow's hand. During these ruthless proceedings the poet of his drunken ménage gleefully promises to "write thy life my sonne of pleasure, equall with *Nero* or *Caligula*" (2.3.110–11). The captain glosses this classical allusion by explaining to the uncomprehending, because presumably uneducated, younger brother that it refers to "two roring boyes of *Rome* that made all split" (2.3.113). Young Loveless is indeed a "roaring

---

[8] Weber, quoted by Dyce, *Works of Beaumont and Fletcher*, 1:13n., glosses the last phrase thus: "i.e., according to the thought that first strikes me."

boy," if not quite a Nero or Caligula. The most frequent epithet applied to him is "wild," his manner and that of his followers is "uncivil." What they most abhor is the bourgeois injunction to "consider" before they act:

> *Savil.* Good Sir consider.
> *Young Loveless.* Shall we consider gentlemen. How say you?
> *Captain.* Consider? that were a simple toy ifaith.
>   Consider? whose morrals that? The man that cries
>   Consider, is our foe: let my steele know him.
>
> (2.2.27–31)

Reckless incivility enables Young Loveless to outwit the usurer and win the rich widow. At the same time Elder Loveless's sober civility and witless tricks bring him a succession of humiliating defeats. As *The Scornful Lady* develops, it becomes increasingly clear that the organizing principle and the chief impact of the play spring from a running contrast between two ways of behaving. In the fourth act the lady extracts from the elder brother the abject confession, "I cannot live without you" (261). One scene later the widow, just before their marriage, tries to persuade Young Loveless to turn away his disreputable companions, but his response is notably different: "I will be short and pithy: I had rather / Cast you off" (4.2.49–50). His lady—a grocer's widow with aspirations to gentility—had hoped that after marriage he would keep a "civill house" and follow "a course / Farre from your old carrire" (4.2.5–7). These sentiments, very similar to those of Mrs. Merrythought in *The Knight of the Burning Pestle* (3.3.487–90), inspire a series of obscene jokes by Young Loveless's followers at the expense of "civil" manners. They also provoke one of the funniest speeches in the play, a spirited, fanciful defense by Young Loveless of his comrades' monastic simplicity of life, reduced as it is to one indispensable, purifying aliment, ale:

> In this short sentence Ale, is all included:
> Meate, Drinke, and Cloth. . . .
> .   .   .   .
> Ale is their eating, and their drinking surely,
> Which keeps their bodies cleere, and soluble.
> Bread is a binder, and for that abolisht
> Even in their ale, whose lost roome fills an apple,
> Which is more ayrie, and of subtiller *Nature*.
> The rest they take, is little, and that little,
> As little easie: For like strict men of order,

They doe correct their bodies with a bench,
Or a poore stubborne table. . . .

(4.2.62–84)[9]

The irreverent wit that sees a connection between "strict men of order" and lazy, disorderly leeches who sprawl drunkenly wherever
they chance to fall is reminiscent of speeches by Lords of Misrule at
college or Inns of Court revels. Young Loveless is not charming; he
is not the good-natured man of sentimental comedy. He is a relaxed
amoralist with a good eye for the main chance. As such, he is a model
for an impoverished younger son at Blackfriars and even for his
older brother.

By the magical workings of the double plot, Elder Loveless in act 5
suddenly shifts his attitudes and methods. As if he had received tu-
telage from his more successful sibling, he now speaks of his Petrarchan Lady in strictly sensual, animalistic terms, as a thing to be
beaten, mastered, overreached. It almost seems like a valid response,
considering her perverse cruelty. Even her own sister admits that
Lady lacks civility (5.2.256) and does not respond to gentle treatment.
The older brother adopts the rather implausible stratagem of dis-
guising his former rival Welford as his fiancée and announcing that
he intends to marry "her" unless Lady will marry him instantly. She
falls for the trick, perhaps because she is afraid that her cruelty has
jeopardized her chances of ever getting him (5.2.1–21). But the important point is the change in Elder Loveless's tactics. When he appears at the opening of the play, he addresses his beloved with stuffy
humility, "Mistres, for me to praise over againe that worth, which all
the world, and you your selfe can see—." Of course, she interrupts
him by feigning boredom (1.1.68–88). By the end of the play the single aim of the lovers—it gives an extra dimension to the name "Loveless"—is to trap their prey, any prey. Welford, originally a suitor of
the lady, settles for her sister without a moment's hesitation: "I care
not which I have" (5.1.78). After both lovers have achieved their goal,
their language, as we have seen, is that of the hunt, of falconry, and
of eating. No words of love are passed. The conversion to Young
Loveless's methods and manners has taken place, and the connection
is specifically made:

⁹ Here again is a passage suggestive of Beaumont's influence. The tenacious, bohe-
mian jollity of Old Merrythought of *The Knight of the Burning Pestle*, always praising
what gave him his "jolly red nose," qualifies him as the spiritual ancestor of this defender of the moral virtues of ale; and *The Knight's* criticism of the bourgeois values of
the merchant Venturewell and the citizens closely resembles Young Loveless's program
of uncivil, unconsidered wildness. Fletcher created the subplot of *The Scornful Lady*
with the author of *The Knight* at his side or in his mind.

Young Loveless. How doe you finde my brother?
Lady. Almost as wilde as you are.

(5.4.120–21)

But a more surprising conversion makes Young Loveless's function
as a model even more explicit. The usurer Moorcraft, until now the
stereotypical, ruthless skinflint of Elizabethan drama, becomes a reckless spendthrift:

> *Moorcrafte.* [to Young Loveless] Yes faith Knight, Ile follow thy example:
> thou hadst land and thousands, thou spendst, and flungst away, and
> yet it flowes in double: I purchasde, wrung, and wierdraw'd for my
> wealth, lost, and was cozend: for which I make a vowe, to trie all the
> waies above ground, but Ile find a constant meanes to riches without
> curses.

(5.3.51–56)[10]

At the comic conclusion Moorcraft gives all the newly married couples jewels while evangelizing for his new creed of unconsidered
recklessness: "Come be mad Boyes" (5.4.209). Only servants are excluded from the pleasures and profits of wildness. The steward Savile
is strongly chastised for his momentary indulgence in drink and
women and is restored to favor only on the promise of future temperance.

In Fletcher's later solo work and in collaboration with others, he
produced a series of roaring boys and wild gallants in a direct line of
succession from Young Loveless. They are frequently presented as
vital and attractive, but one is also shown that they pose a problem to
"civil" society, as in *Monsieur Thomas*, or that they are essentially
coarse of nature, as in *The Wild Goose Chase. The Scornful Lady* portrays
a wild gallant with none of this admixture of criticism. Thus there are
many ugly moments, like the baiting by the "wits" (led inevitably by

---

[10] Dryden in the "Essay of Dramatic Poesy," *Essays of Dryden*, 1:66, misses the point
of Moorcraft's change:

> the conversion of the Usurer in *The Scornful Lady* seems to me a little forced; for,
> being an Usurer, which implies a lover of money to the highest degree of covet-
> ousness (and such the poet has represented him), the account he gives for the
> sudden change is, that he has been duped by the wild young fellow; which in
> reason might render him more wary another time, and make him punish himself
> with harder fare and coarser clothes, to get up again what he had lost: but that he
> should look on it as a judgment, and so repent, we may expect to hear in a sermon,
> but I should never endure it in a play.

Moorcraft does not convert to a moral life; he changes his tactics to gain more material
success.

Young Loveless) of the foolish but pleasant curate after his marriage to the Lady's much-reviled maid Younglove:

> *Welford.* Sir *Roger*, what will you take to lie from your sweeteheart to
>   night?
> *Roger.* Not the best benefice in your worships gift Sir.
> *Welford.* A whorson, how he swels.
> *Young Loveless.* How many times to night Sir *Roger*.
> *Roger.* Sir you grow scurrilous:
>   What I shall doe, I shall doe: I shall not neede your helpe.
> *Young Loveless.* For horse flesh *Roger*.

(5.4.192–99)

In this example of the "language of gentlemen," one looks in vain for the "quickness of wit" Dryden admires; its "repartee" more nearly resembles the unlamented last days of vaudeville. This exchange is symptomatic of a deeper coarseness in the play that feeds off the exhausted tradition of antifeminine humor, particularly in the many tedious (but probably popular) exposures of the ugly, aging Younglove's sex hunger.

The vein of coarseness in this amusing play springs mainly out of its simplistic admiration of Young Loveless's methods. The play's great popularity brings to mind the failure of *The Knight of the Burning Pestle* with its much subtler presentation of the attractions and defects of "carelessness." Beaumont and Fletcher are frequently accused of having achieved their legendary success by "catering" to their audiences. While I usually disagree with this viewpoint, in *The Scornful Lady* I see a nearly total identification of values between the authors and a significant portion of the Blackfriars audience. It is a play about and for young gallants, imitating and sanctioning without much criticism their very tones and manners, their crass vulgarity as well as their liveliness and wit. It particularly encourages that vast and bitter underclass of which both Beaumont and Fletcher were members, the younger sons, by making the actions and attitudes of Young Loveless exemplary. They make a case for his carelessness by reminding one that the "plans" and "consideration" of the usurer involves living off the suffering of others. Were the widow to marry the usurer, asks Young Loveless,

> Is it fit
> One of such tendernes, so delicate,
> So contrary to things of care, should stirre
> And breake her better meditations,
> In the bare brokage of a brace of Angels?

. . . .
Eate by the hope of forfeits, and lie downe
Onely in expectation of a morrow,
That may undoe some easie harted foole,
Or reach a widowes curses? Let out money,
Whose use returnes the principall?

(3.2.2.84–88, 90–94)

But to account for the immense popularity of this play, one must probably look beyond the pleasures of recognition and celebration that it so obviously possesses. Its deeper fascination, as Shirley's preface suggests, must have sprung from its operation as an exemplum: a stripped, bare depiction of how a hopeful young heir should talk and act in order to win a fortune or subdue a lady.

The Scornful Lady is the most popular example of a kind of play, in fact the largest single group of private theater plays, that has come to be called "city comedies." Usually set in contemporary London or a barely disguised version of it, their central concerns are the economic, social, and sexual problems of young gentry. By their very nature they would appeal to a restricted audience—Inns of Court residents, affluent country visitors, court hangers-on, and the like. In the preface to one such play, *The Roaring Girl*, Middleton said that he was writing "for the times and the termers."[11] City comedies carp at courtiers and citizens, assume habitual recourse to prostitutes and usurers, make elaborate jokes in technical legal language, often assume a university education. Above all they revere wit as the weapon that will ensure survival in a society where traditonal values seem obsolete. As Brian Gibbons says in his study of this kind of play, "The essential dynamic of the plays in City Comedy is the conflict between order and authority on the one hand, and intelligently aggresssive insubordination on the other."[12] The one constant element is a disordered world that denies traditional pieties. In their last scenes one finds none of the harmony, music, or assurance of a revivified, healthy society we have been taught to expect by Shakespeare's comedies of the 1590s. Marriage promises no union of true minds, only the hope of large unearned incomes. Characterizations are notably flat because social interaction is conceived primarily as a battle between raw appetencies. Hobbes rather than Hooker describes best the "world picture" of these plays. In style and values the Jacobean private city comedies anticipate Wycherley and recall nothing of Lyly.

[11] A. H. Bullen, ed., *The Works of Thomas Middleton* (New York, 1964), 4:7.
[12] *Jacobean City Comedy* (Cambridge, Mass., 1968), p. 202.

The Scornful Lady is a prime example of the type; it at once described and formed the "young spirits of the time."

AFTERWORD ON *THE CAPTAIN*

Another example will illustrate Beaumont and Fletcher's enormous talent for conveying the very form and pressure of the Jacobean period. *The Scornful Lady* was first produced by a children's company, but it would take a detector not yet devised to determine how it suited the tastes of its audience better than *The Captain* (1609–12), written more or less simultaneously for the King's Men.[13] Of course, this is in large part because the King's Men then occupied Blackfriars, where the audience was indistinguishable from that at any of the private theaters.

The Captain is a double plot play built on a heavily moralistic theme. In the main plot, much indebted to Marston's *Dutch Courtesan*, two young men are bewitched and enchanted by the very beautiful Lelia, whom they know to be a dissolute whore. Eventually they discover the ugliness of her true nature and are freed of her power. In the farcical, humors-style subplot, the title figure Captain Jacamo is as honest and ugly as Lelia is depraved and beautiful. However, he attracts a sympathetic, wealthy young girl who eventually convinces him despite his nearly pathological distrust that she admires even his face. In both plots virtue overcomes "outward things." Even Lelia eventually repents—under duress, it is true—and claims to possess "a heart / As pure as any womans" (5.5.104–5).[14]

Such, then, is the trite outer framework of this play. There is, however, another, more interesting play struggling to appear, one that the authors seem scarcely aware of writing. In *The Scornful Lady* the success of Young Loveless's calculated incivility provides an amusing, infectious fantasy, but *The Captain* with its picture of the necessity and rewards for taming natural instincts presents its realistic complement. Captain Jacamo is both worthy and animalistic, honorable and untameable. This character type composed of polar opposites reappears in many Beaumont and Fletcher plays, but more often in those Fletcher wrote alone. Sometimes the wild gallant cannot be socialized and must leave the civilized world, for example, the title figure in *The Mad Lover*; sometimes he is accepted on his own terms, as is the title figure in *Monsieur Thomas*; and frequently, as in this play, he is assim-

---

[13] It is a collaborative work with many difficulties about precise ascription of responsibility.

[14] All references in the text are to the edition of L. A. Beaurline in Bowers, gen. ed., *Dramatic Works*, vol. 1.

ilated into the world, his claws manicured if not totally clipped. In a wild conclusion, Jacamo must be doused with a bucket of urine and tied down before he will listen to his mistress plead her love. Convinced of her sincerity he agrees to become part of the community of gentlemen: "Slight I'le have my head corld, and powderd" (5.4.62). As he says, he has been "beatten to some understanding" (5.4.92–93). A parallel process of enforced socialization occurs to the utterly depraved Lelia after she tries to seduce her own father. Exposed for what she is, she is carried away kicking, scratching, and screaming. When she next appears, she is completely "penitent" (5.1.11) and domesticated, prepared to be a faithful wife to the fool her father has tricked her into marrying.

Thus the action of *The Captain* shows how society naturalizes and civilizes by extinguishing "natural" instincts. The play takes place in a period of peace, much like the inglorious peace of King James's reign that rankled so many of his high-spirited subjects. Fletcher himself, as seen in chapter 1, was to express the hope some years later to the countess of Huntingdon that England would go to war with Spain.[15] In *The Captain* the honest soldiers are convinced that peace is harmful to the moral fiber of the state:

> *Jacamo.* Pox a peace.
>   It fills the Kingdome full of holydayes,
>   And onely feedes the wants of whores and pipers;
>   And makes the idle drunken Rogues get Spinsters.
>
>   . . . .
>   . . . it is the surfet of all youth,
>   That makes the toughnesse, and the strength of nations
>   Melt into women. 'Tis an ease that broodes
>   Theeves, and basterds only.
>
>   (2.1.32–44)

Clearly, there is no outlet in a peaceful world for one's deeper impulses:

>   cold dull rusty peace makes us appeare
>   Like empty Pictures, onely the faint shadowes
>   Of what we should be.
>
>   (2.1.8–10)

In a nearly perfect exemplification of civilization and its discontents, as soon as Jacamo and Lelia have been tamed and dragged into soci-

---

[15] S. A. Tannenbaum, "An Unpublished John Fletcher Autograph," *Journal of English and German Philology* 28 (1929): 35–40, l. 19.

ety, a legitimate outlet is discovered for the captain's, if not Lelia's, "angry" nature. Just after the marriages Jacamo's brother-in-law Fredrick appears with some happy news:

> *Fredrick.* First joy unto you all; and next I think
>   We shall have warres.
> *Jacamo.* Give me some wine, I'le drinke to that.
>
> (5.5.126–28)

Unbounded mirth erupts. Beatings, showers of urine, moral conversions with a sword, subdue those unable or unwilling to join society. In the modern world men are permitted to "looke like men" (2.1.7) only when their energies are employed against outside enemies. Soldiers here and elsewhere in Fletcher are the supreme "sort of men":

> they are people . . .
> . . . .
> Of all the old world, only left to keepe
> Man as he was, valiant and virtuous.
> They are the modell of those men, whose
>   honours
> We heave our hands at when we heare recited.
>
> (1.2.121–26)

The heroic age was within easy memory while Raleigh was languishing in the Tower and the *Golden Hind* was rotting at anchor as a tourist attraction. All around London angry young would-be heroes were brawling, duelling, drinking, whoring, and gambling away fortunes, while the proud kingdom seemed to be decaying in impotent, alien hands. Vital spirits yearned for some opportunity to distinguish themselves. As Fabritio observes, it is nearly "malitious, / To curse the faire peace of my Mother Countrey" (2.1.29–30); yet the frustration and desperation were there. It is not hard to understand why Beaumont and Fletcher were so immediately popular. Despite the uproarious and artificial exterior of plays like this, they describe a real psychological and moral dilemma.

Chapter Six

CUPID'S REVENGE: PURITY AND PRINCES

IF SCHOLARS are correct in their dating, *Cupid's Revenge* (1610–12) is the first product of the collaboration to exhibit most of the characteristics of a "Beaumont & Fletcher" play: an improbable plot set in a distant time and exotic place; realistic characters who seem intermixed with archetypes out of dreams; high-pitched rant alternating with gentlemanly conversation.[1] In short, it is a far cry from *The Knight of the Burning Pestle* and *The Faithful Shepherdess*. The chemistry of the collaborators' "strange unimitable Intercourse"[2] produced a compound that differs radically from what either had made separately.

One striking example is Fletcher's shift from the puritanical attitude toward chastity he held in *The Faithful Shepherdess*. Combining two stories from Sidney's *Arcadia*, the fantastic plot of *Cupid's Revenge* depicts the disasters that occur when, at the entreaties of his daughter and son, the king of the Arcadian kingdom of Lycia suppresses worship of the country's tutelary deity, Cupid.[3] The god, in a choral role similar to that of Revenge in *The Spanish Tragedy*, implacably avenges this affront by causing the death of all three members of the royal

---

[1] The first quarto (1615) attributes the play to Fletcher alone; the second quarto (1630) adds Beaumont. Cyrus Hoy, "The Shares of Fletcher and his Collaborators in the Beaumont and Fletcher Canon," *Studies in Bibliography* 11 (1958): 90–91, sees it as a collaboration but does not find his linguistic methods very useful in distinguishing between the authors. It was written no later than 1612, the date of a court performance, but how much earlier is unclear. James E. Savage, "The Date of Beaumont and Fletcher's *Cupid's Revenge*," *ELH* 15 (1948): 186–94, argues for a date as early as 1607–8 on the basis of what he believes to be three topical references, but all would still have been recognizable in 1612. H. N. Hillebrand points out in *The Child Actors* (New York, 1964; orig. publ. 1926), pp. 320–21, that in 1613 Philip Rossiter as director of the Children of the Queen's Revels was paid for a court performance of this play. He adds, "If it was written for Rossiter's Queen's Revels company, then it belongs in or after 1610, when he came into the company." Therefore, based strictly on documentary evidence, the date must be 1610–12. Savage makes a persuasive case for the priority of *Cupid's Revenge* to *Philaster*. 1610 would still allow for the possibility that *Cupid's Revenge* was *written* before *Philaster*, whose terminus ad quem is 1610.

[2] Prefatory poem by John Pettus in 1647 folio, Arnold Glover and A. R. Waller, eds., *The Works of Francis Beaumont and John Fletcher* (Cambridge, 1905–12), 1:xx.

[3] See James E. Savage, "*Philaster* and Sidney's *Arcadia*," *ELH* 14 (1947): 194–206, for a thorough study of the relationship of *Cupid's Revenge* to *The Arcadia* and *Philaster*; also, Lee Bliss, *Francis Beaumont* (Boston, 1987), pp. 57–69.

family as well as four others associated with them. The authors, it should be noted, took pains to show (in 1.2) that the religion of Cupid with its tolerant attitude toward sex is happy and natural.

From the opening moments it is clear that the king and his children are themselves to blame for their tragic fate. King Leontius is a ranting, foolish dotard whose absolute trust in his daughter's wisdom (1.5.32)[4] leads to ruin. The princess Hidaspes, renowned for her chastity and virtue, has a puritanic abhorrence—expressed in language reminiscent of Pan's priest, the authorial spokesman in *The Faithful Shepherdess*—for what she calls "selfe-pleasing bold lasciviousnes" (1.1.51). Cupid's revenge on the princess is particularly horrible. Her model in *The Arcadia* falls in love with a man "so meane, as that he was but the sonne of her Nurse."[5] In place of this rather mild punishment, the authors invent as the object of the princess's passion the court dwarf Zoilus. Her love language is a black humor mixture of the grotesque, the pathetic, and the lyrical, worthy of the author of the "Elegy on the Lady Markham":

> Is he deformed? looke upon those eyes,
> That let all pleasure out into the world,
> Unhappy that they cannot see themselves.
> Looke on his hayre, that like so many beames,
> Streaking the East, shoote light ore halfe the world.
> Looke on him all together, who is made
> As if two Natures had contention
> About their skill, and one had brought foorth him.
>
> (1.4.39–46)

The princess feels her "bloud" so "inflamed" by him that she demands the dwarf in marriage. Horrified, the king responds by executing this hapless pawn of Cupid's revenge, whereupon the princess dies of grief. "This comes of Chastitie" (1.5.78), remarks a courtier as he watches the fateful events unfold. The wisdom of virgins and the ideal of chastity are as pernicious in Lycia as they were curative in the Thessaly of *The Faithful Shepherdess*.

The story of Cupid's revenge on the princess is concluded by the end of the second act. Her brother, Prince Leucippus, having collaborated in the suppression of the worship of Cupid, is equally deserving of punishment by the love god. For this the authors tack on a

---

[4] All quotations are from the edition by Fredson Bowers in Bowers, gen. ed., *The Dramatic Works in the Beaumont and Fletcher Canon* (Cambridge, 1966–), vol. 2.

[5] Sir Philip Sidney, *The Countess of Pembroke's "Arcadia,"* ed. Albert Feuillerat (Cambridge, 1962), p. 232.

second story from *The Arcadia*. The hitherto chaste Prince Leucippus[6] under Cupid's baleful influence becomes romantically involved with a notoriously loose but beautiful widow named Bacha. His interest in her is strictly sexual, but a misplaced sense of chivalry engendered by his innocent idealism and unworldliness drives the prince to lie prodigiously to his father in defense of her honor:

> If any of thy great, Great-grandmothers
> This thousand yeeres, had beene as chaste as she,
> It wou'd have made thee honester.
>   . . . she is by heaven
> Of the most strict and blamelesse chastitie
> That ever woman was.

In an aside he adds, "good gods forgive me" (2.2.153–58), but his high-pitched rhetoric is all too effective. His senile father—also, of course, under Cupid's curse—is instantly smitten by the corrupt widow's beauty. In quick succession the king orders his son abroad, woos the widow in scenes of broad comedy that depict his geriatric preening, and marries her at the end of act 2, so besotted by his love that he is indifferent to the fact that his beloved daughter, the princess, has just died.

As soon as the new queen is alone with Prince Leucippus, she informs him that she expects them to resume their sexual relationship. This dialogue, with its invitation to incest and its incredulous, "noble" responses, has its counterpart in many subsequent Beaumont and Fletcher plays:

> *Bacha.* . . . Come, kisse me.
> *Leucippus.*   Kisse you?
> *Bacha.*   Yes, be not ashamde:
>   You did it not your selfe, I will forgive you.
> *Leucippus.* Keepe you displeased gods, the due respect
>   I ought to beare unto this wicked woman,
>   As shee is now my Mother, fast within mee,
>   Least I adde sins to sinnes, till no repentance
>   Will cure mee.
>
>   (3.2.153–59)

Bacha persists, even begging him on her knees, but Leucippus remains true to his chivalrous ideals:

---

[6] His original in *The Arcadia* is not related to the royal family and does nothing to offend Cupid.

Leucippus. Tis your will Heaven:
  But let me beare me like my selfe,
  How ever shee does.

                                        (3.2.178–80)

Not for a moment is the prince tempted, but in a dilemma typical of Beaumont and Fletcher's Fools of Honor he cannot reveal Bacha's vile conduct to his father: she is, after all, his mother! His wicked stepmother, transformed into a hellish woman scorned, then plots his destruction. First, she makes the king jealous by her inordinate praise of his son; then she suggests that he is plotting to usurp the crown. When she so arranges circumstances that Leucippus appears on the verge of patricide-regicide, his foolish father condemns him to death.

Like his prototype in *The Arcadia*, about whom Sidney says that he is "subject to that only disadvantage of honest hearts, credulitie,"[7] Leucippus repeatedly puts his trust in a patent villain who acts as Bacha's tool. In the last act, when the prince has Bacha totally at his mercy, the prince tells his "mother" that he will not punish her but (echoing Hamlet's father) will "leave [her] . . . to heaven" (5.4.156). Even after she has fatally stabbed him, he tries in his last words to make one more noble gesture: "Last, I beseech you that my Mother-in-Law / May have buriall according to——[*Dyes*]" (5.4.219–20). The absolute purity of Leucippus inspires the loyalty of a friend, Ismenus, and love-unto-death from Bacha's innocent rustic daughter, Urania, who interposes herself between him and an assassin's knife. The citizens, too, admire him so much that they spontaneously mount an insurrection to save him from execution. Even a group of courtiers who act as a cynical, sophisticated chorus revere the hero's manifold virtues (3.3).

These admirers regard Leucippus with such uncritical reverence that it has blinded readers from seeing that Beaumont and Fletcher have injected an element of priggishness and pride into Leucippus's purity. When his friend Ismenus warns him not to trust Bacha's treacherous accomplice Timantus, Leucippus loftily suggests that he is a coward: "So much of man and so much fearefull; fye" (4.1.218). In impotent fury Ismenus can only respond, "Goe, and let your owne rod whip you: I pity you" (223). But it is difficult to pity someone so filled with a sense of his own righteousness. Ismenus's warning is justified, for Timantus leads Leucippus into the compromising situation that convinces the king that he must execute his son. The uprising by the admiring citizenry saves him, but as soon as he has been freed,

---

[7] *Countess of Pembroke's "Arcadia,"* p. 248.

he cavalierly dismisses his followers. After Ismenus reproaches Leucippus for once more being at the mercy of his enemies, Beaumont
and Fletcher offer their clearest criticism of the prince's rigid "nobility":

> *Leucippus.* To what end should I keepe em [his troops]. I am free.
> *Ismenus.* Yes, free o'th Traytors, for you are proclaymed one.
> *Leucippus.* Should I therefore make my selfe one?
> *Ismenus.* This is one of your morall Philosophy is it? Heaven blesse me
>   from subtilties to undo my self with; but I know, if reason her selfe
>   were here, she would not part with her owne safetie.
> *Leucippus.* Well, pardon *Ismenus*, for I know
>   My courses are most just; nor will I staine em
>   With one bad action.

$$(4.5.23–32)$$

One may be moved by Leucippus's rhetoric while feeling the validity
of Ismenus's criticism: there is something oversubtle, contrived, and
inhumane in Leucippus. His refusal to act like a rebel even though
he has been unjustly branded a traitor by a totally immoral enemy
may be "noble," but it is also irrationally self-destructive.

His "morall Philosophy" leads Leucippus to practice further casu-
istical tricks on himself, as when he justifies his lies in behalf of
Bacha's chastity:

>   it is lawfull
> To defend her, that onely for my love
> Lov'd evill.

$$(2.2.137–39)$$

His inflexible adherence to what is "lawfull" causes him to perpetuate
the situation his lie has engendered. The realization that Bacha is
now his "mother" renders him as impotent as the word "king" does
the literal-minded, royalist hero of *The Maid's Tragedy*, Amintor. Leucippus's virtues, Bacha perceives, so trap him that they can be manip-
ulated for his "undoing" (3.2.247–48). In the earlier part of the play
Beaumont and Fletcher are primarily concerned with dramatizing
the dehumanizing effects of puritanical attitudes toward sex. But as
with the ironic gibe at "morall Philosophy," they shift their criticism
to courtly targets, in particular to the kinds of priggish conduct enforced by an over-rigid construction of the honor code.

It is the failure to realize that figures like Leucippus are simultaneously objects of admiration and of criticism that, more than any
other single factor, has provoked a basic misunderstanding of the
work of Beaumont and Fletcher. Thus Una Ellis-Fermor comes very

close to seeing what the authors are attempting without realizing its implications:

> [Leucippus' scruples are] of so fantastic, ungrounded and strained a loyalty that he submits with patience and reverence to the insults, hostility and plotting of his own cast mistress Bacha simply because, by hoodwinking the old king Leontius, she has married him and become Leucippus's queen and mother. Here is a character rooted in unreality, with motives that seem to rest upon words only, with no perception of the nature of fact . . . , paying a ridiculous respect to a woman who, for seducing his own father, should be doubly hideous to him, and for her plans to undo the kingdom should be stamped out like any other contagious disease. The salt of common sense that meets us on every page of Ben Jonson, and that stayed by the major Jacobean dramatists at all but their wildest moments, has vanished from the fairy-land of Beaumont and Fletcher.[8]

Ellis-Fermor fails to notice—probably through an a priori sense of what Beaumont and Fletcher are like—that the authors share her view of Leucippus. All the points the critic scores against the prince are made either explicitly by commentators like Ismenus, who possess the "salt of common sense," or implicitly by the clearly displayed, disastrous consequences of Leucippus's actions. The "fairy-land" was not the construction of Beaumont and Fletcher but of their over-idealistic characters, nor was conduct like Leucippus's merely a figment of the authors' imaginations. In fact, the most "Sidneyan" aspect of this play is not its dramatization of two stories from *The Arcadia* but the resemblance of Leucippus's character to Sidney's (or more precisely, to that of contemporary legend), especially to his self-destructive, self-conscious "nobility." Leucippus, too, would have offered his water to the dying soldier and taken off his armor to share the danger of his friend. Sidney was not an isolated example but a model for the conduct of Jacobean cavaliers. Beaumont and Fletcher had only to look around Jacobean London to see serious and intelligent men impelled to foolhardy actions by the hollow absolutes of "honor" and "nobility" and "divine right." Lord Herbert of Cherbury and Sir Kenelm Digby come instantly to mind because they recorded their confused idealism in autobiographies, but there were many others. Dreams of knight-errantry were not confined to grocer's apprentices.

But the similarity between knights and grocer's apprentices also reminds one of the large changes in English culture in the brief interval

---

[8] *The Jacobean Drama: an Interpretation* (London, 1936), p. 209.

since Sidney's death. Beaumont and Fletcher show what is admirable about Leucippus while making it impossible to take him seriously as a tragic hero. His undeviating credulity or, more precisely, his inability to learn from experience, often makes him look simply foolish. Further, he lacks the power and energy of a true hero; he constantly appears hopeless and devitalized, a patient rather than an agent. His response to Bacha's attempt to discredit him to his father is typical. Instead of confuting her, he withdraws from the confrontation into a noble but passive querulousness:

> I am weary of my life,
> For Gods sake take it from me: it creates
> More mischiefe in the State then it is worth.
> The usage I have had, I know would make
> Wisedome her selfe run frantick through the streetes,
> And Patience quarrell with her shaddow.

(4.1.34–39)

As one hears in an admiring description of his conduct on the scaffold, he comports himself better as a martyr than a hero:

> His houre was come
> To lose his life, he ready for the stroke,
> Nobly, and full of Saint-like patience.

(4.4.43–45)

This tired nobility finally costs him his life. Through his usual unwary trustfulness he manages to receive a fatal wound from his ferocious "mother," though she is his captive. He himself points out the ignominy of the manner of his death:

> *Leucippus.* . . . what is man?
>   Or who would be one, when he sees a poore
>   Weake woman can in an instant make him none.

(5.4.200–202)

As a tragic hero Leucippus is badly miscast, but in him Beaumont and Fletcher, consciously or not, created a character type, the antihero, deeply appropriate to the Jacobean and Caroline age. A figure of great public esteem, but weak-willed, life-hating,[9] given to extreme, self-defeating, impressively noble gestures, he seems to have been conceived with Hamlet in mind. But his ethical confusions are only superficially related to Hamlet's problems because Beaumont and

---

[9] Among Beaumont and Fletcher's antiheroes Leucippus is atypical in not even once attempting suicide.

Fletcher concentrated on the manners and morals of a particular group at a certain time, the high gentry and aristocracy of Jacobean London. To the audience, figures like Leucippus and his more deeply etched successors, Philaster, Amintor, and Arbaces, would have had a familiar quality. Their ultimate successor was that literal-minded, code-constricted, noble figure, the Royal Martyr. Like Leucippus, King Charles had his greatest moment on the scaffold.

Chapter Seven

THE CONTEMPORARY "APPLICATION" OF
THE NOBLE GENTLEMAN

No PLAY by Beaumont and Fletcher is given a firmer "local habitation" than *The Noble Gentleman* (1611–15).[1] Just offstage, glamorous Jacobean courtly activities are occurring:

> a maske, or Barriers,
> Or tilting or a solemn christning,
> Or a great marriage, or new fire-works,
> Or any bravery.
>
> (2.1.183–86)[2]

One hears about but does not see such occurrences because the play deals with figures on the outer fringes of the court. Ostensibly set in France, the play portrays that moment in Jacobean London when the king's foolish generosity in awarding titles, honors, and money created a gold rush atmosphere in London. Elizabeth created 878 knights and 18 English peers during her forty-five-year reign; in twenty-two years James created 2,712 knights—934 in his first nine months—and 65 peers.[3] As news of the monarch's prodigality seeped into the countryside, a swarm of greedy hopefuls came to town. Since barbers and innkeepers had been made knights, it was not unnatural for a country gentleman with a few acres of land and fewer wits to dream of much more, perhaps (in Beaumont and Fletcher's satiric extension) even of a dukedom.

Such was the historical context for this play about a wealthy fool's quest for titles and honors. One sees the "Noble Gentleman" selling off his land bit by bit to maintain his extravagant life and ingratiate himself with courtiers who are ostensibly assisting his efforts to obtain a title or place. He infects his country cousin and even his servant

---

[1] This date is my suggestion. Its accuracy is of prime importance to the argument of this chapter, but it requires such detailed justification that I consign it to appendix A. The theater of origin is unknown.

[2] All quotations are from the edition of L. A. Beaurline in Fredson Bowers, gen. ed., *The Dramatic Works in the Beaumont and Fletcher Canon* (Cambridge, 1966–), vol. 3.

[3] Lawrence Stone, *Crisis of the Aristocracy* (Oxford, 1965), p. 755.

with similar ambitions, especially after the courtiers trick him into believing that his quest has been successful.

At times it appears that the point of the play is to evoke an older and better, if simpler, way of life disrupted by the infectious extravagance of the court. At one uncharacteristic moment of self-scrutiny the foolish protagonist muses,

> The country life is best, where quietly
> Free from the clamour of the troubled Court,
> We may enjoy our own greene shadowed walkes,
> And keepe a moderate diet without art.
> Why did I leave my house and bring my wife,
> To know the manner of this subtile place?
> I would when first the lust to fame and honour,
> Possest me, I had met with any evill
> But that.
>
> (2.1.2–10)

Moreover, the court is even uglier than that of *The Woman Hater*, where courtiers were merely walking stomachs. Here the inflated language of the play's first words, reminiscent of the glutton's paeans to his fishhead, promises a familiar kind of satire:

> What happiness waits on the life at Court,
> What dear content, greatness, delight and ease?
> What ever-springing hopes, what tides of honour,
> That raise their fortunes to the height of wishes?
> What can be more in man, what more in nature,
> Then to be great and fear'd? A Courtier,
> A noble Courtier? 'Tis a name that drawes
> Wonder, and dutie, from all eyes and knees.
>
> (1.1.1–8)

As this would suggest, one quickly finds that the reality of the court is far otherwise. In the next scene, two "noble" courtiers argue over who is the greater "Whore-master" (1.2.11). One revels in being "pointed at to be a noble wencher" (1.2.16). The other smugly enunciates a "noble theory of luxury" (1.2.59):

> This it is:
> When your desire is up, your blood well heated
> And apt for sweet encounter, chuse the night
> And with the night your wench, the streets have store,
> There seize upon her, get her to your chamber,

Give her a cardecew, 'tis royall payment;
When ye are dull, dismisse her, no man knows
Nor she her selfe, who hath encountered her.

. . . .

The night allows her equall with a Dutches,
Imagination doth all.

(1.2.64–74)

By comparison, the "young man carbuncular" of *The Waste Land* is a Petrarchan lover. With such gross exemplars of the "noble" and the "royall," the play seems embarked on a harsher attack on the court than *The Woman Hater*.[4] Then, quite abruptly, the focus shifts; the dark political satire dissolves into harmless farce. The court awards no honors, and the noble sexual expert is tricked into marriage with one of the apparent victims of his "theory."

The subplot seems to touch even more explicitly on political matters. A noble courtier named Shatillion has gone mad after having been rebuffed in his proposal of love to his "Love," as she is always designated.[5] He believes that invisible, malign forces are imprisoning his mistress because she is next in the line of succession to the throne and, further, that he is being tricked into treasonable activity in her defense. At the end of the play Shatillion snaps back to sanity and is united with his mistress. All his fears are revealed as fantasies, the product of temporary madness with no basis in fact. The court of *The Woman Hater* employed "intelligencers," but they do not exist here. Instead of Shatillion being persecuted, the authors make his fears totally a product of love melancholy, and his madness even becomes material for raucous comedy.

Baldwin Maxwell has suggested that this subplot contains many resemblances to events in the life of the Lady Arabella Stuart (1575–1615).[6] As daughter of Charles Stuart, earl of Lennox, younger brother of Lord Darnley, Arabella because of her birth in England was thought by some to have a stronger claim than James to the English throne. Nonetheless, she was welcomed to James's court and for some years was treated generously by him. Unfortunately, Arabella

[4] Like *The Woman Hater* it may even contain one of the few allusions in Jacobean drama to homosexuality at court: "*Shatillion*. . . . Pertaine you to his chamber? / *Love*. No indeed Sir, / That place is not for women" (1.3.43–44).

[5] Dyce's modernization of the spelling to "Chatillion" in his edition, *The Works of Beaumont and Fletcher* (London, 1843–46), vol. 10, makes clearer the apparent intention to suggest a noble French family of a prominence comparable to that of the English Seymours. The "Noble Gentleman" of the title is named "M. Mount Marine," a version of another prominent noble name, Montmorency.

[6] *Studies in Beaumont, Fletcher, and Massinger* (Chapel Hill, N.C., 1939), pp. 149–54.

like all Stuarts was headstrong and politically inept. She exacerbated her potentially threatening dynastic situation by becoming romantically involved with the sorts of men who made James suspect her intentions. One of these was Stephen Bogdan, prince of Moldavia. Their relationship was sufficiently notorious to provoke a comment in a play (apparently by Jonson), and Arabella managed to have it suppressed.[7] In 1610 she made the defiant and ultimately fatal gesture of secretly marrying William Seymour, the least acceptable man in the kingdom to King James as her husband. As grandson of Edward Seymour, earl of Hertford, and of Lady Catherine Grey, younger sister of Lady Jane Grey, he also had a strong claim to the throne. When James heard of the marriage, he ordered the couple imprisoned. Both escaped separately in June 1611, intending to rendezvous in France. Seymour reached the Continent safely, but Arabella was soon captured and spent the remaining years of her life in the Tower. On her death in 1615 it was rumored that she had gone insane.

Maxwell notes several passages in *The Noble Gentleman* that resemble Arabella's story. In act 1, scene 2, someone mentions that Shatillion in his madness believes his loved one "stood very near the Crowne" (93) and that she "remaines close prisoner by the Kings command, / Fearing her title" (97–98). In scene 3 Shatillion claims that his love is fated to die because "she stands too neare a fortune" (61) for "there is no jesting with a Princes title" (62). A speech by Shatillion in act 4, scene 3 would appear to touch precisely on Arabella's story:

> But if his Majesty had suffered me
> To marry her, though she be after him,
> The right heire generall to the Crowne of *France*,
> I would not have convayed her into *Spaine*,
> As it was thought, nor would I ere have joyn'd,
> With the reformed Churches to make them
> Stand for my cause.
>
> (4.3.20–26)

Since the play is set in France, for "Spain" one must read "France." As for a possible role for the "reformed Churches," Sir Ralph Winwood, James's knowing diplomat at the Hague, thought for "many pregnant reasons" that the couple would be "most pitied by the Puritans."[8] Another parallel cited by Maxwell occurs in the fifth act

---

[7] See E. K. Chambers, *The Elizabethan Stage* (Oxford, 1923), 3:370–71.
[8] Quoted by P. M. Handover, *Arbella Stuart* (London, 1957), p. 279.

when Shatillion says: "Let him release my poor love from her torment, / From her hard fare and strict imprisonment" (5.1.339–40).
Arabella's imprisonment was indeed strict, and she complained about
her poor food. In addition to what Maxwell has noted, L. A. Beaurline points out that just as Arabella's and James's claims to the throne
derived from Margaret Tudor, Shatillion's Love's royal pedigree
"Springs from a female" (3.4.111). To these I would add a few more
parallels. The madman pleads, "If he will warrant me but publique
tryall, / I'le freely yeild my selfe into his [the king's] hands" (4.3.37–
38). In the same way Arabella implored the legal authorities "to enquire by an habeas corpus or other usual form of law what is my
fault; and if, upon examination by your Lordships, I shall therefore
be justly convicted, let me endure such punishment by your Lordships' sentence as is due to such an offender."[9] And since Shatillion is
not married, his reference to "my loves true title, mine by marriage"
(3.4.95) would seem to apply more to Seymour than to him.

   In light of the parallels he has detected, it comes as a surprise to
hear Maxwell explain,

> I am not, of course, suggesting that the subplot of *The Noble Gentleman* is
> based upon the unhappy affair of Arabella and Seymour, or even that
> the two are parallel. But I do believe that the situation in the play would
> have been sufficiently suggestive of Lady Arabella's misfortune as to give
> offense, and that such lines as those already quoted, together with ex-
> pressions of sympathy by other characters, would never have been tol-
> erated upon the public stage during 1610–1615.

It is curious that Maxwell takes such an absolute position about censorship when he has noted that there had already been a play on the
London stage alluding to Arabella.[10] The unnamed play may have
been suppressed, but the important point is that a company had been
willing to take its chances by inserting the reference and that (as was
almost invariably the case) no serious consequences ensued. In any
case, Maxwell's argument leads him to the view that the play must
have been presented before or after Arabella's imprisonment, 1610–
1615. He prefers a pre-1610 date because on subjective grounds he
detects the hand of Beaumont, who would not have been available
after 1615.[11]

   [9] Ibid., p. 271.
   [10] On February 18, 1609/10, the Venetian ambassador in London wrote that "Lady
Arabella is seldom seen outside her rooms and lives in greater dejection than ever. She
complains that in a certain comedy a playwright introduced an allusion to her person
and the part played by the Prince of Moldavia. The play was suppressed" (Maxwell,
Studies, p. 153).
   [11] If it is agreed that the story of Shatillion and his love touches on Arabella and

For a variety of reasons I believe that Maxwell was too timid in his use of the Arabella material he had unearthed. My prime reason is that the language of some of Shatillion's speeches—notably 4.3.20–26, in which he speaks of his Love as "after him [the king] / The right heire generall to the Crowne of *France*," of the notion of conveying her out of the country, and of the possibility of support from the "reformed Churches"—is simply too close to the real circumstances and too specific in language to be explained as merely coincidental. Second, as I argue in appendix A, the date admits of the possibility. Third, as I have argued elsewhere, one should not be deterred a priori from entertaining such hypotheses out of an assured sense that Jacobean censorship was an efficient and rigorous mechanism. If one were daring and foolhardy and had little to lose, one could say almost anything—at least briefly—without getting into very serious trouble.[12]

But would the authors of *The Noble Gentleman* have been punished if the play did contain explicit parallels to the life of Arabella Stuart? I would argue that they might not if it were played at a time relatively close to the marriage, escape, and imprisonment—the earlier in the imprisonment the better, while the couple was still in the limelight and no final disposition of the case had been reached. According to Sir Ralph Winwood, there were public disagreements about how to handle the situation. The English faction at court held

> that if this couple should have escaped, the danger was not like to have been very great, in regard that their pretensions are so many degrees removed, and they ungraceful [i.e., ungrateful] both in their persons and their houses, so as a hot alarm taken at the matter will make them more illustrious in the world's eye than now they are, or (being let alone) ever would be.

The Scots lords, on the other hand, "aggravated the offences in so strange a manner, as that it might be compared to the powder treason; and so it is said to fill his Majesty with fearful imaginations, and with him the Prince, who cannot easily be removed from any settled opinion."[13] In the play the Stuart–Seymour-like situation is presented in a good-natured tone, as the fantasy of a deranged creature. The couple is pitiable, of no particular danger to the state. Hence the aim of introducing such material might have been a plea for good sense

---

Seymour, a date for the play after Arabella's death is equally difficult to accept. James continued to be uneasy about Arabella because of a rumor that she had borne a son. For refusing to deny the rumor, the king kept Lady Shrewsbury, Arabella's aunt, in prison for life (ibid., p. 152, n. 13).

[12] Once again I must cite my " 'The Comedians' Liberty': Censorship of the Jacobean Stage Reconsidered," *English Literary Renaissance* 16 (1986): 123–38.

[13] Quoted by Handover, *Arbella Stuart*, p. 283.

and tolerance (like *The Rape of the Lock*) about a matter the authors believe to be of no serious danger to the kingdom, a reminder to James that, as someone says of the French king, "there is mercy / As well as justice in his Royall heart" (3.2.155–56).[14] James, of course, traumatized by his terrifying childhood and the plotting of his many mortal enemies, could not be persuaded to view Arabella's marriage as harmless. In fact, the play was first licensed for performance on February 3, 1625/26, so it may be that the play in its present form was prohibited and never played until after James's and Fletcher's deaths in 1625.

I do not claim that it is possible to sort out all the problems raised by *The Noble Gentleman*. The important elements of the Arabella story are present, but in a form that allows its "deniability" should the authorities object. The same is true of the main plot, where the Jacobean world of promiscuous awards is evoked, but somehow no honors are awarded. One is left with the strong feeling that something *very* topical is being played with in ways that modern readers cannot hope to decode. But it seems important to realize that Beaumont and Fletcher may have written a play that touched on such matters and that such involvement is always a possibility in Jacobean drama. In an understandable reaction against the irresponsible scholarship of some Victorians, most modern literary historians have observed the austere dictum, "Whereof we cannot speak, thereof we must be silent." But even if we cannot be certain of the details, does it not falsify the nature of Jacobean drama to ignore its concern with what was happening in the world, to imply, by ducking ultimately insoluble problems like the one this play poses, that it was a generalized art of platonic forms?

I would like to propose a history for the text (with the brillant if somewhat cranky precedents of J. Dover Wilson and Empson behind me) wherein initially a slim, perhaps Inns of Court version concentrated on the Noble Gentleman's aspirations to a title. Throughout his life Beaumont maintained his ties with the Inner Temple, which as late as 1613 commissioned him to write a marriage masque, and he is known to have participated in the Inn's revels. It happens that many of the standard elements in the reign of such Christmas princes as the Inner Temple's "Prince of Sophie" appear in *The Noble Gentleman*: the ceremonial creation of a mock-duke (act 2), the formal justification of his title and challenge by a stranger knight in behalf of

---

[14] Why might Beaumont and Fletcher have concerned themselves with Lady Arabella Stuart's pitiable plight? It should at least be mentioned that Beaumont's maternal uncle, Sir Henry Pierrepoint, was married to Arabella's maternal aunt, Frances Cavendish, and that during her many years of residence at Hardwick Hall in Derbyshire she lived close to Beaumont's home in Grace Dieu.

the reigning monarch (act 5),[15] his progress through the town (act 3),[16] and his formal deposition in act 3. In fact, the Noble Gentleman is described as just this kind of figure:

> 'tis the finest fellow
> That ere was Christmas Lord, he carries it
> So truly to the life, as though he were
> One of the plot to gull himselfe.
>
> (2.2.152–55)[17]

Such an origin for the play would be consistent with Hoy's view (as mentioned in appendix A), based on internal, linguistic evidence, that it was among Beaumont's earliest work, with revisions by Fletcher. It could have been lengthened later for public performance by grafting the court-centered material onto a play about the war between the sexes and adding the Shatillion material.

Whether or not my theory of its evolution is literally true, it is a way of describing the immiscibility of the play's elements. Not only a credulous gull, the Noble Gentleman is a henpecked cuckold. His witty wife, determined to maintain her pleasure-filled life in the city, tricks her husband into believing that the king has authorized his creation as a duke. After he receives his honors, he acknowledges to her that "all thy counsell / Hath been to me Angelicall' (2.2.218–19) and with a fabliau-like touch the new "duke" gives her an appropriate reward:

> here in token that all strife shall end
> 'Twixt thee and me, I let my drawers fall
> And to thy hands I do deliver them:
> Which signifies, that in all acts and speeches,
> From this time forth my wife shall wear the breeches.
>
> (2.2.233–37)

The gentleman's wife pursues her jest so remorselessly that one of her accomplices remarks on "the fierce masculine spirit, / Of this

[15] Such playfully impossible dating of the "Defense" as "the 37. of *February* stilo novo" (5.1.268–69) has its precedents, and February may have been chosen because the revels often concluded on Candlemas, February 2.

[16] See the description of such progresses by Inns of Court Christmas princes through London in Gray's Inn's *Gesta Grayorum 1688*, ed. W. W. Greg, Malone Society Reprints (Oxford, 1914), p. 55; and in Sir Benjamin Rudyerd's account of the Middle Temple's festivities, *Le Prince d'Amour* (London, 1660), p. 86.

[17] See my *John Marston of the Middle Temple* (Cambridge, Mass., 1969), chap. 3 and 4, for a detailed description of the Inns' revels; see also William Dugdale, *Origines Juridicales* (London, 1671), pp. 153–57, for a detailed account of the Inner Temple's revels.

dread Amazon" (4.2.1–2). She is given motives that sound program-
matic and theoretical:

> That woman is not worthy of a soule
> That has the soveraign power to rule her husband,
> And gives her title up.
>
> (3.2.103–5)

Throughout the play the wife expresses her sense of her own superiority and her right to rule. The words with which she closes the play
leave one with the feeling that the manner of her treatment of her
husband has been the central point:

> Now all my labours have a perfect end
> As I could wish: let all young sprightly wives
> That have dull foolish Coxcombs to their husbands,
> Learn by me their duties, what to doe,
> Which is to make 'em fooles, and please 'em too.
>
> (5.1.446–50)

The wife certainly demonstrates the superiority of her wit, but at a
price. As R. Warwick Bond rightly observes, "it could not escape the
audience that the 'perfect end' which her closing speech claims to
have reached is, in reality, the speedy ruin of her husband and herself."[18] The wife has been transformed by her experience in town
from a simple country lady to a corrupt and amoral wanton. Since
this is so, what is one to make of the feminism she espouses so vigorously? *The Scornful Lady* similarly exhibits a woman's urge to domi-
nate, humiliate, even destroy a male. This vision of female power and
superiority intermixed with a cruel, even self-destructive perversity
belongs to the collaborative plays. It may well be a Beaumont finger-
print, for Fletcher's unaided plays like *The Woman's Prize* are altogether more sympathetic to women and their plight.

   In the midst of all its confusions and incoherencies, *The Noble Gentleman* manages to be entertaining primarily because of the comic title
figure. He is so possessed by dreams of glory that he is not particularly surprised to be created in successive moments knight, baron,
earl, and finally duke of Burgundy.[19] There is nothing remotely cred-

---

[18] "Six Plays in *Beaumont and Fletcher, 1679*," *Review of English Studies* 11 (1935): 275.
[19] In Arthur Collins, *Peerage of England*, augmented by Egerton Brydges (London,
1812), 3:127ff., there is a story by the unreliable and scurrilous Osborne that King
James bestowed on the earl of Montgomery during his period as the favorite (ca. 1606)
four titles in one day. This was untrue, yet it could well have been a rumor or a joke
around London.

ible about his ceremony of investiture, but once installed he instantly sounds every inch a duke:

> It pleased the King my Master
> For sundry vertues not unknown to him,
> And the all-seeing state, to lend his hand
> And raise me to this Emminence; how this
> May seeme to other men, or stir the mindes
> Of such as are my fellow Peers, I know not;
> I would desire their loves in just designes.
>
> (3.2.64–70)

He is a comic counterpart to the title figure in Pirandello's *Henry IV*, at once immersed in his role as a duke—tolerant and generous to his underlings, yet dignified and austere—while still a cowardly, silly coxcomb. The authors' master touch is the duke's heroic refusal to cast aside his title once he believes he has obtained it: "Not all the water in the river *Sene* / Can wash the blood out of these Princely veines" (5.1.238–39). There is something grand, even Richard II-like, in this and in his farcical heroic affirmation when he rises from a trouncing by the mad Shatillion to assert, "Then by your favors Gentlemen I rise, / And know I am a Duke still" (5.1.377–78). Such figures as the Hungry Courtier, the mock-duke, and the Madman are in the grips of absurd but obsessive fantasies. The special note of the so-called tragicomedies is sounded when similarly afflicted figures are heroes.

Chapter Eight

PHILASTER, OR LOVE LIES A BLEEDING:
THE ANTI-PRINCE

Tragicomedy?

Philaster (1608–10) was, according to Dryden, the first play that brought Beaumont and Fletcher "in esteem" in the London theater.[1] Perhaps this occurred merely because it was the first of their plays performed by the King's Men, whose great prestige, superior actors, and large audiences doubtless guaranteed a certain level of success. But *Philaster* also represents a "breakthrough" to a new level of artistic achievement, and it was soon followed by *The Maid's Tragedy* (1610) and *A King and No King* (1611). To this day these three plays are generally regarded as the best work Beaumont and Fletcher wrote in collaboration.

Each of the three plays has a separate identity, and there is no external evidence that the authors conceived them as a group. But they have many important similarities and interrelationships: *Philaster* depicts the follies of three mercurial princes; *A King and No King* shows a court in disarray because a vain prince is consumed by incestuous longings; and *The Maid's Tragedy* concerns an absolute monarch whose adulterous love affair provokes his assassination. Whether or not consciously designed as such, they constitute a trilogy about the public and private consequences of princely intemperance.

I am not the first to see political matter in *Philaster*. In 1946 Mary G. M. Adkins pointed out that it presents an unfavorable portrait of a king who espouses divine right doctrine very similar to that of King James and that the play shows the citizenry to be a distinct and desirable check on regal power.[2] Some years later Peter Davison elabo-

---

[1] "An Essay of Dramatic Poesy," *Essays of John Dryden*, ed. W. P. Ker (Oxford, 1900), 1:81. The date derives from a mention of the play by John Davies of Hereford in *The Scourge of Folly* (1610); some evidence makes possible a date as early as 1608. The title page of the first quarto of 1620 mentions production by the King's Men as well as collaborative authorship. Internal evidence gives Beaumont the larger share of the writing: see Cyrus Hoy, "The Shares of Fletcher and His Collaborators in the Beaumont and Fletcher Canon," *Studies in Bibliography* 11 (1958): 95–96.

[2] "The Citizens in *Philaster*: Their Function and Significance," *Studies in Philology* 43 (1946): 203–12. Adkins is reluctant to make broad claims for her argument: "The aristocratic sympathies of Francis Beaumont and John Fletcher are a commonplace of

rated on Adkins's claims by displaying many parallels between the political ideas in the play and James's writings. He also suggested that the "characterization of [the hero] Philaster . . . is designed to comment upon human fallibility, a fallibility which princes are shown to share."[3]

One scene in particular in this popular play—staged, one must recall, by the supposedly cautious King's Men and presented at court twice in 1612–13[4]—seems as politically freighted and hostile to divine right dogma as almost anything staged by the private theaters. A king is expressing extreme agitation at the disappearance of his daughter while hunting:

> *King.* . . . I am your King,
>   I wish to see my daughter, shew her me:
>   I doe command you all, as you are subjects,
>   To shew her me: what, am I not your King?
>   If I, then am I not to be obeyed?
> *Dion.* Yes, if you command things possible, and honest.
> *King.* Things possible and honest? Heare me, thou, —
>   Thou traytor, —that dar'st confine thy King to things
>   Possible and honest.
>
> (4.4.24–32)[5]

The Revels edition editor, Andrew Gurr, finds a

> resemblance . . . between Lord Dion's standing up to the King in IV.iv and Sir Edward Coke's clash with King James on 13 November 1608. . . . It is inconceivable that Beaumont could not have been concerned with the issue; his father was a Common Law judge, and he himself was a member of Coke's own Inn of Court, the Inner Temple.[6]

---

criticism. . . . The purpose of this paper is not to dispute the dictum but to analyze *Philaster* as an exception" (203). How they could normally have had aristocratic sympathies but became democrats for one play she does not explain.

[3] "The Serious Concerns of *Philaster*," *ELH* 30 (1963): 1–15.

[4] I state the situation thus to reiterate how little we really comprehend about the nature of Jacobean censorship.

[5] All quotations are from the edition of Robert K. Turner in Fredson Bowers, gen. ed., *The Dramatic Works in the Beaumont and Fletcher Canon* (Cambridge, 1966–), vol. 1.

[6] *Philaster* (London, 1969), pp. lv–lvi. Gurr also points out "the coincidence between the stage King and James as rulers of two kingdoms," but adds that the play "does not really make use of its two kingdoms as a parallel to the Stuart position in 1609" (p. liv). Davison, "Serious Concerns of *Philaster*," 8–9, says, "By making the King a usurper Beaumont and Fletcher are tactfully (or expediently) masking the true state from the Master of the Revels and of course the usurping king fits admirably into the conventions of romantic tragicomedy. In any case the distinction [as *Richard II* illustrates] between a usurping but *de facto* king, and a living, but deposed, *de jure* king, was a fine one."

The passage from the fourth act quoted above continues the confrontation with the king, who now describes himself as one

> whose breath can still the Winds,
> Unclowd the Sunne, charme downe the swelling Sea,
> And stop the flouds of heaven: speake, can it not?
>
> (39–41)

When the courtier Dion denies these and further absurd claims, the king threatens him:

King.   Is it so? Take heed.
Dion. Sir, take you heed, how you dare the powers
    That must be just.

> (44–46)

The king quickly reverses himself and concedes that he has been making excessive claims:

> Alas, what are we Kings?
> Why doe you gods place us above the rest,
> To be serv'd, flatter'd, and ador'd, till we
> Beleeve we hold within our hands your thunder?
> And when we come to try the power we have,
> There's not a leafe shakes at our threatenings.
>
> (46–51)

In a play with three intemperate and irrational princes this criticism of absolutist pretensions is obviously central.

But the political aspect of *Philaster* is rarely considered important enough to mention. For example, Eugene M. Waith in his influential *The Pattern of Tragicomedy in Beaumont and Fletcher* ignores it completely because he is interested in showing how the play conforms to Fletcherian tragicomedy, described thus:

> Sensational situations abound, each one fully developed as the basis of an intense emotional experience. . . . [Tragicomedy] tends . . . to nullify the total meanings which either comedy or tragedy may have and to substitute for them a more rarefied aesthetic satisfaction in purely formal relationships. Here is a direct appeal to tastes both cultivated and jaded. The emphasis falls upon a rhetoric which is itself formal in its reliance upon conspicuous patterns of sound and which is the chief means of projecting the emotion of the dramatic moments. Both the extravagance and the formality of this style were aptly designed to appeal to the Jacobean audience.[7]

[7] (New Haven, Conn., 1952), p. 198.

Consistent with this formulation Waith sees *Philaster* as a succession of scenes at a pseudohistorical court that, he claims, "alternate with woodland scenes, reflecting pastoral Sicily, to form a combination of pseudo-history and romance."[8] The atmosphere in the play appears to be evil, but in keeping with the generic requirement of tragicomedy's middle mood, the play, according to Waith, concludes happily: "The dark atmosphere of the play is dissipated, and Philaster is shown that the evil which most affected him . . . was no more than a false hypothesis" (p. 18).

Waith wrote with a conviction that the plays of Beaumont and Fletcher were "superb examples of dramatic art" (p. 201), and he justified this heretical judgment by placing these plays in a genre that immunized them from the conventional view that they were unserious, sensationalistic, and salacious:

> The conventions of realistic tragedy and comedy have led the modern theater audience to expect something totally unlike Fletcherian tragicomedy. In our times the attitudes necessary for an enjoyment of this kind of artistic achievement have become attached exclusively to other arts—to music, for example, and to painting. There the most dramatic contrasts, the boldest designs, the purest abstractions, the most powerful emotional stimuli are frankly acknowledged and admired. Only in ballet, in opera, and in the more recent "musical drama" do such techniques enter the theater. One may speculate that if a modern audience approached Beaumont and Fletcher with the expectations it has on going to the opera, it would find much to enjoy, for it would accept the contrivance of the play more readily and would await the more declamatory passages as eagerly as the famous arias, duets, or quartets of grand opera. (P. 201)

"COMEDY OF BLOOD"

As useful as Waith's definition of "tragicomedy" certainly is for some of Fletcher's later work, central features of *Philaster* are obscured when one insists on its generic resemblance to plays like *The Faithful Shepherdess*.[9] None of the plays I am now discussing was labeled a "tragicomedy," much less a "pastoral tragicomedy." Certainly there are definitions of the genre that could cover both *The Faithful Shep-*

[8] P. 16. The claim that such scenes "alternate" is rather inaccurate. The only "woodland" scenes occur in act 4. The rest of the play is set at court.

[9] While the one tragicomedy so-called during the period of the collaboration was by Fletcher, all internal and external evidence suggests that the trilogy was largely written by Beaumont. When Fletcher wrote by himself, Waith's definition seems to fit better.

herdess and *Philaster*,[10] but every treatment of *Philaster* as a tragicomedy has tended to ignore or slight scenes like the one about the king's limited power because it does not fit generic specifications. Therefore, convinced that *differentia* are as important as *genus*, I propose to create for *Philaster* a subgenre of tragicomedy and name it "comedy of blood" to emphasize what is unique about the play. Such a term may help one to recognize that the opening play of the trilogy on intemperate princes is related to the "tragedy of blood" since it portrays the dislodgment of a usurper-king; to emphasize and therefore to ponder the significance of its twenty-eight "blood" images—almost as many as in *Macbeth*; and to alert one to its curious ending, near to the "comic" tone of *All's Well That Ends Well* and far more equivocal than Waith would have it.

According to Waith and the many commentators influenced by him, *Philaster* depicts a romantic love triangle that (like the incest dilemma in *A King and No King*) is used as a pretext for the display of much high rhetoric about faithless womankind, untrustworthy friends, and the like. Once it is revealed that the hero Philaster's apparent rival for the hand of his beloved Arathusa, the young page Bellario, is really a disguised girl named Euphrasia, any moral ramifications melt into thin air. Thus the political material of Adkins and to a lesser extent that of Davison can be ignored since they scarcely touch the romantic love story. But a much different play emerges if the love plot is connected to the political overplot. The "prince" (his title is endlessly mentioned) Philaster is the son of a deceased king of Sicily whose kingdom was usurped by the king of neighboring Calabria, who now rules both countries. Naturally, Philaster and many of his countrymen are displeased by the present state of affairs, and so is the king because—as in *Cupid's Revenge*—the common people revolt every time he tries to imprison the popular prince. The standoff between the two factions is summarized by one of Philaster's court followers:

> the King (of late) made a hazard of both the Kingdomes, of *Cicilie* and his owne, with offering but to imprison *Philaster*. At which the City was in Armes, not to bee charm'd downe by any State order or Proclamation, till they saw *Philaster* ride through the streetes pleasde, and without a guard; at which they threw their hats and their Armes from them; some to make bonfires, some to drinke, all for his deliverance. Which (wise

[10] See especially the rigorous discussion by John T. Shawcross, "Tragicomedy as Genre, Past and Present," in Nancy Klein Maguire, ed., *Renaissance Tragicomedy* (New York, 1987), pp. 13–32.

men say) is the cause, the King labors to bring in the power of a forraigne Nation, to awe his owne with. (1.1.31–39)

This monarch, who claimed that he "can still the Winds, / Unclowd
the Sunne, charme downe the swelling Sea," must call in Spain, the
most odious of foreign powers (at least from an English Protestant's
point of view), in a vain effort to subdue the common people. Later
in the play he finds legitimate grounds for imprisoning Philaster—
nothing less than the hero's admission that he had tried to murder
the king's daughter—but once again the people rebel until Philaster
is freed, in the process taking as hostage the very prince who had
been imported from Spain to "awe" them. Eventually realizing that
he cannot control the people of Sicily, the king resigns his claim to its
rightful ruler, Philaster. It is clear where power is based in this particular monarchy.

As his speeches on absolute power indicate, the king is presented
as an ineffectual ranter whose only redeeming feature is a Claudius-
like conscience that slightly troubles him about his unjust usurpation
of the Sicilian crown. But like Claudius he is incapable of genuine
repentance:

> *King.* . . . I have sind, tis true, and here stand to be punish'd;
>   Yet would not thus be punish'd; let me chuse
>   My way, and lay it on.
> *Dion* [*aside*]. He articles with the gods; would somebody would draw
>   bonds, for the performance of covenants betwixt them.
>
>   (4.4.52–56)

As Peter Davison points out, the emphasis in Dion's comment is on
the word "performance": "The inference of [this] is that if a bond for
the *performance* of a contract between God and king might be drawn
up, the king could not break his part of the contract yet demand that
his people, nevertheless, adhere to their part of the contract." Gurr
adds, "This, of course, is precisely what James did demand."[11]

Dion's wry comment is part of a pattern of antiregal sentiments
sustained in large and small elements of the play. Some are merely
verbal pinpricks at princes, as when the king (as he is always called,
thus underlining his representative quality) speaks of "sickly promises (which commonly / In Princes finde both birth and buriall / In
one breath)" (1.1.79–81). This undercuts the assurances a moment
later of the Spanish prince Pharamond: "Gentlemen, / Beleeve me in
a word, a Princes word" (1.1.134–35). Similarly, one hears scepticism
about the possibility of a member of the nobility being penitent: "Is't

[11] Gurr, *Philaster*, quoting Davison, p. 80n.

possible this fellow should repent? Mee thinkes that were not noble in him" (4.1.18–19).

But the more biting political satire appears in the characterization and actions of the various princes who inhabit Sicily. In addition to the king, there is the Spanish prince Pharamond. At the start of the play, in a scene reminiscent of the opening of *King Lear*, he is formally promised the king's daughter and succession to the thrones of Sicily and Calabria. Pharamond's speech in response, as an unsympathetic courtier remarks, "calls him *Spaniard*, beeing nothing but a large inventory of his owne commendations" (1.1.152–53). He is also a shameless lecher whose uncontrollable sexual appetite triggers the difficulties that occupy the romantic plot. What most critics have been reluctant to concede is that the puzzling, fascinating Prince Philaster, the ostensible hero and central figure in the play, is the object of similar satire and criticism.[12]

THE CHARACTER OF PHILASTER

From the moment Philaster first bursts onto the stage in a torrent of wild and whirling words, one notices a disparity between his reputation and his actions. As the heroine says, "the whole Court / Is bold in praise of him" (1.2.11–12). In addition to the common people, a group of courtiers admire his virtues so much that they plan an insurrection to restore him to his rightful position. He attracts the undying loyalty and love of both his page and the king's daughter. Yet one cannot fail to notice fundamental weaknesses in Philaster's character and, what is more, the commission by him of acts that would normally be considered the work of a madman. Several critics have argued that irreconcilable inconsistency in Beaumont and Fletcher's characters was a necessary byproduct of an art in which everything was sacrificed to the necessities of the dramatic situation. This viewpoint has a long tradition, starting with Dryden's remark in his preface to his "Troilus and Cressida" that characters in Beaumont and Fletcher's plays "are either good, bad, or indifferent, as the present scene requires it."[13] Similarly, Waith describes Fletcher's tragicomic figures as "protean," radically inconsistent in character from one scene to the next. But as Clifford Leech wisely observed, Beaumont and Fletcher "show more understanding of a human being's range of

---

[12] In some details (especially the interpretation of the Country Fellow in act 4), my reading was anticipated by Clifford Leech in *The John Fletcher Plays* (Cambridge, Mass., 1962), esp. pp. 78–94. But Leech's emphasis on the tragicomic and mine on the comic and satiric elements lead to very different conclusions.

[13] *Essays*, 1:217.

behaviour than is common among his critics."[14] In the case of Philaster, at least, a consistent subtext may be discerned beneath the apparent inconsistencies of his volatile behavior.

Philaster has nothing of Hamlet's complexity; the resemblance is to relatively simple characters like Leontes in *The Winter's Tale* and to Marston's father-and-son team of hysterics, Andrugio and Antonio in the *Antonio* plays. Still, various echoes of *Hamlet* shape one's early responses to Beaumont and Fletcher's hero. Although Prince Pharamond calls "mad" (1.1.193) Philaster's disruptive tirade against the king's decision to name the Spaniard as his successor, the Hamlet resemblance leads one to feel that one is hearing a distraught but noble mind unsettled by his ill fortune. His vein is angry and full of obscure threats until the king loses patience and threatens him, upon which Philaster echoes Hamlet, but with a subtle difference:

> I am dead sir, y'are my Fate: It was not I
> Said I was wrong'd: I carry all about me
> My weake starres leade me too; all my weake fortunes.
> Who dares in all this presence speake, (that is
> But man of flesh, and may be mortall)? Tell me,
> I doe not most intirely love this Prince,
> And honour his full vertues.
>
> (1.1.261–67)

When Hamlet apologizes to Laertes by saying that he was not himself, he conveys an innate courtesy of spirit. Here Philaster simply seems to be disowning, as if in fright, his previous brave, if obscure, words.[15] A moment later he begins to speak bitterly of his plight, but once again concludes amicably by taking his rival's hand. When left alone with his admiring court followers, he continues to act in a distracted manner, and he responds most tepidly to their plans for an uprising against the usurper:

> Friends, no more;
> Our eares may be corrupted: Tis an age
> We dare not trust our will to.
>
> (1.1.315–17)

Often this hero sounds as languid and worldweary as Tennyson's Marianna.

The passive, will-less quality of Philaster (perhaps, as he says, in-

---

[14] *Fletcher Plays*, p. 104.

[15] The last sentence of the quoted speech is ambiguous. Most modern editors solve the ambiguity by eliminating the comma after "Tell me," but perhaps the old punctuation suggests an equivocal pause in Philaster's expression of his love.

herent in the age he lives in, but also certainly his own) is developed further in the second scene. The princess summons him to her chamber, where it is she who makes overtures of love: "I must have them [both Calabria and Sicily], and thee" (1.2.82), to which Philaster, though reciprocating her passion, responds with a tentativeness and suspicion one begins to recognize:

> Madam, you are too full of noble thoughts,
> To lay a traine for this contemned life,
> Which you may have for asking: to suspect
> Were base, where I deserve no ill; love you,
> By all my hopes I doe, above my life:
> But how this passion should proceed from you,
> So violently, would amaze a man,
> That would be jealous.

(1.2.89–96)

J. F. Danby brilliantly constructs the subtext of this contorted utterance:

> Philaster sees the chaste and hitherto inaccessible model of womanhood suddenly proposing to him. He is overwhelmed, but of course ready to accept. In the midst of his confusion he is able to note the possible ambiguity of Arathusa's behavior for an interpreter that "*would* be jealous." His 'amazement' is another stroke of wit, and an oddly serious one. He loved Arathusa apart from any hope of reciprocation: in spite of her impossibility and almost because of it. . . . Now that the Impossible She is so possible, the possibility might itself argue an imperfection. . . . The conception in this scene prepares us to accept Philaster's subsequent misbelief of Arathusa.[16]

Before the artistic quantum leap that this play represents for them, the dramatic poetry of Beaumont and Fletcher rarely invites this kind of close reading. Here they successfully created a slippery language that suggests the confusions of a character troubled by warring, obscure impulses rising uncontrollably to the surface.

The "misbelief" of Arathusa to which Danby refers occurs after the lecherous Spanish prince is found by his would-be father-in-law, the

---

[16] *Poets on Fortune's Hill* (London, 1952), p. 171. While I cannot agree with every word of this (for instance, how does Danby know the nature of Philaster's past love for her?), I wish I could admire the rest of Danby's discussion as much as I do this passage. I cannot understand why he sees Philaster as a complex characterization only in the first act. It may be that he felt further analysis unnecessary because in his view the play is highly repetitive. In any case, he fails to discuss Philaster's actions in acts 4 and 5, which are to my mind the most interesting, subtly conceived part of the play.

king, in compromising circumstances with a lascivious court lady named Megra. Megra instantly retaliates by accusing Arathusa of fornication with Philaster's page. The outrageous lie is delivered with such conviction and effrontery that everyone, including the king— Philaster is not present—is stunned into silent belief as act 2 concludes. At the opening of act 3, the lie has become a universally accepted fact. The first words, uttered by one of Philaster's followers, are, "Nay, doubtlesse tis true" (3.1.1). Convinced that Philaster has been reluctant to lead a revolt out of love for their enemy's daughter, his strategists decide to remove this obstacle by reporting Megra's accusation to him.

As one who "would be jealous," it takes only the movement from one line to the next to change Philaster, the "King of Courtesie" according to his admirers (5.4.141), from angry denial to tentative belief in the misconduct of the two people he claims to love most: "Tis false, by heaven tis false: it cannot be, / Can it?" (3.1.95–96). This use of the comic "double-take" device at the inception of Philaster's jealousy suggests that Beaumont and Fletcher want the audience to respond to their hero's overeasy credulity not with sympathy but with scornful laughter. After the seemingly trustworthy Dion flatly asserts a few lines later, "I tooke them [i.e., in flagrante delicto]: I my selfe" (3.1.111), Philaster is completely convinced and totally devastated, and he begins his loud ranting against womankind.[17] Not until after the courtiers depart does he notice an important omission: "I had forgot to aske him where he tooke them, / I'le follow him." But in another broadly satiric touch he decides not to hear the evidence on the grounds that "more circumstances will but fan this fire" of fury in his breast (3.1.133–34, 136). His mind is closed, the issue settled on the basis of hearsay evidence against those he professes to love.

This much admired hero, one comes to realize, is not Prince Hamlet; at times he is ridiculous, at times almost the Fool. And like his two counterparts in the play, always a prince. The parallel to Hamlet operates by contrast. Philaster responds to an implausible accusation by unpacking his heart with words, with rant. What he cannot do is turn his brain about—the notion barely enters his head—to gain grounds for belief more "relative" than Dion's bald assertion. At the same time the authors emphasize the implausibility of the accusation by making the accused women perfectly virtuous, more adoring and faithful than any of the many comparably ill-treated figures in their subse-

---

[17] Philaster is often compared to Leucippus in *Cupid's Revenge*. Both are passive, credulous heroes. But Leucippus trusts unworthy people because he is idealistic and believes the best of them; Philaster believes the worst. Their differences are as important as their similarities.

quent work. Even as Philaster carves them up with his sword, they pray for him and shield him from punishment for his mad actions. The subtitle "Love lies a Bleeding" can refer to either of them; both are virtually allegorical figures of love.

Rather than a passionate but still rational Hamlet, Philaster becomes an undignified Othello. He tries to trap princess and page into confession, threatens murder, pities himself, castigates womankind endlessly. While both of the accused instantly realize that he has been made the dupe of a plot, to him everything, however flimsy, proves their guilt:

> *Arathusa.* The pretty boy you gave me—
> *Philaster.*   What of him?
> *Arathusa.* Must be no more mine.
> *Philaster.*   Why?
> *Arathusa.*   They are jealous of him.
> *Philaster.* Jealous, who?
> *Arathusa.*   The King.
> *Philaster.*   Oh my misfortune,
>   Then tis no idle jealousie.
>
>   (3.2.55–59)

Here the weakness of the logic is particularly laughable, but nothing that Philaster does in the third act after his jealous rage erupts reveals the overthrow of a mind that has previously seemed noble. His actions are simply a natural extension of the weak, erratic figure of the first two acts. The upshot is that Philaster becomes progressively more distasteful, particularly in contrast to his dignified, much put-upon, ever-loyal loved ones.

In act 4 Beaumont and Fletcher shift the action from the court to the countryside, where courtly manners and morals are subjected to pastoral, hence political, criticism. It is in the country that the king finds that nature will not respond to his absolutist commands, that huntsmen speak irreverently about the morals of the maids of honor, and that country folk are baffled by court behavior. Just when Philaster seems to have realized that his judgments may have been intemperate (4.5.18–21), he stumbles upon his page Bellario ministering to Arathusa, who has fallen ill. Completely at the mercy of appearances and chance events, Philaster conforms to Bergson's classic description of comic figures in the machinelike predictability of his response. He immediately assumes the worst and in his melodramatic, stagy way, offers himself up to be killed: altogether in the play he makes a ges-

ture toward suicide or asks to be killed on five occasions![18] When this
is refused, he decides to kill or, more precisely, to execute Arathusa.
He proceeds in a formal, ceremonious manner reminiscent of
Othello:

> *Philaster.*   Then guide
>   My feeble hand, you that have power to doe it,
>   For I must performe a peece of Justice. If your youth
>   Have any way offended heaven, let prayers
>   Short, and effectuall, reconcile you to it.
> *Arathusa.* I am prepared.
>
> (4.5.69–74)

A "Country Fellow" who has been hoping to get a glimpse of the king
now comes onstage.[19] He is already a bit puzzled by the way the court
comports itself: "These Kings had need of good braines, this whoop-
ing is able to put a meane man out of his wits" (4.5.79–80). Suddenly
he notices "a Courtier with his sword drawne ... upon a woman"
(80–81). Unaware of his presence Philaster continues:

> *Philaster.* Are you at peace?
> *Arathusa.* With heaven and earth.
> *Philaster.* May they divide thy soule and body.
>
> Philaster *wounds her.*
>
> *Countrey Fellow.* Hold dastard, strike a woman!
>   th'art a craven: I warrant thee, thou wouldst bee loth to play halfe a
>   dozen venies at wasters with a good fellow for a broken head.
> *Philaster.* Leave us good friend.
> *Arathusa.* What ill-bred man art thou, to intrude thy selfe
>   Upon our private sports, our recreations?
> *Countrey Fellow.* God uds me, I understand you not; but I know the
>   rogue has hurt you.
> *Philaster.* Persue thy owne affaires; it will be ill
>   To multiply blood upon my head, which thou
>   Wilt force me to.

[18] 3.1.122–23; 4.5.45, 62; 5.5.79, 124.

[19] The centrality, or at any rate the notoriety, of this episode is attested to by an
illustration on the title page of the first quarto and by the subtitle ("Love lies a Bleeding"), both of which refer to events therein. However, the picture of the Country Fellow is misleading because it shows him dressed as a gentleman and even labels him "A
Cuntrie Gentellman." This dignifies him too much and hence diminishes the humiliation the prince himself acknowledges having suffered by being outfought by someone
variously described as "a meane man" (4.5.80), "ill bred" (89), a "Boore" (101), and a
mere "Fellow" (138); his lower-class speech confirms that (e.g., 86–87). As Turner
demonstrates in his edition, 1:389, the first quarto has no authority in this matter.

Countrey Fellow. I know not your rethoricke, but I can lay it on if you
touch the woman.

They fight
(4.5.82–97)

The mixture of tones here provides one of the richest moments in
Beaumont and Fletcher's plays: Philaster's sanctimonious cruelty,
Arathusa's noble resignation mixed with the hauteur of a grande
dame toward the "fellow," and the Country Fellow's unsophisticated
incomprehension of the latest in courtly recreation and rhetoric.[20]
Any lingering doubts about how one is to regard this hero are dissipated when Philaster ("the bravery of his age" [3.1.6], according to
admiring courtiers) is bested by the Country Fellow in their fight and
runs off. Fearful that he will be punished for wounding the princess,
he rationalizes his flight by claiming that he is preserving his life in
order "to lose it, rather by my will then force" (4.5.104), by suicide
rather than execution. Soon one sees that this is an insincere ration-
alization, that self-preservation was his sole motive.

This scene, as Arthur Kirsch rightly observes, "constitutes a paradigm of Fletcherian dramaturgy." But the "paradigm" Kirsch sees
differs so radically from mine that I question whether we are observ-
ing the same object. As Kirsch sees it, in language reminiscent of
Waith's, the scene "is entirely contrived to allow for striking if not
sensational contrasts of emotion. The whole situation is false and improbable, and since we know it is, we consciously follow the ebb and
flow of Philaster's passion, responding to his diatribes and laments as
declamatory exercises."[21] To me the scene is no more improbable
than twenty others in Jacobean drama, beginning with *Othello*. An
easily jealous man finally "sees" that his worst suspicions are "true,"
and he reacts as any sword-carrying cavalier might, by taking justice
into his own hands. Someone blunders onto the scene, is appalled by
the attack on a helpless creature, intervenes, and bests the pretentious bully. What is shown as "false and improbable" here and
throughout the Beaumont and Fletcher canon is the honor code that
dictated such behavior.

Since my reading of this scene deviates so much from received
opinion and is so crucial to the central point of this book, I want to
clarify further my differences by showing how Kirsch concludes his
interpretation of this scene:

[20] Consistent with this courtly usage, in 5.3.103–4 Philaster reaches a point of total
despair and tells the king: "it is a joy to die, / I find a recreation in't."

[21] *Jacobean Dramatic Perspectives* (Charlottesville, Va., 1972), p. 41.

The intervention of the country fellow italicizes the wholly self-regarding theatricality of the scene even further. In the peculiar dialectic of Fletcherian dramaturgy the country fellow would seem to represent a popular ideal of honor which Philaster at that point lacks, but at the same time his emphatic outlandishness serves to qualify any serious apprehensions we might develop about Philaster and Arathusa and thus to preserve the mood of tragicomedy. His honorable uncouthness is finally an urbane joke, a conceit which paradoxically insulates the boundaries of Beaumont and Fletcher's world of gay sights and protects its private sports and recreations. His appearance not only assures us that any wound Arathusa receives has been made with a pasteboard sword, but absolutely compels us to become conscious of the preciousness of the entire scene.[22]

As I view this moment, what the Country Fellow "italicizes" (to employ Kirsch's metaphor) goes to the heart of the politics of the play, the difference between "court" and "country" values (which in this case also includes the city). The court uses real swords for "bloody" recreations that the country quite sensibly finds incomprehensible and pernicious. Just as the city's citizens protect Philaster's throne from a usurper and a Spaniard, so the Country Fellow protects Arathusa when Philaster acts like the two other intemperate princes.

Philaster's subsequent actions reinforce this interpretation. In his next appearance, he seems to have fallen into a state of temporary sanity:

> I have done ill, my conscience calls me false,
> To strike at her, that would not strike at me:
> When I did fight, me thought I heard her pray
> The gods to guard me. She may be abusde,
> And I a loathed villaine.
>
> (4.6.9–13)

---

[22] Ibid., pp. 41–42. Waith, Kirsch, and Bliss use James Shirley's introductory epistle to the 1647 folio to buttress their view of Beaumont and Fletcher's work as self-conscious and artificial. The most important passage says that the plays offer the reader "passions raised to that excellent pitch and by such insinuating degrees that you shall not chuse but consent, & go along with them, finding your self at last grown insensibly the very same person you read, and then stand admiring the subtile Trackes of your engagement" (Arnold Glover and A. R. Waller, eds., *The Works of Francis Beaumont and John Fletcher* [Cambridge, 1905–12], 1:xii.) This is true of any compelling work of art: first one is caught up in it, then, once free of its spell, one notices the artistry. An artist like Shirley would be particularly disposed to such an approach.

Philaster certainly sounds as though he has recovered his senses;[23] he may even feel some guilt, but in a brilliantly conceived bit of perverted logic, the line continues: "If she be, / She will conceale who hurt her" (13–14). Sublime assurance that a true lover of Philaster will be infinitely forgiving! As he talks, he comes upon the sleeping Bellario and hears the cries of his pursuers. He invents a scheme, cunning but crazed, to shift the blame to his page for the stabbing of Arathusa:

> I'le take this offerd meanes of my escape:
> They have no marke to know me, but my wounds,
> If she be true; if false, let mischiefe light
> On all the world at once. Sword, print my wounds
> Upon this sleeping boy; I ha none, I thinke
> Are mortall, nor would I lay greater on thee.
>
> *Wounds him.*
> (4.6.20–25)

The hero wounds his page while "he" is sleeping! Lest any director be misled by Philaster's last words into making these wounds appear like minor razor nicks, it should be noted that Bellario loses enough blood to make "him" fall down (4.6.50). Without hesitation and in spite of the wounding, Bellario protects Philaster by lying to his pursuers about his actions while the hero cowers nearby. Finally, shamed and deeply moved by his page's loyalty, he "*creepes out of a Bush*" (according to the stage direction [4.6.82]) where he has been hiding. In his usual style of extravagant rant, Philaster now extols Bellario's matchless virtues and acknowledges his crimes and errors:

> Tis not the treasure of all Kings in one,
> The wealth of *Tagus*, nor the rocks of pearle,
> That pave the Court of *Neptune*, can weigh downe
> That vertue. It was I that hurt the Princesse.
>
> (4.6.86–89)[24]

[23] I state it thus to express my disagreement with Gurr's gloss on this speech: "It is a measure of Philaster's being out of his right mind that he should follow his wounding of a woman with an attack on a sleeping boy" (*Philaster*, p. 88). Philaster may be mad here, but no more so than in the rest of the play. Gurr believes that Philaster comes to "himself" in 5.4. I try to show that his actions in 5.5 reveal that "recovery" to be as specious as several previous ones.

[24] Throughout their work, when Beaumont and Fletcher begin a speech of high praise in the form of a denial with the words "tis not," they are announcing a speech of extreme, exhibitionistic rant. In this case the effect is redoubled by a nearly precise repetition a few lines later ("Tis not . . . ," 112ff.).

Now the king has sufficient grounds to order Philaster's execution. As the prince is led off at the conclusion of act 4, his political followers assess the damage to his "image":

Clermont. [to Dion]. I pray that this action loose not *Philaster* the hearts of the people.
Dion. Feare it not, their overwise heads will thinke it but a tricke.

(4.6.144–46)

Next to Arathusa's imperious dismissal of the Country Fellow as he is trying to save her from being stabbed, this exchange is the funniest moment in an act filled with ironic humor. Dion sounds like a knowing public relations man assessing the damage his client has done to himself. He is sure Philaster's actions will not harm his reputation because the truth is too incredible to be accepted by the "streetsmart" people.

The swift whirl of events in act 5 manages to produce an ending that, as noted earlier, leaves the same sort of taste in one's mouth as does the "happy" conclusion to *All's Well That Ends Well*. In scene 2. the imprisoned and sheepish Philaster apologizes for suspecting "a paire of the most trusty ones / That ever earth bore" (5.2.7–8). In scene 3 he and Arathusa announce to the infuriated king their prison marriage, and in scene 4 Philaster (like Leucippus in *Cupid's Revenge*) is freed through a revolt by his loyal followers. He appears to be a calm, regal figure then, someone who has found himself, and in scene 5 he is promised his rightful position on the throne. With an embrace from his new father-in-law, the king, with Arathusa already his and Pharamond forgiven, all that is left is for Bellario to be unmasked and paired off.[25] Indeed, this sequence of events is the ending the play should have, had it the didactic purpose that Gurr claims for it: to demonstrate how "Philaster ultimately attains his honour and becomes himself through love."[26] But one last witty turn in the plot makes one doubt that Philaster has changed in the slightest. It is a moment ignored by all commentators, perhaps because—to repeat my polemical point—it ought not to occur in the platonic ideal of tragicomedy they have constructed. With the world stabilized and Philaster apparently "cured," the entire absurd cycle of Philaster's jealousy is renewed yet again. The lady who concocted the lie about Arathusa and Bellario repeats it. The "new" Philaster seems to have

[25] This is precisely what happens in the corrupt first quarto, a sound text except at the start and finish, where it appears to be a memorial reconstruction. It reflects what someone with a knowledge of conventional plays would guess the outcome to be.
[26] *Philaster*, p. lxvi. This is the sort of "happy ending" Waith and Bliss describe.

learned something and disdainfully denies the charge, but the king, who has shown himself to be equally passionate and credulous, is not so certain. He tricks Philaster into permitting Bellario to be tortured to extract the truth; Philaster, feeling dishonored by his inadvertent responsibility for Bellario's plight, responds in the only way he knows: not by defending his page but by making for the fourth time one of his reflex gestures toward suicide: *"Offers to kill himselfe"* (5.5.79). After he is forcibly restrained, Bellario decides that she had better reveal her gender and finally stifle all rumors. She draws Dion aside and discloses her identity. The following exchange instantly provokes a *fifth* suicide attempt:

> *Dion.* Alls discovered.
> *Philaster.*   Why then hold you me?
>   All is discovered, pray you let me go.
>
> > *He offers to stab himselfe.*
> > (5.5.123–24)

If this does not produce the sort of laughter one hears at a Marx Brothers movie, the director has failed to convey the sort of game Beaumont and Fletcher are playing. After all that has happened, one word can still rekindle Philaster's jealousy! The most primitive kind of recognition device—the revelation that Bellario is a female—is required to convince him that his two loved ones have been virtuous. He responds with characteristically hysterical joy to complement his usual hysterical despair, screaming out, "It is a woman" three times (5.5.130, 131, 133). Only then can he say to Arathusa, as though he had been impervious to the false aspersions against her, "thou art faire / And vertuous still to ages, in despight / Of Malice" (5.5.133–35).

Philaster is unchangeable, a sophisticated variant on the long line of insecure husbands and lovers in Jacobean drama who live in terror of the cuckoo's song and sprouting horns. He is loved by the constant Arathusa, who does justice to the allusion implicit in her name to an incorruptible Sicilian wood nymph. He is also loved by Bellario, whose female name Euphrasia means "mind-gladdening."[27] Her love is shown as extravagant, theatrical hero-worship that is placed in a three-way comparison with Philaster's and Arathusa's. Once she has revealed her identity, the king promises her a worthy marriage, but she refuses and requests instead the chance to devote her life to the

---

[27] With all the other important names having meanings, it is likely that Philaster's does too. Is it patterned after Renaissance Latin coinages like Jonson's "poetaster," Marston's "parasitaster," and Burton's "philosophaster," which had been used for the titles of plays, making him a "phil-aster," not quite the lover he seemed to be?

service of Philaster and Arathusa. The prospect of being attended for life by a pretty lady madly in love with her husband does not daunt the mature princess. The authors make plain the difference between her self-assured, clear-eyed manner of loving, Euphrasia's teenage hero worship ("I saw a God / I thought, but it was you" [5.5.157–58]), and Philaster's incurable jealousy:

> Arathusa.   I, *Philaster*,
>   Cannot be jealous, though you had a Lady
>   Drest like a Page to serve you, nor will I
>   Suspect her living heere: come live with me,
>   Live free as I do; she that loves my Lord,
>   Curst be the wife that hates her.

(5.5.191–96)

Amoret in *The Faithful Shepherdess*, Viola in *The Coxcomb*, perhaps Luce in *The Knight of the Burning Pestle*, and certainly both of the ladies here deserve better than the "philasters" they love with such generosity. More such uncritically loving heroines would follow: Aspatia in *The Maid's Tragedy*, Panthea in *A King and No King*, and many in Fletcher's subsequent work.

Bloody, Bawdy Princes

It is clear that all three princes in *Philaster* act intemperately, but no one seems to have noticed that this general resemblance is reinforced and given a sharper significance by a pattern of images.[28] What these princes share is an impulse to shed blood and thereby to do harm to various parts of the body politic. Sometimes they draw blood in wars, as the king did in his invasion of Sicily (1.1.25–26). His policies precipitate a revolt that someone predicts will

> bury the lives of thousands
> That must bleed with thee like a sacrifice
> In thy red ruins.

(5.3.17–19)

His usurpation has given Philaster "a general purge already, / For all the right he has, and now he meanes / To let him blood" (1.1.204–6).

---

[28] The normal view is that the overplot and the romantic plot have little connection. Thus Lee Bliss says, "[Philaster's] importance lies in his private, emotional relationships, and state concerns are handed over, after 1.1 to the court lords for interpretation and to the citizens for active intervention." The lovers "interrelations . . . belong to a different realm, that of pastoral romance"; the public and private world are kept separate, "folded one within another" (*Francis Beaumont* [Boston, 1987], pp. 74, 78).

Bloodletting is the king's natural response to private as well as public problems, as when his daughter is lost:

> shew her me,
> Or let me perish, if I cover not
> All *Cicelie* with blood.
>
> (4.4.32–34)

In the same vein, when displeased with his daughter's marriage he warns, "Bloud shall put out your [marriage] Torches" (5.3.58). Although he is hardly the one to chastise others for bloodletting, it seems just for Philaster to state, "Y' are a Tyrant, and a savage Monster, / That feedes upon the bloud you gave a life to" (5.3.78–79).

The Spanish prince is mainly depicted as a buffoon, but in his own way he too causes trouble through the shedding of blood. The witty Lady Galatea warns him to "flie *Phlebotomie*" (2.2.37), but according to the physiology of the day that considered semen a distillation of the essence of blood, Pharamond precipitates the major trouble of the play by "phlebotomizing" himself through his self-indulgent lechery. He induces the vicious Megra to sleep with him by saying "if I doe not teach you to doe it as easily in one night, as you'l goe to bed: I'le loose my royall blood for't" (2.2.99–101). In fact, it is the princes' constant belief, shown to be illusory, that there is something special about "royall blood" that empowers them to be so bloody.[29]

Philaster's propensity for bloodletting can thus be seen as a normal princely activity. Even without his sword his mere presence seems to affect Bellario's blood:

> *Philaster.* . . . It troubles me
>   That I have call'd the blood out of thy cheekes,
>   That did so well become thee.
>
> (3.1.276–78)

Again Bellario, reminiscing about her first view of Philaster says,

> My bloud flue out and backe againe as fast
> As I had puft it forth and suckt it in
> Like breath.
>
> (5.5.159–61)

He can cause the same reaction in kings, as Dion reports:

> . . . How he shooke the King,
> Made his soule melt within him, and his blood,

---

[29] See also 1.1.86, 2.2.15–16, 5.4.30, 5.4.95.

> Run into whay: it stood upon his brow,
> Like a cold winter dew.
>
> (1.1.293–96)

Arathusa too associates Philaster with blood loss:

> If a bowle of blood
> Drawne from this arme of mine, would poyson thee,
> A draught of his would cure thee.
>
> (1.2.27–29)

Like the king, Philaster first responds to challenges by shedding blood, whether his own, as in his constant gestures toward suicide, or the blood of the various creatures who cross his path. As he warns the Country Fellow,

> Persue thy owne affaires; it will be ill
> To multiply blood upon my head, which thou
> Wilt force me to.
>
> (4.5.93–95)

Bloodletting is the sport of princes. One's revulsion is heightened by the authors' insistence that the creatures Philaster has left bleeding are of more than mortal stature. As I mentioned earlier, the subtitle suggests an allegorical dimension to his devoted victims: either could represent Love.[30] But when the bleeding Arathusa is found in the woods, this Sicilian wood nymph (as her name suggests) is metamorphosed by Pharamond's exclamation—"O sacred spring of innocent blood" (4.5.115)—into a sacramental object, something like a saint in a poem by Crashaw. This rarefied conception is reinforced when Arathusa announces that she has the "power to pardon sins as oft / As any man has power to wrong me" (5.5.143–44). Only such a godlike creature could pardon Philaster.

The play constantly shows the danger from "your heated bloud when it rebels / Against your reason" (5.5.49–50); kings are turned into enemies of their people. The chastened king acknowledges this with his didactic closing words, which fuse the main, romantic plot and the political overplot and leave an admonition for magistrates like the one who may have seen the two court performances in the winter of 1612–13:

---

[30] Furthermore, as Stephen Booth has suggested to me, the subtitle might be punning on the fact that two embodiments of love lie and tell lies while bleeding.

. . . Let Princes learne
By this to rule the passions of their blood,
For what Heaven wils can never be withstood.

(5.5.216–18)

Princes, as this play and the others in the trilogy make clear, are not gods and should conduct themselves accordingly. If they do not, the play suggests, heaven may provide an answer from the people.

With *Philaster* Beaumont and Fletcher suddenly became the fresh new voice in the London theater. It is possible to imagine even King James enjoying this play with its sensational plot and perspicuous language—its suave, easy, knowing manner was the very essence of what is called "aristocratic" and "courtly." At the same time what is happening in the play seems so at odds with its manner that one keeps wondering whether the authors realize the implications of what they are doing. But the remainder of the trilogy shows that they do indeed. They resemble that legendary executioner whose victims didn't know they'd been decapitated until they laughed their heads off.

Chapter Nine

A KING AND NO KING: THE CORRUPTION
OF POWER

IF *Philaster* portrays an intemperate, dispossessed prince whom Fortune restores to his birthright, *A King and No King* (1611)[1] might for
purposes of symmetry be described as the story of an intemperate
king whom Fortune deposes from a throne to which he has no natural right. Admittedly, this is an unorthodox way of describing this
exotically situated, exciting romance about a man who becomes consumed by an incestuous passion for his sister and is saved from dam-
nation only by the revelation that they are not really kin. This play is
often singled out to exemplify what is most superficial or pernicious
in the work of Beaumont and Fletcher. Arthur Mizener's much-cited
article, "The High Design of *A King and No King*," anticipating Eugene Waith's argument in *The Pattern of Tragicomedy in Beaumont and
Fletcher*,[2] used *A King and No King* to show that their tragicomedies
were entertaining but meaningless well-made plays. According to
Mizener, the plot does not have "a morally significant pattern, and its
great complexity is not determined by any complexity of meaning but
exists because a complex narrative is itself exciting, as well as the
means of providing the maximum number of exciting moments."[3]
Others who have found "meaning" in the tragicomedies see harmful,
meretricious ones, and for them the treatment of incest in *A King and
No King* is a prime example. In Robert Ornstein's view, "Instead of
seeking a genuine ethical solution to [the hero] Arbaces' conflict, he
[Fletcher] falls back on the over-useful trumpery of romance. . . . vice
becomes virtue by a simple twist of the plot."[4] Robert J. Turner
strongly concurs:

> Not only was it [*A King and No King*] titillating, but it must have been
> rather a relief to be told that there was a world where the standards of

[1] The date 1611 is established by Sir George Buc's allowance for its performance;
the earliest evidence of joint authorship is the title page of the first quarto of 1619.
Most scholars give Beaumont the larger share of the composition. See Cyrus Hoy,
"The Shares of Fletcher and his Collaborators in the Beaumont and Fletcher Canon,"
Studies in Bibliography 11 (1958): 91 for the best estimate.

[2] New Haven, Conn., 1952.

[3] *Modern Philology* 38 (1940): 133–54.

[4] *The Moral Vision of Jacobean Tragedy* (Madison, Wisc., 1960), p. 169.

Christian humanism did not hold—where technicalities existed that permitted one to lie with one's sister or perhaps to gorge on such other exotic emotional confections as suited one's palate without having to pay with a moral illness that might last an eternity.[5]

KINGSHIP AND THE *CYROPAEDIA*

Statements like Ornstein's and Turner's tend to confirm Lee Bliss's recent observation that *A King and No King* "is the Beaumont-Fletcher play most antipathetic to modern sensibilities."[6] In the seventeenth century, on the other hand, it was one of their most popular plays, "always . . . acted with applause," according to Langbaine; Dryden thought it the "best of their designs."[7] Perhaps this difference in valuation stems from a dimension of the play that was of contemporary importance but faded away as the years went by. *A King and No King*, I suggest, is not primarily a play about incest but one about a *king* with incestuous longings. The status of the protagonist is noted in the very first words and stressed in the typography of the first quarto: "*Bessus*, the KING has made a fayre hand on't, has ended the warres at a blow" (1.1.1–2).[8] The word "king" echoes through the script on no fewer than seventy-one occasions, including the last word of the play, and kingship is alluded to in thirty related words such as "royal," "prince," and "your majesty."

The emphasis on kingship coheres with the fact that although no single source for the plot has been discovered, the names of many of the characters and some of the most important situations have been traced to Xenophon's *Cyropaedia*, a book much revered in the Renaissance for its idealized portrait of a king, Cyrus.[9] Xenophon says Cy-

[5] *A King and No King*, Regents Renaissance Drama Series (Lincoln, Neb., 1963), pp. xxv–xxvi.

[6] *Francis Beaumont* (Boston, 1987), p. 121.

[7] Both quotations are from *The Critical Works of Thomas Rymer*, ed. Curt A. Zimansky (New Haven, Conn., 1956), p. 206. Subsequent citations from Rymer refer to this edition.

[8] Quotations are from the edition of George Walton Williams in Fredson Bowers, gen. ed., *The Dramatic Works in the Beaumont and Fletcher Canon* (Cambridge, 1966–), vol. 2. Of course, it is not known who is responsible for the play's typography.

[9] Among the admirers of Xenophon's Cyrus were Castiglione, Sidney, Spenser, and Milton. For a discussion of the influence of the *Cyropaedia* on Renaissance poetry, see O. B. Hardison, Jr., *The Enduring Monument: a Study of the Idea of Praise in Renaissance Literary Theory and Practice* (Chapel Hill, N.C., 1962), pp. 72ff. The use of the *Cyropaedia* in *A King and No King* was first briefly noted by R. Warwick Bond in A. H. Bullen, gen. ed., *The Works of Francis Beaumont and John Fletcher* (London, 1904–12), 1:246–47. Waith, *Pattern of Tragicomedy in Beaumont and Fletcher*, expanded somewhat on Bond, and Lee Bliss in her *Francis Beaumont*, pp. 107–8, first observed that in some sense King Arbaces may be viewed as (in her term) an "anti-Cyrus" figure.

rus "believed that he could in no way more effectively inspire a desire for the beautiful and the good than by endeavoring, as their sovereign, to set before his subjects a perfect model of virtue in his own person."[10] This perfect king took pains to be devout in his observance of religion, upright and considerate in his dealings with friends and allies, and generous to those who obeyed him. Above all, according to Xenophon,

> By making his [Cyrus's] own self-control an example, he disposed all to practise that virtue more diligently. For when the weaker members of society see that one who is in a position where he may indulge himself in excess is still under self-control, they naturally strive all the more not to be found guilty of any excessive indulgence. . . . And he thought that temperance could be best inculcated, if he showed that he himself was never carried away from the pursuit of the good by any pleasures of the moment, but that he was willing to labour first for the attainment of refined pleasures. (8.1.30–31)

The *Cyropaedia* mattered so much to King James that he commissioned Philemon Holland to translate it for Prince Henry's edification.[11] Beaumont and Fletcher's "trilogy" may therefore have been an effort to remind a great man who professed to admire the *Cyropaedia* that he would do well to emulate Cyrus's example. Both *Philaster* and *The Maid's Tragedy* conclude as if written in the shadow of Xenophon, with summarizing speeches by a king that state that the highest wisdom for princes is to act in an unimpassioned, temperate way. And *A King and No King* is a continuous display of what happens when "one who is in a position where he may indulge himself in excess" does so.

The First Two Acts: "Sudden Extremities"

For the first two acts, fully one-third of the play, Beaumont and Fletcher show King Arbaces wandering home from the wars while his court awaits his arrival. Almost nothing "happens" but a series of conversations that serve primarily to establish the king's character. Only then do the authors explicitly introduce the incest plot. One learns that there is much to admire about this king. The forthright captain Mardonius tells him that he possesses most of the virtues he esteems in a friend:

[10] *Cyropaedia*, trans. Walter Miller, Loeb Edition (Cambridge, Mass., 1914), bk. 8, chap. 1, l.21. Subsequent citations in the text are to this edition.
[11] Hardison, *Enduring Monument*, p. 72.

should I chuse a companion for wit and pleasure, it should bee you; or for honesty to enterchange my bosome with, it would be you; or wise-dome to give me counsel, I would pick out you; or vallor to defend my reputation, still I would find out you; for you are fit to fight for all the world, if it could come in question. (1.1.367–73)

Many of these positive attributes are shown. Arbaces can be an amusing companion (1.1.394–412), a gentle captor (1.1.201–2), a magnanimous son to a mother who for mysterious reasons is constantly trying to have him murdered (2.1.99–102).

But Mardonius prefaces his tribute to Arbaces by saying that his many virtues are diluted by his propensity to "wilde moodes" (1.1.368). Before one first sees the king, Mardonius describes him as "vain-glorious, and humble, and angrie, and patient, and merrie, and dull, and joyfull, and sorrowfull, in extreamities in an houre" (1.1.81–83). The cranky seventeenth-century critic Thomas Rymer properly comments, "Should we find underwritten *This is a King*, yet could not reason give way to our belief" (p. 42). Rymer's views on regal decorum are notoriously simplistic, but with one's first glimpse of Arbaces, one feels that in some metaphoric sense, at least, Rymer is correct in saying that this king is "no king." He is still basking in the victory in single combat over King Tigranes of Armenia that concluded the war and made Tigranes (a name out of the *Cyropaedia*) his prisoner. Arbaces tries to treat his fellow-king, a member of his entourage, in a manner befitting his rank, but he cannot open his mouth without revealing himself as a shameless braggart:

> Thy sadnesse (brave *Tigranes*) takes away
> From my full victorie; am I become
> Of so small fame, that any man should grieve
> When I orecome him? They that plac't me here,
> Intended it an honour large enough
> For the most valiant living, but to dare
> Oppose me single, though he lost the day.
> What should afflict you, you are as free as I:
> To be my prisoner, is to be more free
> Then you were formerlie.
>
> (1.1.87–96)

Again Rymer offers a useful comment:

Arbaces . . . no sooner comes on the stage, but lays about him with his tongue at so nauseous a rate, Captain Bessus is all Modesty to him, to mend the matter his friend Mardonius shaking an empty skull, says *'Tis pity that valour should be thus drunk.* Had he been content to brag only amongst his own Vassals, the fault might be more sufferable, but the King of *Armenia* is his prisoner, he must bear the load of all; he must be swagger'd at, insulted over, and trampl'd on without any provocation. We have a *Scene* of his sufferings in each *Act* of the Play: *Bajazet* in the *Cage* was never so carried about, or felt half the barbarous indignities which are thrown on this unfortunate Prince by our monster of a King. (P. 43)

Arbaces is completely wrapped up in himself and his endeavors; his mercurial temperament constantly impels him to erratic, "sudden extremities" (1.1.507), in clear contrast to the temperate behavior of Tigranes. The authors make it plain through Tigranes' response that they regard the old 1580s style of vaunting, the sort Tamburlaine employed on Bajazet, as uncivilized behavior:

> Is it the course of
> *Iberia*, to use their prisoners thus?
> Had Fortune throwne my name above *Arbaces*,
> I should not thus have talkt, for in *Armenia*
> We hold it base: you should have kept your temper,
> Till you saw home agen; where tis the fashion
> Perhaps to brag.
>
> (1.1.111–17)

The use of the captain Mardonius as a kind of chorus also firmly regulates one's attitude toward the braggart king:

> *Arbaces.* . . . Should I that have the power
>   To teach the Neighbour world humility,
>   Mix with vaine glory.
> *Mardonius.* [*aside*] In deede this is none?
>
> (1.1.130–33)

Throughout the play Mardonius attempts to reform Arbaces, warning him that his temperament is leading him to disaster. Sometimes Arbaces acknowledges the validity of this criticism:

> Thou hast spoake truth, and boldly, such a truth
> As might offend another. I have bin
> Too passionate, and idle, thou shalt see
> A swift amendment.
>
> (1.1.378–81)

But as they did with Philaster, Beaumont and Fletcher show that for Arbaces "swift amendment"—any amendment—is difficult. In the last scene of the play Mardonius still finds it necessary to admonish the intemperate monarch: "You are more variable than you were" (5.4.22). Unlike the Cyrus of the *Cyropaedia* for whom it was a matter of policy to give credit to his entire army for his victories, Arbaces claims all the glory for himself, a habit particularly galling to the noble Mardonius:

> You told *Tigranes*, you had won his Land
> With that sole arme propt by Divinity:
> Was not that bragging, and a wrong to us
> That daily venturde lives?
>
> (1.1.275–78)

Arbaces talks like Tamburlaine, but he is not the scourge of God, merely a valiant leader dependent on his strong arm, his loyal soldiers, even on the exploits of a cowardly captain who while running away from a battle unintentionally gains a victory (1.1.71). He is another of Beaumont and Fletcher's flawed, postheroic age heroes.

The first section of the play concludes with the victorious king arriving back in his kingdom, where he is met by his admiring people. Despite constant admonitions he once again humiliates Tigranes publicly and shows that he has learned nothing:

> See all good people, I have brought the man,
> Whose very name you fear'd, a captive home:
> Behold him, tis *Tigranes*; in your hearts
> Sing songs of gladnesse, and deliverance.
>
> (2.2.101–4)

Thus incited, the people want to hang the noble Tigranes, who complains that he is being made "a scorned spectacle" (109), whereupon Arbaces apologizes and, as Tigranes says, makes "amends . . . with a speech in commendation of himselfe" (125–26)! The people (quite like Eliot's parade crowd in *Triumphal March*) have flocked to this great event, confused about what is happening or what it signifies. As he thanks them for their "love," the narcissistic king speaks in the timeless tones of a self-congratulatory politician. He tells them that as "payment" for their "expences to maintaine my warre" he brings them "such a word / As is not to be bought without our blouds; / Tis peace" (2.2.83–88). In a deadpan comment on the overblown rhetoric, Beaumont and Fletcher make the grateful people anticipate with pleasure the peck of peas each will receive "for all our money" (2.2.153). Xenophon's Cyrus was known as "father" not only to his nobles but even to his country's slaves and to the people he had subdued in war, "for he provided for them well" (8.1.44; 8.2.9). Perhaps in an ironic echo of that model, Arbaces leaves his beloved people on a note of patently insincere, unctuous paternalism:

> when there is
> A want of anything, let it be knowne
> To me, and I will be a Father to you:
> God keepe you all.

(2.2.137–40)

Not only a father to his people, Arbaces soon shows himself to be a loving brother as well.

INCEST: THE REGAL VICE

After the careful preparation of the first two acts, the "sudden extremities" of the king's behavior when he first sees his sister in act 3 are not surprising. He acts like the aptly named title figure of Fletcher's *The Mad Lover* (1616), who seems to go into a trance on his first view of a beautiful princess (1.1). As soon as Panthaea comes into his presence, Arbaces appears oblivious of her attempts to address him, delivers a eulogy about her as though she were dead, declares her not his kin by regal fiat, and wishes he were a beast so that his desire for her would not be constrained by the laws of civilization. He notices that Tigranes, to whom he has promised Panthaea, has been similarly smitten. In a jealous fury he sends Tigranes to prison, kneels in apology to Panthaea, ardently kisses her, then suddenly makes her a prisoner, accusing her of being a witch and of having poisoned him with a kiss. As this brilliant, wild scene concludes, the king acknowledges in a prayer that "Incest is in me / Dwelling alreadie," and that only divine power can pull him from it (3.1.330–32). Two scenes later (3.3) he is still obsessed by his desire for Panthaea, but in a fit of moral revulsion he ends the third act determined to control himself:

> I will not doe this sinne.
> Ile presse it here till it doe breake my breast;
> It heaves to get out: but thou art a sinne
> And spight of torture, I wil keep thee in.

(3.3.190–93)

It is an impressive moment, but Arbaces does not have the strength to maintain his resolution. He arranges a private interview with his sister—the most famous scene in the play—in which one comes to fear that an act of incest may well be performed onstage before it concludes. Arbaces believes that he is under control, that he has "collected all thats man" (4.4.21) about him to withstand his lawless impulses, but he soon admits to Panthaea that he has

>   lost
> The onely difference betwixt man, and beast,
> My reason.
> *Panthaea.* Heaven forbid.
> *Arbaces.* Nay it is gone,
>   And I am left as farre without a bound,
>   As the wild Ocean that obeyes the winds;
>   Each suddaine passion throwes me as it lists,
>   And overwhelmes all that oppose my will.
>
>   (4.4.64–70)

Earlier he had conceived his power to be, like the sea's, indisputable (3.1.164); now he says that even the ocean is at the mercy of the winds. When he informs Panthaea directly of his desire, he describes what he feels as blind lust. He makes no pretense of "love":

> I have beheld thee with a lustfull eye:
> My heart is set on wickednesse, to act
> Such sinnes with thee, as I have beene afraid
> To think off: If thou dar'st consent to this,
> (Which I beseech thee doe not) thou maist gaine
> Thy libertie, and yeeld me a content:
> If not, thy dwelling must be darke, and close
> Where I may never see thee; For God knowes
> That layd this punishment upon my pride,
> Thy sight at some time will enforce my madnesse
> To make a start ene to thy ravishing:
> Now spit upon me, and call all reproaches
> Thou canst devise together; and at once
> Hurle um against me: for I am a sicknesse
> As killing as the plague, ready to seize thee.
>
>   (4.4.71–85)

In spite of her brother's frank expression of a loveless lust and yet another threat of rape ("I shall force thee, though thou wert a Virgin / By vow to Heaven" [100–101]), Panthaea becomes infected by his diseased passion. Before the scene is over it is unclear who is the seducer:

> *Panthaea.*   But is there nothing else
> That we may doe, but onely walke: me thinkes
> Brothers and sisters lawfully may kisse.
>
>   (4.4.151–53)

And so they do, twice, barely managing to separate as the fourth act ends on a terrifying note.[12]

Beaumont and Fletcher add to the tension and suspense by delaying the climax with the insertion of three longish scenes, totalling over three hundred lines, that say nothing about Arbaces. Finally, in the fourth and final scene of a play whose genre has become increasingly unclear, the desperate Arbaces comes onstage to deliver a soliloquy, holding a sword:

> It is resolv'd, I bore it whilst I could,
> I can no more, Hell open all thy gates,
> And I will thorough them; if they be shut
> Ile batter um, but I will find the place
> Where the most damn'd have dwelling; ere I end,
> Amongst them all they shall not have a sinne,
> But I may call it mine: I must beginne
> With murder of my friend, and so goe on
> To an incestuous ravishing, and end
> My life and sinnes with a forbidden blow
> Upon my selfe.
>
> (5.4.1–11)

The hero-king has become a helpless prisoner of his criminal passion.

Arbaces' desire to commit incest provides Beaumont and Fletcher with the ultimate metaphor for lack of self-control. A straightforward passage in the normative *Cyropaedia* underscores the universality of the taboo he wants to violate: "A brother does not fall in love with his sister, but somebody else falls in love with her; neither does a father fall in love with his daughter, but somebody else does; for fear of God and the law of the land are sufficient to prevent such love" (5.1.10).[13] But unlawful as this form of desire is for mankind generally, Beaumont and Fletcher remind us, its appearance in a king has special implications. First, kings may violate even the most sacred prohibitions with impunity. As Shakespeare's Pericles says in considering the incest of King Antiochus, "Kings are earth's gods; in vice their law's their will; / And if Jove stray, who dares say Jove doth ill?" (1.1.103–4). This claim is amply illustrated by Arbaces' actions. Once he is smitten by his unlawful passion, Arbaces repeatedly employs his regal status to pursue his unlawful ends, as when he declares his sister

> no kinne to me, nor shall shee be;
> If shee were any, I create her none,

[12] A virtuous woman named Panthaea in the *Cyropaedia* (6.1.31–34, 7.3.14) resists a seducer and on the death of her husband commits suicide nobly.

[13] Bliss, *Francis Beaumont*, p. 108, first noted the relevance of this passage to this play.

And which of you can question this? my power
Is like the Sea, that is to be obey'd,
And not disputed with: I have decreed her
As farre from having part of bloud with me,
As the nak'd Indians: Come, and answer me,
He that is boldest now; Is that my Sister?

(3.1.161–68)

Mardonius dares to criticize him for this absurdity ("O this is fine"
[3.1.169]), but only in an aside. From his position of power the king
demands instant obedience to his most outrageous decisions:

Away with him to prison. . . .
. . . You shall know my word
Sweepes like a wind, and all it grapples with,
Are as the chaffe before it

(3.1.254–57)

Arbaces is reminded that "This is tyrannie / . . . subtiller then the
burning Buls, / Or that fam'd Tyrants bed" (3.1.264–66), but in his
helpless abandonment to his passion he repeatedly exploits his position to pursue his perverse longing. Intermittently he realizes the
harm his status has done to him, surrounded as he is by amoral flatterers: "If there were no such Instruments as thou, / We Kings could
never act such wicked deeds" (3.3.183–84). When at the conclusion
Arbaces learns that he is "no king," Mardonius makes explicit the
point that power has harmed his character: "Indeed twere well for
you, / If you might be a little lesse obey'd" (5.4.266–67).

But beyond the harm to himself is that which his mercurial temperament and narcissistic self-indulgence may inflict upon his kingdom. As Mardonius warns Arbaces, were he to rule as an unchecked
tyrant,

Then you may talke, and be beleevd, and grow,
And have your too selfe-glorious temper rock't
Into a dead sleepe, and the kingdome with you,
Till forraigne swords be in your throats, and slaughter
Be every where about you like your flatterers.

(4.2.178–82)

Nor can an immoral king rule with any authority. As Mardonius is
made to say, "if you doe this crime, you ought to have no lawes; For
after this it will bee great injustice in you to punish any offendor for
any crime" (3.3.97–99).

Indirectly as well as directly, the authors criticize the king's character. I have already noted the contrast between Arbaces and his fellow king Tigranes, who falls in love with Panthaea at the very moment Arbaces does. Overwhelmed by her attractions, he attempts to woo her in the presence of his faithful and jealous betrothed, Spaconia. But by the next time he appears, he has mastered his passion and berates himself for his "unmanly, beastly, sudden doting / Upon a new face" (4.2.28–29). He shamefacedly confesses his lapse and assures his love that he has gained "a new strong constancie, / Not to be shooke with eyes" (5.2.88–89). The ease with which Tigranes overcomes his momentary temptation, caused by the "passions of a man" (5.2.90), makes a heavily didactic point at Arbaces' expense.

There is much more of the same: an "untemperate" (4.3.107) cowardly swordsman, a short-tempered "intemperate" (5.1.110) ambassador, and most important, the utterly amoral, cowardly Captain Bessus. As Arthur Mizener first suggested, just as Mardonius seems to be an external representation of the king's good side, the cowardly, amoral Bessus serves almost like his "bad angel" in a morality play.[14] It is a useful way to look at Arbaces: he begins the play as the soulmate of Mardonius but is forced to cashier his conscience and employ Bessus when he needs a pander to pursue Panthaea. The vile Bessus is glad to serve and helpfully adds, "when this is dispatcht, if you have a minde to your Mother tell me, and you shall see Ile set it hard" (3.3.167–69). The authors underline the parallel by constructing the action so that Arbaces' big scenes are preceded by ones featuring Bessus. In act 4, scene 3, Bessus and some consultants on the subtleties of honor concoct a formula that argues that the coward's ability to suffer all his beatings proves him a "valiant man" (4.3.136).[15] Cowardice is valor. By similar doublespeak in the following scene, Arbaces almost proves to his satisfaction that moral law is a question of "meere sounds" (4.4.113) and that brothers and sisters "lawfully" (153) may kiss. In the fifth act Bessus and his swordsmen attempt to convey their dubious conclusions about his valor to a sceptic who doubts the coward's right to "honorable" status. They claim that "his honour is come off cleane, and sufficient" (5.3.39–40), and for their

[14] Mizener's idea was elaborated by Robert K. Turner in "The Morality Play of *A King and No King*," *Renaissance Papers* (1961): 93–103 and in his preface to his edition of the play.

[15] In this debate among a group of cowards about whether one is honor-bound to avenge a beating by one's prince, it is agreed that "we subjects must . . . / Be subject to it" (4.3.46–47). Passive obedience was integral to the doctrine of divine right to which James was so attached. It is not surprising that the authors make these disreputable cowards subscribe to it. It is touched on lightly at a few points in this play about a king becoming a tyrant, but as I shall show, it is a prime concern of *The Maid's Tragedy* as well as of Fletcher's later plays, *Valentinian*, *The Loyal Subject*, and *A Wife for a Month*.

outrageous casuistry receive a thorough beating. In the scene that follows, the last in the play, Arbaces' honor comes off "cleane and sufficient" by an equally dubious path.

But he does not get beaten. All that has been diseased, poisonous, and against divinity in Arbaces' passion is apparently sanctioned. He may marry his "sister": she is a legitimate but late child of the king and queen, while he is the son of a commoner who was reared as the heir when the queen feared she was sterile.[16] Arbaces has come off "cleane and sufficient," but the parallel to Bessus makes one realize the cynical tone of the happy conclusion. It is incredible and outrageous, one is made to feel, for nothing has changed and no one has learned anything.

A TRAGEDY AND NO TRAGEDY

Every commentator on *A King and No King* describes the ending as unambiguously happy, with Arbaces regaining his title and power by marrying Panthaea. Certainly the stage is filled with joy because Arbaces will not have to commit rape, murder, and suicide, and because an atmosphere of good will is created by the freeing of Tigranes. But those who see Arbaces' status as unchanged are speaking legalistically and not responding to what actually transpires on the stage. When he learns the truth about his life and realizes that he may legally marry the object of his dark lust, Arbaces conducts himself as much unlike a king as ever. Precisely like the unstable Philaster jumping around the stage exclaiming "It is a woman" when Bellario-Euphrasia's gender is revealed (5.5.130, 131, 133), Arbaces repeatedly raves in manic exultation that he is no longer king (5.4.264, 270, 276–82, 291, 327–28, 353). Mardonius, in one of the play's most telling lines, responds, "Indeed twere well for you, / If you might be a little lesse obey'd" (5.4.266-67). The nonking does not seem to notice this crucial observation but continues, "*Panthaea* is the Queene, / And I am plain *Arbaces*" (5.4.269-70). He insists that no man should any longer pay homage to him by taking off his hat in his presence and adds, "I am *Arbaces*, we all fellow subjects" (5.4.281, 291). Then Bessus makes literal the point developed throughout the play—their similarity—by calling his former king "fellow subject *Arbaces*" (293). It is the first time anyone except King Tigranes calls him by his proper name. With everyone on a first name basis, their hats on, the general good feeling of the ending seems to be a by-product of the diminution of

---

[16] It is virtually impossible to deduce this history from the obscure hints the authors plant throughout the play. In a careful first reading (hence, even truer of a stage performance) none of the hints leads us to doubt the kinship of Arbaces and Panthaea.

Arbaces' power. Whatever the legalities of the situation, the effect is like a shift from absolute to constitutional monarchy.

As the play concludes, the joy-maddened Arbaces makes exorbitant promises of gifts to his former captives, Tigranes and his fiancée, Spaconia—"Chariots easier then ayre / That I will have invented" (5.4.314–15) and a "Horse cut out of an entire Diamond, / That shall be made to goe with golden wheeles" (318–19)—"I know not how yet" (320), he admits. Rymer with his vigilant nose for regal indecorum strongly disapproves of Arbaces' conduct in these final moments: "Might not a Poet as well describe to us how the King eats and drinks, or goes to *Stool*; for these actions are also *natural*: but observe the behavior of *Arbaces*, after that he is found to be *no King*" (p. 45). Again Rymer fails to see that Beaumont and Fletcher would have agreed with his observation. They make Mardonius comment sardonically on Arbaces' extravagant behavior (313), and in Arbaces' implicit contrast of himself to Tigranes he shows that he has acquired at least one piece of self-knowledge: "Maist thou be happie / In thy faire choice; for thou art temperate" (342–43). Temperate, Arbaces could never be, and hence never "king" over himself.

There is no reason to believe that Fletcher (Beaumont was dead) had anything to do with the production of the first quarto of *A King and No King* (1619), but on the title page is a woodcut of great interest because it suggests how some contemporary interpreted the ending of the play.[17] The woodcut seems to corroborate my claim that a deposition of some sort occurs. The silly smile on Arbaces' face apparently represents his final mood of hysterical happiness. Some have said that it is unclear whether the crown is being placed on his head or taken from it, but the fact that his scepter is already lying on the ground makes it certain that Fortune (or Heaven) is removing the crown. Deprived of scepter and crown in an empty hilly landscape, Arbaces is now a fellow man. He who had appeared every inch a "KING" at the opening has by the action of the play been, in the last words, "prov'd no King" (5.4.353). In the words of James Shirley's great poem, Fortune may determine when "Scepter and crown / Must tumble down," but a monarch watching this play might well decide that he would fare better by modeling himself on Cyrus than on Arbaces.

---

[17] The publisher of the 1619 quarto, Thomas Walkley, prefaces it with a letter of thanks to Sir Henry Nevill for having provided him with the manuscript. Charles Gayley, *Beaumont, the Dramatist* (New York, 1914), pp. 145–48, claims that Sir Henry's father (also named Sir Henry) was a member of the Mermaid Tavern circle, hence connected to Beaumont and thus the source of the manuscript, but I. A. Shapiro, "The 'Mermaid Club,' " *Modern Language Review* 45 (1950): 8, shows that the Sir Henry of the Mermaid was not the father of the owner of this manuscript.

A King and no King.

Acted at the *Globe*, by his Maie-
sties Seruants.

Written by *Francis Beamount*, and *Iohn Flecher*.

AT LONDON
Printed for *Thomas Walkley*, and are to bee sold
at his shoppe at the Eagle and Childe in
Brittans-Burse. 1619.

Title page of *A King and No King* quarto of 1619. (Reproduced by permission
of the Houghton Library, Harvard University.)

As I have described *A King and No King,* the term "tragicomedy" does not fit. Through most of the action every generic signal points toward tragedy. Suddenly an ending occurs that can only be called comic. It is a mixture that does not display the pure "middle mood" that Una Ellis-Fermor claims to be "the contribution of Beaumont and Fletcher to the subsequent drama."[18] Dryden seems to me exactly on the mark in classifying *A King and No King* as "of that inferior sort of tragedies, which end with a prosperous event."[19] To this kind of tragedy, portraying "a bad man passing from adversity to prosperity," Aristotle objects that "nothing can be more alien to the spirit of Tragedy; it possesses no single tragic quality; it neither satisfies the moral sense, nor calls forth pity or fear."[20] But may not a play enrich the moral sense by displaying rewards to the undeserving? Is this not a recurrent, regrettable pattern in life? Intent on rape and murder at the moment he learns about his background, Arbaces has few redeeming qualities, but he gets the girl of his perverse dreams. That does not mean that the authors excuse or approve of him or celebrate the capriciousness of the universe. Like the bloody Philaster, Arbaces is a dangerous example, not to be admired, however much he may prosper. Clearly Beaumont and Fletcher's aesthetic motto for the trilogy was "make it new." They aimed for a form of implication that made novel demands on their audience. But is the ending of *A King and No King* outrageous? Does it not propose a "genuine ethical solution," an antiromantic one, that meets "the standards of Christian humanism" (to use Turner's moralistic terms), to suggest that one does not look to the sublunary world for a just distribution of rewards and punishments?

In arguing for the purity of its moral purpose and the legitimacy of its surprise ending, I do not want to suggest that I believe *A King and No King* to be an artistic success. Dyce remarks about the authors' presentation of Arbaces' changeableness in the first two acts: "the mechanism is too apparent; the reader almost feels as if he were present at a puppet-show, and saw more than a spectator ought to see,— the master of the exhibition pulling the wires that govern the motions of his puppet."[21] I would extend Dyce's remarks to the entire play. Compared to its two companion plays, *A King and No King* is too ex-

18 *The Jacobean Drama: an Interpretation* (London, 1936), p. 205.
19 "Preface to *Troilus and Cressida,*" *Essays of John Dryden,* ed. W. P. Ker (Oxford, 1900), 1:212.
20 "The Poetics," in James H. Smith and Edd W. Parks, eds., *The Great Critics* (New York, 1932), pp. 40–41.
21 *The Works of Beaumont and Fletcher,* ed. Alexander Dyce (London, 1843–46), 1:xxxvi.

plicit, too insistently didactic in its ironic presentation of a king whose misconduct demonstrates the desirability of behaving in the opposite manner. Dryden may be correct in his judgment that Arbaces, that "strange mixture of man," is the best characterization by Beaumont and Fletcher,[22] but he stands in a world of pasteboard figures. Nonetheless, the excessive clarity of *A King and No King* makes it a useful confirmation of the central tendencies of the other two parts of the trilogy.

[22] "Preface to *Troilus and Cressida*," 1:220.

Chapter Ten

THE MAID'S TRAGEDY: HONORABLE TYRANNICIDE

THE MASQUE: FLATTERY AND POWER

Beaumont and Fletcher wrote *The Maid's Tragedy* (1610–11) during the same span of time in which they wrote *Philaster* and *A King and No King*;[1] its links to the other two plays are clear. Its concluding words, uttered by the king, offer the same moral as its two companion pieces. He vows "to rule with temper" and thereby avoid the fate of his "lustfull" predecessor (5.3.293).[2] The title, however, seems to suggest that the center of interest is not a king but a "maid," and Rymer was only the first of many to claim that the "conduct" of the play is "all at random, since not directed to any one certain end."[3] It is true that there are two segments to the plot. In that referred to by the title, the betrothal of Aspatia (the "maid") to Amintor is broken by the king's order so that Amintor may marry Evadne. The grief-stricken "maid," determined to die, manages to trick her former fiancée into killing her; upon discovering this, he commits suicide. But first, in the other part of the plot, Amintor discovers that his marriage is a sham contrived to hide the affair between his new bride and the king. As an obedient subject he tries to keep silent about this humiliating situation, but he finally reveals it to his close friend Melantius. Since Evadne is his sister, Melantius feels personally dishonored. He contrives a revenge plot that results in Evadne's murder of the king and her suicide.

Thus, returning to Rymer's objection that the "conduct" of the play is "all at random," some have suggested that there are really two

---

[1] There are some reasons for believing that it was written just before *A King and No King*, but nothing is certain about the date except that it must be before October 31, 1611, when Buc mentions a *Second Maid's Tragedy*. It is first mentioned as a collaboration in the third quarto of 1630. On the basis of internal evidence most scholars conclude that Beaumont wrote most of the play but that Fletcher was responsible for some of the most important scenes. See Cyrus Hoy, "The Shares of Fletcher and his Collaborators in the Beaumont and Fletcher Canon," *Studies in Bibliography* 11 (1958): 94.

[2] All quotations are from the edition by Robert K. Turner in Fredson Bowers, gen. ed., *The Dramatic Works in the Beaumont and Fletcher Canon* (Cambridge, 1966–), vol. 2.

[3] *The Critical Works of Thomas Rymer*, ed. Curt A. Zimansky (New Haven, Conn., 1956), p. 61. Page references in the text refer to this edition.

maids, ironically including Evadne with Aspatia.[4] And I would suggest the presence of a third maid, the innocent, virginal husband Amintor.

Rymer asks another crucial question about the "conduct" of the plot: "If Amintor's falsehood and its fatal consequence are to be noted, what occasion have we for a King in this tragedy? Cannot *Corydon* deceive his *Amaryllis* (for such is Aspatia) but the King must know of it, the King must be murder'd for't?" (p. 64). A frequent answer has been that one ought not to look to Beaumont and Fletcher for coherence of plot or a central, unifying action; and some, notably Danby, would say that the illusion of coherence is all that a play by Beaumont and Fletcher requires. Certainly it is a play with stunning individual scenes—probably more than in any other of their plays.[5] Rymer has once again raised a fruitful problem, but what is clearest about the maid Aspatia is that she is not an Amaryllis, nor is Amintor a Corydon; they are members of a royal court. And the king "must know" of Amintor's falsehood because he has caused it, as, in fact, he has caused everything else in his court. One sees very little of the king. What Beaumont and Fletcher concentrate on, what unifies the action, are the responses of a variety of victims to the dictates of a monarch with divine right pretensions.[6]

Comparatively speaking, the arena of action of *Philaster* and *A King and No King* is spacious. Each includes court and country, courtiers and citizens, country folk, foresters. *The Maid's Tragedy* is set in the

---

[4] Peter Holland made this suggestion in a review of a production of the play, "The Case for Regicide," *Times Literary Supplement*, May 23, 1980, p. 581; William Shullenberger also suggests this in " 'This For the Most Wrong'd of Women': a Reappraisal of *The Maid's Tragedy*," *Renaissance Drama*, n.s., 13 (1982): 131–56. Long ago Alexander Dyce in his edition, *The Works of Beaumont and Fletcher* (London, 1843–46), 1:xxxii, n. b, pointed to a historical justification for this possibility: "from P. Cunningham, *Extracts from the Accounts of the Revels at Court, &c.*, it appears that the title has a reference to Evadne; 'Shrove Tuesday A play called *the proud Mayds Tragedie*' " (p. 211).

[5] As with *The Knight of the Burning Pestle*, the other widely known play in the canon, *The Maid's Tragedy* has produced many excellent commentaries, notably those by John F. Danby, *Poets on Fortune's Hill* (London, 1952), pp. 184–206; Robert Ornstein, *The Moral Vision of Jacobean Tragedy* (Madison, Wisc., 1965), pp. 173–79; Howard B. Norland's preface in his edition for the Regents Renaissance Drama Series (Lincoln, Neb., 1968); and Lee Bliss, *Francis Beaumont* (Boston, 1987), pp. 87–106.

[6] The best book on the subject is still that by John N. Figgis, *The Divine Right of Kings* (Cambridge, 1934). Figgis shows that there were good and sufficient reasons for such a doctrine to arise in order to counter the power of the church, but for the purposes of this study it is important to remember that many of James's contemporaries, particularly the lawyers, could not view this apparent encroachment on the common law sub specie aeternitatis.

court of Rhodes, an island kingdom; its characters are either courtiers or their servants. It is a parochial, inward-turned world preoccupied with itself and, at the center of everyone's consciousness, the king. Obsession with the royal presence, his wishes and whims, causes the word "king" to be uttered almost as frequently and centrally as in *A King and No King*, no less than sixty-four times, often in contexts that endow the word itself with nearly sacramental significance.

The king-centered nature of this world is established in the remarkably leisurely opening act. Events seem to occur in real time as courtiers await the start of a wedding masque. In the informal "language of gentlemen," they are casually discussing the nature of masques when the general Melantius appears, ordered back from the wars to attend the wedding. The king's brother's welcome sounds the keynote of the play: "The breath of Kings is like the breath of gods, / My brother wisht thee here, and thou art here" (1.1.15–16). Melantius, now greeted by his own brother, reprimands him for not coming to his military camp when summoned. He is told, "my excuse / Is my Kings strict command" (31–32). As the subject shifts to the virtues of the bridegroom Amintor, the jilted maid Aspatia suddenly crosses the stage. Uninformed about her situation, Melantius congratulates her for having just married Amintor. Then he learns that, in fact, his own sister Evadne is the bride: "The King my brother did it / To honour you, and these solemnities / Are at his charge" (76–78), to which Melantius replies in a phrase that reverberates ironically through the play, "Tis royall like himselfe" (78). When Amintor appears, Melantius greets him warmly but chastises him for fickleness to his fiancée. Amintor's excuse summons up the same ubiquitous presence: "She had my promise, but the King forbad it" (135). As the masque is about to start, Calianax, father of Aspatia, is forced as the king's officer to "doe service" at the celebration of the wedding that has "neere kild" his daughter (1.2.18–19). Everything in Rhodes is done at or for "the Kings pleasure" (5.1.3).

Consistent with the leisurely pace of the opening, Beaumont and Fletcher then present to the audiences at the Globe and Blackfriars, as well as to the assembled court at Whitehall and at Rhodes, the complete masque celebrating the marriage of Amintor and Evadne. It is not unusual, of course, to insert such entertainments into plays; the same acting company, the King's Men, performed a marriage masque in *The Tempest* in the same year. But much is unique about Beaumont and Fletcher's masque. It is longer than any extraneous entertainment included in any Jacobean play, longer even than the "real" masque Beaumont wrote to celebrate Princess Elizabeth's marriage in

1613.[7] It is also quite elaborate for a masque not subsidized by the court, requiring some of the spectacular effects—such as a rock that opens and closes—and the lavish costumes for which such "toys" (as Bacon called them) were notorious. Moreover, the masque is presented with none of the interruptions that punctuate similar offerings in *A Midsummer Night's Dream, Hamlet*, or *The Tempest*; and there are no comments about it at its conclusion. Most notably, the authors chose to place it after a very harsh appraisal of the conventions of the masque:

> *Lysippus. Strato* thou hast some skill in poetrie,
>   What think'st thou of a maske, will it be well?
> *Strato.* As well as masks can be.
> *Lysippus.*   As masks can be?
> *Strato.* Yes, they must commend their King, and speake in praise
>   Of the assembly, blesse the Bride and Bridegroome,
>   In person of some god, there tied to rules
>   Of flatterie.
>
>   (1.1.5–11)

The masque that follows observes Strato's "rules" religiously. In it the seamy court of Rhodes is described as a place of such importance that the "immortall great" gods themselves (1.2.221) come to honor the wedding of two of its members. These gods are awed by the beauty of the women in the audience and by the majesty of the king. In addition to such self-parody (as it must seem after Strato's formulation), the masque expresses conventional sentiments about wedding nights on which brides are expected to be blushing virgins who make weak denials to lusty bridegrooms. The "real" world of the next scene reveals a very different kind of marriage.

Thus the masque contributes to the ironic presentation of the world of Rhodes. But thanks to two recent studies, it is now beyond dispute that something altogether more subtle is also occurring.[8] For example, the three pretty songs about the married couple's impending sexual activity express none of the conventional hopes for a fruitful marriage. The deity connected with such matters, Hymen, is barely mentioned. In his place as the presiding deity is the goddess Night, who ominously appears out of a mist to which she ultimately returns. Her prime characteristic is hatred of the light and the sun

---

[7] Beaumont's Inner Temple masque has 171 lines, that in *The Maid's Tragedy*, 199 lines.

[8] Michael Neill, " 'The Simetry which Gives a Poem Grace': Masque, Imagery and the Fancy of *The Maid's Tragedy*," *Renaissance Drama* 3 (1970): 111–35; and Shullenberger, " 'This For the Most Wrong'd of Women.' "

god. For this entertainment she enlists a Cynthia whose virginity—
stressed by her denial of any relationship with Endymion—makes her
a dubious celebrant of marriage. This Cynthia in turn asks Neptune's
help in bringing certain mild winds to sing, but in the process the
"rebellious" (190) north wind Boreas breaks his chain and threatens
to flood the island. In the abrupt ending Neptune does not capture
this wild, unruly force; the distinctly unpleasant, "dead" (263) Night
expresses hopes that the sun have "another wild fire in his axeltree, /
And all fall drencht" (1.2.269–70); there is no final dance joining
masquers and audience. Traditionally and through the imagery of
the masque, the sun is portrayed as the heavenly analogue of the king
(e.g., 273). As William Shullenberger writes,

> The masque leaves two dramatic loose ends. One is the realization of
> Night's apocalyptic fantasy, the acting out of her murderous rage against
> the sun. The other is the chaining of Boreas, the containment of the
> chaotic energies he personifies. In a brilliant subterranean dramatic con-
> ceit, the dramatists tie these loose ends with a single climactic action,
> Evadne's binding and murder of the king. (P. 140)

The masque thus ironically exemplifies Strato's "rules" and acts as
a commentary on the events in the marriage chamber of Amintor
and Evadne. But since events occur in the play proper after destructive symbolic forces like Boreas are unleashed, the masque also serves
a magical function, as Michael Neill first suggested:

> The sleight of hand is possible only because the dramatists are juggling
> with two levels of illusion: in life mundane reality conventionally tran-
> scends stage reality at the conclusion of a masque (the presence of the
> king visibly affects the actions of the masquers), but when the mundane
> reality is itself a play there is no felt reason why the relationship should
> not be reversed and the masque "determine" the fate of its audience.
> Queen Night and Cynthia, after all, who control the revels and see the
> stage audience as their "servants" (1.2.141), are as "real" to the theater
> audience as Amintor and Evadne themselves. (P. 116)

It is as though the disease that infects the court emanates from the
masque.

Today masques, those expensive exercises in self-congratulation,
have many ardent admirers:

> The masque presents the triumph of an aristocratic community; at its
> center is a belief in the hierarchy and a faith in the power of idealization.
> Philosophically, it is both Platonic and Machiavellian; Platonic because it
> presents images of the good to which the participants aspire and may

ascend; Machiavellian because its idealizations are designed to justify the power they celebrate. . . . The democratic imagination sees only flattery in this sort of thing, but the charge is misguided, and blinds us to much that is crucial in all the arts of the Renaissance.[9]

Misguided as the charge may seem to some, Strato's remarks indicate that it is not only modern democrats who detect flattery as the central activity of masques, especially those of Ben Jonson.[10] To monarch and courtiers it must have been a great satisfaction to see one's milieu idealized, to play at being gods and goddesses in gorgeous masquing apparel, to believe however briefly in the reality of the "insubstantial pageant." Masques may be seen not merely as justifications of power but as forces that helped maintain the political status quo. In this play it was a politic notion on the part of the king to present a masque, and so to remind the court and a certain honest young bridegroom of the divinity and majesty of kings. It was an equally politic notion for Beaumont and Fletcher to show the audience at the Globe and Blackfriars what those notorious, intramural occasions look like. Fletcher, one may recall, expressed reservations about them in his verse letter to the countess of Huntingdon. He lists for his correspondent in the country some of the bits of gossip then floating around London that he will not discuss:

> nor whether ytt bee true
> we shall have warrs with Spaine: (I wold wee might:)
> nor whoe shall daunce I'th maske; nor whoe shall write
> those brave things done: nor summe up the Expence;
> nor whether ytt bee paid for ten yeere hence.
>
> (16–22)[11]

The associational links in this passage are ones that any knowledgeable Jacobean would recognize. The possibility—or, for Fletcher, the hope—of another war against papist Spain leads him to think of masquing, that practice that best epitomized all that a good "Commonwealthsman"[12] detested about the dominant Spain-placating, cryptopapist court faction with its self-glorifying ways that were bleeding the country dry. Whether consciously intended or not, this unabridged masque brought into the daylight for everyone to see one

---

[9] Stephen Orgel, *The Illusion of Power* (Berkeley, Calif., 1975), p. 40.

[10] See Philip Edwards, *Threshold of a Nation* (Cambridge, 1979), esp. pp. 149ff., for a generous but refreshingly candid discussion of this point.

[11] S. A. Tannenbaum, "An Unpublished John Fletcher Autograph," *Journal of English and Germanic Philology* 28 (1929): 35–40.

[12] See *OED*, entry 2. Its earliest citation is from 1658, but the term was used much earlier in the century to describe the general position I ascribe to Fletcher.

of those private sports and recreations that were undermining England in the way (as the subterranaean imagery suggests) this one harmed Rhodes. But as we shall see, much of the politics of this play is far from subterranean.

AMINTOR: HIGH-FLYING TORY BRIDEGROOM

By a seemingly random selection of material, the first act displays the polity and religion of the court of an absolute monarch. Despite glimpses of private outrages, one senses that the government runs smoothly, thanks to the active cooperation of subjects like the bridegroom Amintor. His is a simple character, but one must not miss the many subtle touches in his characterization. Everyone at court agrees that in addition to being an attractive young man, he has all the social virtues. He is "valiant" but "temperate," a loyal friend, and above all "honest."[13] Beaumont and Fletcher exploit some of the inherent richness of this last word in building Amintor's character. Here it connotes not merely Amintor's apparent integrity and his youthful guilelessness, but also the tractability that results from his strict conformity to society's code of behavior. The king explains to Amintor that he was selected as Evadne's spouse precisely because he was "honest / As thou wert valiant," to which Amintor bitterly responds, "Gods, take your honesty againe, for I / Am loaden with it" (3.1.263–67). Late in the play, humiliated by his role as the king's cuckold, Amintor tries to enlist Melantius's aid in assassinating his oppressor. Disturbed that such precipitate action would ruin his own revenge plot, Melantius charms the sword from his friend's hand by thrice invoking the magic word "king." In an aside he adds, "I know hees honest, / And this will worke with him" (4.2.310–11). Amintor's ordinarily unquestioning honesty makes him the perfect subject of an amoral tyrant since absolute obedience sanctions even the dishonest actions of an honest man. We have already seen a portion of Amintor's glib answer to Melantius's charge of being fickle. It will be useful to consider the entire speech:

> She [Aspatia] had my promise but the King forbad it,
> And made me make this worthy change, thy sister,
> Accompanied with graces about her,
> With whom I long to loose my lusty youth,
> And grow olde in her armes.
>
> (1.1.135–39)

[13] The complexity of this epithet has been brilliantly analyzed by William Empson in his chapter "Honest in *Othello*" in *The Structure of Complex Words* (Norfolk, Conn., n.d.), pp. 218–49.

One cannot fail to notice the ease with which the young noble has obeyed his master's command to break his promise and the unabashed eagerness with which he anticipates his joys with the beautiful bride he has been forced to marry.[14]

This intellectually dishonest side of Amintor appears again just before he enters the bridal chamber. He meets the jilted Aspatia—pure, faithful, and mortally stricken. Momentarily, he feels his guilt: "It was the King first mov'd me too't, but he / Has not my will in keeping" (2.1.130–31). Quickly he suppresses these honorable feelings with two specious arguments:

> my guilt is not so great
> As mine owne conscience, too sencible,
> Would make me thinke, I onely breake a promise,
> And twas the King that forst me.
>
> (133–36)

With "too sencible" he is criticizing himself for being oversensitive, excessively scrupulous, too rule-adhering. This honest cavalier seems to be saying that promises are made to be broken. Ardent royalist though Rymer was, he is properly scornful of Amintor's excuses:

> If the King commanded Amintor; Amintor should have begg'd the Kings pardon; should have suffer'd all the racks and tortures a Tyrant could inflict; and from Perillus's Bull should have still bellowed out that eternal truth that his *Promise was to be kept*, that he is true to *Aspatia*, that he dies for his Mistress, then would his memory have been precious and sweet to after-ages; and the Midsummer Maydens would have *offer'd* their Garlands all at his grave. (P. 65)

Rymer's alternative of martyrdom is an option often mentioned and sometimes chosen by Beaumont and Fletcher's heroes and, more frequently, their heroines. But that is precisely the point. Amintor is no hero; he is simply an "honest," pliant young man, so saturated in the values of the court that he can be counted on to do what is required of him.

Thus when one views the nightmarish scene in the bridal chamber (2.1) between Amintor and Evadne, one's reaction must be an exceedingly complex one. This is the first of three plays in which Beaumont and Fletcher (or Fletcher alone) show in harrowing detail the failure to consummate a marriage on the wedding night. In *Thierry and Theodoret* (3.1) the husband is impotent, having been drugged by his mother. In *A Wife for a Month* (3.3), as discussed in chapter 11, the

---

[14] For another passage that shows his attraction to Evadne's beauty, see 2.1.138–39.

husband feigns impotence to protect the life of his wife from a brutal prince. In both plays the husband and wife are noble, totally admirable figures whom outside forces have victimized. In *The Maid's Tragedy*, on the other hand, the external evil is represented by the bride herself. In a dazzlingly constructed scene, the incredulous Amintor discovers that Evadne will not go to bed with him, that she is not a virgin, and that the marriage has been arranged to make "more honorable" (2.1.318) her affair with the king. Evadne combines the brittle sophistication of a Scott Fitzgerald heroine with something of Goneril's contempt for milk-livered men.[15] From the contemptuous worldliness of her stunning "A maidenhead *Amintor* / At my yeares?" (2.1.193–94), she can easily move to expressions of ferocious sexual revulsion (208–12), to frank sensuality (284–91), and to the cold remorselessness of her "pity" when Amintor asks her to kill him:

> I must have one
> To fill thy roome againe if thou wert dead,
> Else by this night I would, I pitty thee.
>
> (326–28)[16]

But powerful and sadistic as she is by nature, she derives further self-assurance from the power behind her. Amintor threatens to kill the protector she hints she has until at length she reveals his identity:

Evadne.   Why tis the King.
Amintor.   The King.
Evadne. What will you doe now?
Amintor.   'Tis not the King.
Evadne. What did he make this match for dull *Amintor*?
Amintor. Oh thou hast nam'd a word that wipes away
     All thoughts revengefull, in that sacred name

[15] I find Shullenberger's suggestion that her name is an anagram for Adam and Eve brilliant and most attractive. If it is not literally true—there is no comparable coinage in the canon—it should be. It is certainly the case that Evadne is the preeminent instance in a long line of Beaumont and Fletcher's women infected by the curse of Adam and Eve. But perhaps the common sense suggestion made to me by Professor Stephen Booth that Evadne means "wayward" is best.

[16] Danby, *Poets on Fortune's Hill*, writes with great brilliance on this scene. He sees Beaumont as developing the scene by a succession of witty "moral puns," comparable to metaphysical images in their yoking together of incongruous language and situation. My main—and very large—disagreement concerns his assumption that Beaumont unconsciously identified with such heroes as Amintor and Philaster. My detailed treatment of Amintor aims to demonstrate how detached the author is from his hero. I should add that I have numerous minor disagreements with Danby on matters of fact, that is, about what actually happens in the play.

> The King, there lies a terror, what fraile man
> Dares lift his hand against it? let the Gods
> Speake to him when they please, till when let us
> Suffer, and waite.
>
> (306–11)

There is something rotelike to Amintor's speech, as if he were recit-
ing a divine right catechism.[17] Coming as it does in the best-known,
most anthologized play of the collaboration, this passage is often
wrenched from its context and used to exhibit Beaumont and Fletcher's Tory politics. Nothing is usually said about the mentality of the
character who speaks these lines.

Suddenly this "hopefull youth" of whom, as he sadly says, his "land
was proud" (256, 258) discovers that he is helpless and trapped, the
victim of tyranny. For the rest of the play he can do nothing but "suffer, and waite" until there is nothing to do but commit suicide. Nonetheless, two factors serve to diminish one's sympathy for Amintor.
One is constantly reminded, either by the appearance of the mourn-
ful Aspatia or by his own pangs of guilt, of the dutiful faithlessness
that has placed him in his humiliating predicament. What is equally
distressing, Amintor allows himself to be ruled by Evadne's moral
code. She married him to make her sin "more honorable" (318); for
the same reason he sadly agrees to pretend to be her husband:

> me thinkes I am not wrong'd,
> Nor is it ought, if from the censuring world
> I can but hide it—reputation
> Thou art a word, no more.
>
> (331–34)

One is to hear pathos in this desperate reduction, conceived under
duress, of the concept of honor. The fact remains that he has chosen
the opposite path from that taken by such figures as Leucippus in
Cupid's Revenge. Adherence to a narrow, literal-minded notion of
honor that demanded absolute moral purity eventually caused Leucippus's downfall, but he showed that he was as truly honorable as he
was foolishly self-destructive. Amintor's decision to live a lie in order
to maintain his "honor" involves a tissue of contradictions that Beaumont and Fletcher expose relentlessly.[18] Thus he will mask as a lusty
bridegroom on one condition:

---

[17] Fredson Bowers, *Elizabethan Revenge Tragedy* (Princeton, N.J., 1940), p. 175, says
that the authors "carefully copied James's own utterances" in Amintor's various expressions of absolute obedience to the king.

[18] In his edition of the play, Howard B. Norland does an excellent job of analyzing
this topic.

> Nor let the King
> Know I conceive he wrongs me, then mine honour
> Will thrust me into action, that my flesh
> Could beare with patience.
>
> (338–41)

As long as the king will pretend that he is unaware of Amintor's dishonor, Amintor's honor will not provoke him to revenge. But the
king out of jealous insecurity insists on breaking the silence and ac-
cuses Evadne of cuckolding him with her husband. As he had
warned, Amintor is provoked so seriously by the breach of appearances that he calls the king a "tirant" (3.1.223) and draws his sword,
but once the king reminds him of who he is, the pious Amintor presents his sword to him because his "treacherous hand / [will not]
Touch holy things" (3.1.250–51).

The outer pressure of the king's persecution and the inner pressure of his constricting code of behavior gradually strangle Amintor.
Under sympathetic probing from his friend Melantius in the famous
quarrel scene (3.2), he reveals his humiliating secret and breaks into
tears. Yet even here one must respond with a mixture of pity and
irritation. After gaining a pledge of aid from Melantius, Amintor
suddenly draws his sword and wants his secret back. If Melantius
punishes Evadne and the king, Amintor's own elaborate act will be
exposed: "on me that have walkt / With patience in it, it will fixe the
name / Of fearefull cuckold" (3.2.226–28). This drives Rymer to ex-
claim, "Thou art mad, *Amintor*, Bedlam is the only place for thee."[19]
An uglier side is revealed when the contrite Evadne finally begs forgiveness of her husband. It would be difficult to imagine a more un-
generous, sanctimonious response than what he utters under the in-
hibitions of his code of conduct. He is willing "as far / As honour
gives me leave" to be "thy *Amintor*," but he cannot refrain from adding "would to heaven / The holy Preist that gave our hands together,
/ Had given us equall virtues" (4.1.263–64, 271–73). The inhumanity
of Amintor's virtuous adherence to his notion of honor is particularly
striking when Evadne announces that she has murdered his oppressor. Servile *jure divino* royalist that he is, he recoils in horror; the particular form of his response suggests the care Beaumont and Fletcher
took in his characterization:

> Those have most power to hurt us, that we love,
> We lay our sleeping lives within their armes.

---

[19] P. 73. According to Rymer, this ingenious scene with its endless succession of twists
and turns as the friends draw and sheathe their swords always moved audiences to
applause.

> Why thou hast raisd up mischiefe to his height
> And found one, to out-name thy other faults.
>
> (5.3.129–32)

Amintor is so revolted by the act of regicide that his sympathies are completely transferred to his royal oppressor, whom Evadne murdered in bed. His fanatical obedience places him with figures like Archas in Fletcher's *The Loyal Subject,* who wants to kill his son for presuming to save him from unjust torture by their tyrannical prince. But consideration of his relationship to Aspatia, the jilted "maid," will suggest a less harsh judgment of Amintor's priggish rigidity and remind one of the poignancy of his plight.

THE TWO MAIDS

Despite obvious differences the fundamental similarity of Aspatia and Amintor becomes clear as the play progresses. Before the play began, when Amintor informed her of his marital plans, she had discovered the moral truth that Amintor learned on his wedding night. He refused to believe Evadne "false" because he could not "finde one blemish in . . . [her] face / Where falsehood should abide" (2.1.188–89). Aspatia, viewing Amintor's handsome "shape," knows that it "burie[s] falshood in it" (5.3.35–36). She had erected

> a faith
> Out of the miracles of ancient lovers,
> Such as speake truth and di'd in't, and like me
> Beleeve all faithfull.
>
> (2.2.7–10)

When she lost her faith because she found her lover faithless, she had no more reason to live; in the circumscribed world of Rhodes there are no alternatives. As she wanders through the play, one is doubtless to view her as slightly deranged, reminiscent of the mad Ophelia. Aspatia's talk is all of faithless men, abandoned maids, and her impending death. She fancies herself an expert in the art of grieving and announces to her maids that if some discontent arises in their love,

> Enquire of me and I will guide your mone,
> And teach you an artificiall way to grieve,
> To keepe your sorrow waking.
>
> (2.1.94–96)

She demonstrates her mastery of the art of lamentation in some of the most frequently admired passages in the canon—apparently the

work of the more lyrical Fletcher. Here she gives instructions (similar
to Hieronimo's in the "Painter" addition to *The Spanish Tragedy*) on
how she should be portrayed on a piece of embroidery:

> strive to make me looke
> Like sorrowes monument, and the trees about me
> Let them be dry and leavelesse, let the rocks
> Groane with continuall surges, and behind me
> Make all a desolation,—looke, looke wenches,
> A miserable life of this poore picture.
>
> (2.2.71–76)

Lovely as this passage is detached from context, the language that
surrounds it, casual and colloquial, makes Aspatia's speeches stand
out as self-conscious, contrived, and literary—she is far from the
Amaryllis Rymer claimed her to be. In one passage she shows that
she has given some thought on how to grieve properly:

> come lets be sad my girles,
> That downe cast of thine eye *Olimpias*,
> Showes a fine sorrow.
>
> . . . .
> . . . now a teare.
>
> (2.2.27–31)

And in planning her death she strains for "some yet unpractis'd way
to grieve and die" (2.1.124). Her extended, somewhat self-indulgent
lamentations irritated Rymer, who knew what they sounded like onstage: "At this rate of tattle she runs on, and never knows when she
has said cnough" (p. 68). One may view her "artificiall" grieving with
the guilty impatience that mental disorder frequently provokes, but
her father Calianax reminds one of the essential point: "The King
may doe this, and he may not doe it, / My childe is wrongd, disgrac'd"
(2.2.81–82). She is a helpless victim of the king's absolute power and
selfish lust. Despite his cooperation in his own downfall, so is Amintor. The resemblance, as Rymer scornfully indicates, is noticeable as
early as the wedding night: "As the Scene and provocations work
higher, what Aspatia might have said to him, he whines to Evadne"
(p. 70). Both of them can do nothing but "suffer, and waite"
(2.1.311)—and grieve. He is honor's fool, she is love's fool, but both
are pitiable. His plight has diminished and exhausted him; she finds
she can no longer "endure the miserie / That I have on me" (5.3.6–
7).

As Aspatia promised, her diseased imagination concocts a perfect
and yet "unpractis'd way . . . to die" (2.1.124). She disguises herself

as her younger brother, one of Melantius's soldiers, and challenges
Amintor to a duel to avenge his treatment of her. Because of his
mounting sense of guilt, Amintor must be goaded mercilessly before
he finally consents to fight. Only after he has stabbed her mortally
does he notice that she has opened her arms to accept his thrusts. It
is, indeed, original and highly ingenious to employ the duel of honor
as a way of committing suicide. It compounds Amintor's guilt to have
murdered the innocent victim he has dishonored, and it enables Aspatia to remain true to the "faith" she has constructed out of the examples of those who died for love (2.2.7–10). At the same time, the
perversity of her invention and its phallic symbolism are inescapable:
one way or another, she will "die" (the widely used Elizabethan pun)
from Amintor's thrusts.[20] Amintor has become one of the series of
"heroes" starting with Jasper in *The Knight of the Burning Pestle* and
Perigot in *The Faithful Shepherdess* who draw their swords on defenseless women. It is a personal piece of stage iconology, a trademark of
Beaumont and Fletcher, representing the ultimate degradation of a
cavalier. Strangled by guilt and humiliation, Amintor finally commits
suicide. He has delayed this act too long to inspire "the Midsummer-
Maydens" to offer "their Garlands all at his grave" (in Rymer's
phrase), as they would had he refused to marry Evadne in the first
place. What one finally feels for the two maids—Amintor, it is
stressed, is also a virgin (3.1.125–26)—is not the tragedy of their
plight but the pity of it, not unmixed with criticism of their unquestioning acceptance of the fictions written by "poets when they rage"
(1.2.160): he, the political doctrine of *jure divino* made fictive in the
masque, and she, the romantic fictions in the tales of faithful lovers.

Tyrannicide

To the end of his life Amintor clings to the view that the king has "a
life / The very name of which had power to chaine / Up all my rage,
and calme my wildest wrongs" (5.3.136–38). No political belief in Renaissance England was preached more fervently or frequently than
obedience to the king, whoever he was, whatever he did. It was a
particular obsession of the reigning monarch, who for good and sufficient reasons had an unceasing terror of assassination. In *The Trew
Law of Free Monarchies* King James wrote that the only resistance the
people may offer a monarch is prayer "for his amendment, if he be
wicked; following and obeying his lawfull commands, eschewing and
flying his fury in his unlawfull [commands], without resistance, but

---

[20] This point was made by Ornstein, *Moral Vision of Jacobean Tragedy*, p. 176.

by sobbes and teares to God."[21] On the other hand, as absolute mon-archy and despotic rulers became more entrenched in the sixteenth century and as the Reformation created life-or-death differences be-tween Catholic and Protestant nations and civil factions, the moral legitimacy of tyrannicide became a live issue. Scholars and theolo-gians from James's early tutor (whom he repudiated) George Bu-chanan with his *De Iure Regni Apud Scotos* (1579) to Milton in his *The Tenure of Kings and Magistrates* (1649) showed that there were many honorable precedents and powerful arguments—classical, biblical, and modern—for the assassination of tyrannical kings and magis-trates.[22]

The king in *The Maid's Tragedy* abused his power and infected the life of the commonwealth in a manner that meets Milton's definition of a tyrant—"he who, regarding neither law nor the common good, reigns only for himself"[23]—and his suffering subjects do not shirk from branding him with this title. Before murdering him Evadne ac-cuses him of being "a tyrant, / That for his lust would sell away his subjects" (5.1.93–94). Even the obedient Amintor is driven by the "anguish of . . . [his] soule" into exclaiming, "Y'are a tirant, and not so much to wrong / An honest man thus, as to take a pride / In talking with him of it" (3.1.223–25).

The defense of the murder of the king in this play resembles the sixteenth century justifications of tyrannicide:

> *Melantius.* Dost thou not feele . . . one brave anger
>   That breakes out nobly, and directs thine arme
>   To kill this base King?
> *Evadne.*   All the gods forbid it.
> *Melantius.* No al the gods require it,
>   They are dishonored in him.
>
> (4.1.142–46)

The notion that it is a duty to murder a tyrant and that tyrants give "the gods" a bad name can be found in the writings of various "mon-archomachists" (so-called for the first time in 1600). A particularly influential expression of this view was written by John Knox, then a Marian exile, in urging the English nobility to assassinate their queen:

---

[21] *The Political Works of James I*, ed. Charles H. McIlwain (Cambridge, Mass., 1918), p. 61. McIlwain says that although *The Trew Law* was published in 1598, it remained the best expression of the political philosophy James held throughout his life.

[22] Roland M. Frye provides a judicious summary of the current state of scholarship on this subject in *The Renaissance "Hamlet"* (Princeton, N.J., 1984), pp. 38–75.

[23] "Tenure of Kings and Magistrates" in *John Milton, Complete Poems and Major Prose*, ed. M. Y. Hughes (Indianapolis, Ind., 1957), p. 760.

But this part of their duty [i.e., to assassinate bad rulers], I fear, do a small number of the nobility of this age rightly consider; neither yet will they understand that for their purpose God hath promoted them. For now the common song of all men is, we must obey our Kings, be they good or be they bad; for God hath so commanded. But horrible shall the vengeance be, that shall be poured forth upon such blasphemers of God. . . . For it is no less blasphemy to say that God hath commanded Kings to be obeyed when they command iniquity, than to say that God by his precept is author and maintainer of all iniquity.[24]

In another passage Melantius explains what impelled him to plot the murder of the king:

> Thy brother
> Whilst he was good, I cald him King, and serv'd
>   him,
> With that strong faith, that most unwearied valour,
> Puld people from the farthest sunne to seeke him,
> And buy his friendship, I was then his souldier:
> But since his hot pride drew him to disgrace me,
> And brand my noble actions with his lust,
>
> .   .   .   .
> . . . like my selfe
> Thus I have flung him off with my allegeance,
> And stand here mine owne justice to revenge
> What I have suffred in him.

(5.2.39–51)

Tyrannicide was frequently justified in cases where the monarch failed to fulfill his coronation oath or, as in this case, where he had become negligent in the performance of his duties. One example comes from another of the Marian exiles, Christopher Goodman, in his essay *Of Obedience*: "When kings or rulers become blasphemers of God, oppressors and murderers of their subjects, they ought no more to be accounted kings or lawful magistrates, but as private men to be examined, accused, condemned, and punished by the law of God, and being convicted and punished by that law, it is not man's but God's doing."[25] At the end of *The Malcontent* Marston took a similar line:

---

[24] Quoted by Frye, *Renaissance "Hamlet,"* p. 61.
[25] Quoted by Milton in "Tenure of Kings and Magistrates," p. 776. In *The Trew Law* King James in his crabbed style directly attacked this view that "a contract betwixt two parties, of all Law frees the one partie, if the other breake unto him" when it applies to monarchs (*Political Works of James I*, ed. McIlwain, p. 68).

Yet thus much let the great ones still conceale.
When they observe not Heavens imposd conditions,
They are no Kings, but forfeit their commissions.[26]

In a corrected edition of the third quarto (1604) a vigilant censor saw the dangerous political implications in these lines and changed "Kings" to "men." It remains one of the greatest mysteries in Jacobean censorship that much more severe action was not taken against *The Maid's Tragedy*.[27] The nearest Beaumont and Fletcher came to getting into trouble for writing this play is described in an anecdote by Fuller:

> [The authors] meeting once in a Tavern, to contrive the rude draught of a Tragedy, Fletcher undertook *to kill the King* therein; whose words being overheard by a listener (though his Loyalty not to be blamed herein), he was accused of High Treason, till the mistake soon appearing, that the plot was only against a Drammatick and Scenical King, all wound off in merriment.[28]

The "listener's" suspicions were correct. *The Maid's Tragedy* is as menacing to the institution of kingship as any in Jacobean drama.

Not only did Beaumont and Fletcher make their tyrannicide justify his actions with the sorts of arguments advanced by reputable theologians and politicians at that time; they took unusual pains to paint him in attractive colors and to free him of any blame for his actions. At first glance Melantius looks like a standard Beaumont and Fletcher general: honest, open, free-spoken, brave, a loyal friend. The generals created by Fletcher, most notably Aecius in *Valentinian* and Archas in *The Loyal Subject*, make their highest duty unquestioning obedience to their sovereign, however immoral he may be. But the generals of the collaborative plays, perhaps through Beaumont's influence, are different.[29] As seen earlier, Mardonius in *A King and No King* refused to do Arbaces' bidding when he gave him immoral

---

[26] *Plays of John Marston*, ed. H. Harvey Wood (Edinburgh, 1934–39), 1:214.

[27] In the Restoration someone seems to have noticed its pernicious implications. Waller was commissioned, possibly by the king, to write a new fifth act in which the king is saved, Evadne leaves the country, and Amintor and Aspatia marry. See Arthur C. Sprague, *Beaumont and Fletcher on the Restoration Stage* (Cambridge, Mass., 1926), pp. 58–62, 178–86.

[28] Dyce, *Works of Beaumont and Fletcher*, 1:xxxii, is quoting from Thomas Fuller's *The Worthies of England*.

[29] As will be clear in chapter 11, I do not mean to suggest that Beaumont and Fletcher disagreed on this topic, merely that Fletcher tended to depict generals who were fierce loyalists.

orders: "if all / My heires were lives, I would not be ingag'd / In such a cause to save my last life" (3.3.84–86). In the same vein, Melantius's first words make plain what he values most:

> where I finde worth
> I love the keeper, till he let it goe,
> And then I follow it.
>
> (1.1.23–25)

Unlike Philaster, who dared not trust his will to quick action, decisions are easy for Melantius because moral issues are totally clear. And unlike his friend Amintor, whose conduct is controlled by societal codes, the fiercely independent Melantius trusts his inner impulses completely: "I hope my cause is just, I know my blood / Tels me it is, and I will credit it" (3.2.288–89). Thus the moment he learns that the king he had served so loyally has "whored" his sister while turning his best friend into a cuckold, he decides on vengeance. So much for any divinity-hedging kings, so much for Jacobean passive obedience.

What do the authors do to make this decisive tyrannicide attractive and to present his actions in the best possible light?[30] Unlike most of Beaumont and Fletcher's characters, who seem to operate in what J. F. Danby aptly describes as "monadic self-enclosure,"[31] Melantius is unusually responsive to the feelings of others. In one of his earliest appearances, he is disturbed by the unwitting hurt he inflicted on Aspatia when he congratulated her on her supposed marriage: "I am sad, my speech beares so infortunate a sound / To beautiful *Aspatia*" (1.1.79–80). In the same sympathetic way he instantly detects that his close friend Amintor is trying to hide some "inward miserie" after his wedding night (3.2.47):

---

[30] I totally agree with Shullenberger's view of the politics of this play in " 'This For the Most Wrong'd of Women' ": that "although kingship survives, its myth of sanctity does not. The play seems in retrospect a rehearsal for the Civil Wars; it demystifies the central myth of monarchy" (p. 134). But I arrive at the same conclusion by a remarkably different path. Rather than engage in a point-by-point argument here, I leave it to the interested reader to compare our essays. As I see it, the differences stem from our methodologies. His approach is psychological; he treats characters as if they were people. I view them as instruments for the authors' larger aims, in this case their justification of tyrannicide. Were I to employ Freudian insights (as Shullenberger does), I would apply them not to the characters but to the authors, whose oedipal problems with their very "establishment" bishop and judge fathers might have made them uncomfortable with patriarchies like the one at Whitehall. But I do not know enough about the authors' inner lives or about Freudian methodology to speak responsibly of such matters.

[31] *Poets on Fortune's Hill*, p. 170.

I have observ'd your wordes fall from your tongue
Wildely, and all your carriage
Like one that strove to shew his merry moode,
When he were ill dispos'd: you were not wont
To put such scorne into your speech or weare
Upon your face ridiculous jollity,
Some sadnesse sits heere, which your cunning would
Cover ore with smiles, and twill not be,
What is it?

(3.2.63–71)

Such sensitive and precise observations show that Melantius transcends the stereotype of the honest, gruff soldier. Even at his most ferocious when he bullies his sister into killing the king, he is willing to compromise his rigid standard of honor and forgive her sins because "I have too much foolish nature / In me" (4.1.122–23).

Another factor shaping positive responses toward this tyrannicide is the manner in which the authors shield Melantius from becoming, like Hieronimo and Vindice, a mirror image of the evil object of his vengeance. This they accomplish by making him the instrument of the act but not the actual agent. It feels completely proper for Melantius to force his vicious sister to expiate her sin by personally avenging the dishonor to her and their family. The murder she commits is a particularly bloody affair. Evadne ties up the sleeping king, who awakens with joyous anticipation of some new recherché pleasure, only to have the morally rearmed Evadne carve him up with much sadistic relish. The king's evocation of the magical power of his title at this important moment reminds us that he has forfeited the right to be considered a king:

King.   Heare *Evadne*,
   Thou soule of sweetnesse, heare, I am thy King.
Evadne. Thou art my shame.

(5.1.95–97)

The murder accomplished, Evadne leaves the bedchamber. Her brief sojourn there prompts a sardonic quip by one of the gentlemen of the bedchamber that mischievously demystifies kings of godlike pretensions in another important area: "how quickly he had done with her, I see Kings can doe no more that way then other mortall people" (5.1.117–18).

While Evadne is about her business, Melantius pursues a plot that is unusual in a revenge play. Normally revengers are indifferent to their own survival; revenge is their sole raison d'être. But Melantius has no intention of dying:

> To take revenge and loose my selfe withall,
> Were idle, and to scape, impossible,
> Without I had the fort.
>
> (3.2.290–92)

If he can win the "fort" whose possession guarantees control of the kingdom, he can gain his revenge and survive. Melantius succeeds in doing this by a plot so cunning and amusing that it helps one admire him. It seems that his enemy, the foolish Polonius-like Calianax, father of Aspatia, is the court officer in charge of the fort. Melantius brazenly asks him for the keys because "I would kill the King" (3.2.312), knowing full well that Calianax will report this outrageous request directly to the king. When the king confronts the general with what he has said, Melantius denies the charge with all the righteous indignation he has earned by a lifetime of loyal service while suggesting that his accuser and inveterate enemy Calianax is suffering from senility. As he discredits Calianax out loud, Melantius continues sotto voce to request the keys. The implausibility of the noble Melantius's being a traitor, much less plotting in such a heavy-handed way, puts the laughable but honest old fool in an impossible position: the more he accuses him, the more he destroys his own credibility. Finally, publicly branded a senile dotard and furious at the king for refusing to believe him, Calianax hands the keys over. No disguised masquers, no skulls daubed with poison, no unbated foils, but a commedia dell'arte "sport" (4.2.244) gains Melantius control of the kingdom.

The revenger's hands are free of blood as he stands in possession of the fort after the king's murder, and one hears a courtier express a judgment about him to the new king that seems to have full authorial backing:

> He lookes as if he had the better cause, Sir,
> Under your gracious pardon let me speake it,
> Though he be mightie spirited and forward
> To all great things, to all things of that danger
> Worse men shake at the telling of, yet certainly
> I doe beleeve him noble, and this action
> Rather puld on then sought, his minde was ever
> As worthy as his hand.
>
> (5.2.14–21)

The king agrees: "Tis my feare too, / Heaven forgive all" (21–22). Thus, after hearing Melantius's explanation at the fort of what led him to become his "owne justice" (5.2.50), and after his threat to "un-build / This goodly towne" (58–59) unless he and his followers are given a blanket pardon, the king consents. Moreover, Beaumont and Fletcher make it clear that this is not merely a concession delivered under duress—the new king believes in Melantius's continuing value to the kingdom. In the final moments of the play, fresh from his pardon, Melantius comes upon the dying Amintor. Overwhelmed with grief at the fate of his friend—described in the best tradition of Renaissance friendship as his "Sister, Father, Brother, Sonne, / All that I had" (5.3.266–67)[32]—he makes a gesture toward suicide. This would have provided the conventional stage solution to the problem of the continuing existence of a regicide, and Beaumont and Fletcher's decision not to allow it contributes to the sense that they are condoning tyrannicide. Melantius's ultimate fate is left unclear, since he is so stricken by the death of Amintor that he vows to have nothing "to doe with that / That may preserve life" (5.3.289–90). However, in the final speech of the play it is noteworthy that only after the new king expresses concern for the well-being of Melantius does he deliver his sententious commitment to temperate conduct:

> Looke to him [Melantius] tho, and beare those bodies in.
> May this a faire example be to me,
> To rule with temper, for on lustfull Kings
> Unlookt for suddaine deaths from God are sent,
> But curst is he that is their instrument.
>
> (5.3.291–95)

Melantius's aim was to avenge the dishonor done to him, his family, and his friend; then, somehow, the survivors were to live in amity. With all three "maids" dying, his plans went awry, but Melantius cannot be blamed for any of their deaths.[33] At the end of the play the feeling is that the tyrannicide has the "better cause" and that thanks to him a temperate king who will not act like a tyrant is on the throne.

In his standard study of the topic, *Elizabethan Revenge Tragedy*,

---

[32] Peter Holland, "The Case for Regicide," laments the necessity for a modern director to explain Melantius's motivations as homosexual: "it is only a modern suspicion that all forms of virtue must be covering a guilt-ridden sexuality" (p. 581). Whatever motivated Beaumont and Fletcher at a subconscious level, they were writing at a time when male friendship was idealized and when (as J. W. Lever showed in his *The Tragedy of State* [London, 1971]) the politics of "civic humanism" was a serious matter.

[33] Beaumont and Fletcher's treatment of Melantius may be compared to that in the other Jacobean play in which a tyrannicide survives, Marston's *Antonio's Revenge*. Antonio is half-crazed by his task. After chopping up the villainous usurper's innocent child and serving him up to the king in a Thyestean pie, Antonio murders his enemy in a particularly sadistic way. He is offered high office, but Marston hustles him off to a religious order.

Fredson Bowers does not see anything unique or seriously unorthodox in the conclusion to *The Maid's Tragedy*. His main explanation for
Melantius's treatment is "the fact that Melantius does not execute the
revenge himself but delegates it to his sister Evadne." He admits that
"legally" if not "sentimentally" Melantius, as an "accessory," is as
guilty as his sister.[34] In fact, the authors show that Evadne was less
responsible for the regicide than Melantius. She initially shrank from
killing the king because he was a king (4.1.144–46); only the threat
of physical violence (162-63) induces her to do the deed. After the
king's body is discovered, a search is begun for Evadne as the only
possible murderer. Then Strato enters with the accurate interpretation of events:

>   Never follow her,
>   For she alas was but the instrument.
>   Newes is now brought in that *Melantius*
>   Has got the Fort, and stands upon the wall,
>   . . . .
>   . . . delivering
>   The innocence of this act.

>   (5.1.136–42)

The "alas," an expression of regret at the identity of the true culprit,
is important. If anyone is the "instrument" of God referred to in the
last word of the play, it is the admired Melantius; Evadne was merely
his instrument. Not only does Melantius claim "the innocence of this
act"; the whole weight of the play stands behind the legitimacy of it.
Only the last line affirming the curse on the "instrument" of God has
an orthodox sound, and nothing in the play or in the character of the
speaker is consonant with this. Since the play did receive the approval
of the Master of the Revels, the quandary about Jacobean censorship
remains.

POLITICS AND THE TRILOGY

Whatever the political unorthodoxy and consequent physical risks
from the writing of *The Maid's Tragedy*, Beaumont and Fletcher took
greater artistic risks in this play than anywhere else in their collaboration. I have already noted the unusual decision to include a full-
length masque and to suggest its magical and pernicious power, as
well as their willingness to chance disunity by building a play themat-
ically, around a variety of responses to tyranny. However, it was in

[34] Bowers, *Elizabethan Revenge Tragedy*, p. 174.

the creation of a group of subtly imagined characters that Beaumont and Fletcher most departed from their normal practice. Among the major figures only the king might be described as a "flat" characterization. Beaumont and Fletcher are careful to make the king colorless and unsympathetic, jealous and insecure in love, lacking any sense of guilt for what he does, and convinced that his absolute power is a God-given right. But while the king remains a relatively unknown force, the presentation of his victims takes unexpected directions. Beaumont and Fletcher could have simply shown Amintor as a weak, pitiable victim. Since they also wanted to make credible his selection as Evadne's husband, they made him a priggish, obedient adherent to the doctrine of divine right and the code of honor. It would have been enough for Aspatia to appear helpless and pathetic without suggesting a neurotic and perverted dimension to her response. Even the foolish Calianax gains a surprising life in his bitterly satiric but dignified remark about courtly rhetoric after learning of his daughter's death: "My daughter, dead here too, and you have all fine new trickes to greive, but I nere knew any but direct crying" (5.3.274–75). As for Evadne, Danby's enthusiasm strikes me as exaggeration in the right direction: "As a study in radical perversity, Evadne is more compelling than Lady Macbeth, and more subtle. If she is not a profounder study, that is because Lady Macbeth stands in a perspective of profundities."[35] What the authors attempt after Evadne's cruel performance on the wedding night is equally daring if less certainly successful. After she is forcibly converted by Melantius to virtue, she plays the innocent maiden villainously debauched as she plunges her knife into the helpless king, once for her husband, once for her brother, and one final time "for the most wrongd of women" (5.1.111). Proudly, she displays her bloody knife to Amintor as evidence of her reformation and pleads with him to seal the purification of their marriage by taking her to bed. Only when she receives his horrified refusal does she kill herself, still in the throes of her newfound virtue. She remains the same amoral force, now dedicated with as much passionate intensity to virtue as she had been to vice. Regardless of this, as Robert Herrick noted, her ardent vitality when she "swells with brave rage" makes her "comely every where."[36]

But it is in the the handling of Melantius that Beaumont and Fletcher best exhibit the complexity of their vision in *The Maid's Tragedy*. The whole experience of the play enforces the feeling that the

---

[35] *Poets on Fortune's Hill*, p. 193.

[36] "Upon Master Fletchers Incomparable Plays," Arnold Glover and A. R. Waller, eds., *The Works of Francis Beaumont and John Fletcher* (Cambridge, 1905–12), 1:xli.

king, for the devastation of private lives by public power, deserves to be expunged. And so he is by the impressive and attractive soldier. On the other hand, there must surely be some irony intended when he announces, "[I] stand here mine own justice to revenge / What I have suffred in him" (5.2.50–51). Followed to its logical conclusion, such a position looses mere anarchy upon the world. And in a final reversal, after all the elaborate exoneration and clearing of the path for Melantius's triumphant survival, one is left with the likelihood that he will soon die of heartbreak from the loss of the one person who made life matter to him. The achievement of good governance seems insignificant now that he is alone in the world. This package of contrarieties held in a meaningful tension with one another demonstrates that "negative capability" was not the sole province of Shakespeare.

The precise order among the plays I have been calling the "trilogy" is uncertain; there is no evidence that the authors considered them a separate group, and clearly each play has a distinct identity. Nonetheless, there are striking and enlightening similarities among them. Each, as I have reiterated, depicts the dangers to a kingdom of an intemperate ruler. Each of the rulers gains, and richly deserves, the distinction of being labeled a tyrant.[37] And in one tone or another (depending on the kind of play), each of the rulers is subjected to what may be called a deposition. The main difference from one play to the next is the directness with which it gives the old warning, "Sic semper tyrannis."

BEAUMONT'S MASQUE AND PROTESTANT MILITANCY

The trilogy marks the culmination, if not the conclusion, of Fletcher's collaboration with the short-lived Beaumont. Some of the lesser plays discussed in earlier chapters may have been written after some of the plays of the trilogy; as I mentioned in chapter 1, thanks to Pestell's testimony we know that Beaumont did no more writing after October 1613. But just before Beaumont's profoundly dispiriting if not totally incapacitating stroke, he composed one last work that would seem further to corroborate my arguments here. In celebration of the marriage of the Princess Elizabeth to Frederick V, elector Palatine, in February 1613, the Inns of Court performed two marriage masques. The one for the Middle Temple and Gray's Inn was written by George Chapman. Beaumont was selected to write the other, per-

---

[37] *Philaster*, 5.3.79–80; *King and No King*, 3.1.264–66, 5.4.134; *Maid's Tragedy*, 3.1.223–25, 5.1.93.

formed jointly by his own Inner Temple and Gray's Inn. The marriage was of great political importance. According to Roy Strong, Prince Henry and the anti-Spanish, anti-Catholic Protestants he gathered around him hoped that this marriage would cement "a militant pan-Protestant European alliance to curb Habsburg power."[38] The marriage, in Strong's words,

> was to be marked by the most splendid series of spectacles, expressly designed to establish the Stuart court in the eyes of Europe as the fount of revived Protestant chivalry. The unperformed and half-conceived *fêtes* for the Palatine wedding would have formed the climax of [Prince] Henry's festival policy as it had evolved in 1610. (P. 175)

The project never fully materialized because the prince suddenly died in November 1612, just a month after Frederick had arrived in England for the wedding.

Strong believes that both the form and content of the various marriage fetes were altered once the "prime mover" of the original enterprise was no longer alive. However, he shows that when placed in a context of Henry's various projects and beliefs, the political program is, if dimmed down, still clearly visible. Thus Chapman, who was very closely tied to the prince, presented a masque about Virginia that endorsed the anti-Spanish, anti-Catholic, and Protestant aspects of British imperialistic expansion. Another masque for this occasion has survived (although apparently never performed) that seems to have been composed by a group of Protestant clergymen. The language of its argument suggests the apocalyptic hopes the marriage aroused in certain circles: "the marriage, made in heaven, and consummated on earth . . . had given occasion . . . to believe, that one day, if it pleased God, the world (quitting its errors) would come to give recognition to Truth which resides solely in England and the Palatinate" (p. 181). As David Norbrook describes it, "The governing idea [of the masque] was that the union between Britain and the Palatinate would be an inspiration for the process of preaching the gospel to all parts of the world: when the process had been completed, the apocalypse would be near."[39]

On the surface Beaumont's masque merely seems to be a lavish celebration of the marriage with no relationship to political or religious matters. Partly subsidized by Francis Bacon and utilizing 150 mem-

---

[38] *Henry, Prince of Wales* (London, 1986), p. 177. Further page references to this book are in the text.

[39] "The Reformation of the Masque" in *The Court Masque*, ed. David Lindley (Manchester, 1984), p. 99.

bers of the Inner Temple and Gray's Inn along with some professional actors, it consisted of two antimasques and a main masque.[40]
When the sophisticated courtier at the opening of *The Maid's Tragedy*
spoke in patronizing tones about marriage masques, his main objection was to the inherent limitations of a genre governed by "rules of
flatterie." From the evidence of the "argument" prefaced to the Inner
Temple masque, it would seem that Beaumont attempted to circum-
vent his own objections by devising fresh and novel methods of con-
forming to the old formula. For the first antimasque he invented a
dance "of Spirits or divine Natures: but yet not of one kinde or liverie
(because that had been done so much in use heretofore) but as it were
in consort like to broken Musicke" (4–5).[41] Hence he intermixed
"*Naides* out of the Fountaines, and . . . *Hyades* out of the Cloudes, to
daunce" (10–11). Immediately afterward came another innovative
dance, in which blind Cupids were paired with statues "having but
halfe life put into them, and retaining still somewhat of their old nature, [which] giveth fit occasion to new and strange varieties both in
the Musick and paces" (18–20). The first antimasque was intended to
register approval of the match by the joint dancing of mythological
figures representing the Rhine and the Thames. The second antimasque stressed the diversity rather than the homogeneity of the
dancers through "a confusion, or commixture of all such persons as
are naturall and proper for Countrey sports" (27–29). Their dance
signified the approval of the "Common People" for the marriage.
One is told that "the Musicke was extremely well fitted, having such
a spirit of Countrey jolitie, as can hardly be imagined, but the per-
petuall laughter and applause was above the Musicke" (205–7). This
dance must have been unusually pleasing because the king demanded that it be repeated at the end of the masque, and it was given
further life by insertion into Fletcher and Shakespeare's *The Two Noble Kinsmen.*

   It will be noted that at no point in the masque was there a word of
flattery for king, audience, or even for the married couple. What
Prince Henry wanted to have celebrated—the raw fact of the accom-
plishment of "these wish'd Nuptials" (234)—agreed with what Beaumont wanted to avoid. However, it is in the main masque that one
finds the prince's political message—or what had been retained of it
after his death—in a more direct form. The scene is laid on Mount
Olympus because the underlying fiction is Jupiter's decision to revive

---

[40] Contrary to some claims, it is not certain that the scenery and stage effects were
by Inigo Jones.
[41] *The Maske of the Inner Temple and Grayes Inne*, ed. Fredson Bowers, in Bowers, gen.
ed., *Dramatic Works*, 1:113–144. Line numbers in the text refer to this edition.

the Olympic games. Two sets of masquers costumed as knights and priests appear before two pavilions "trimmed on the inside with rich Armour and Militarie furniture" (249). According to Strong,

> What we are seeing is a vision of Protestant Henrician chivalry, reforming missionary knights and zealous clergy presented in allegorical terms.
>> Behold, *Joves* Altar, and his blessed Priests
>> Moving about it: come you holy men,
>> And with your voices draw these youthes along.
> And they descend and dance reconstituted Olympic Games presaging the glorious future awaiting both bride and groom. (P. 179)

This is the extent of Strong's argument that Beaumont's masque was designed, at least in some putative earlier form,[42] to support Prince Henry's political program. As I have described it for purposes of brevity, his case might seem a bit assertive and flimsy, but I must stress that the passage quoted above appears within a chapter demonstrating Prince Henry's concerted effort to employ fetes, as the Medicis did, as an instrument of education and propaganda. In the case of the marriage masques for Princess Elizabeth's wedding, Strong cites a contemporary source stating that the Inns of Court prepared them "in obedience to the Prince's order" (p. 177). Chapman's masque and that by the anonymous Protestant ministers clearly conform to the underlying scheme as Strong describes it, and the very fact that Beaumont's masque was part of the same group makes Strong's claims about its political dimension all the more plausible.

Once alerted by Strong's claim, one may find further internal evidence to support it. First, its special nature as a masque may be partially described by noting that it has been criticized for its failure to relate "the audience to the masque world."[43] This is true, but it is not a fault because the aim was not glorification or flattery but celebration of an important occasion. Second, Beaumont's description of the main masque is consonant with Strong's theory:

> *Mercurie* by the consent of *Iris* brings downe the *Olympian* Knights, intimating that *Jupiter* having after a long discontinuance revived the *Olympian* games, and summoned thereunto from all parts the liveliest, and activest persons that were, had enjoyned them before they fell to their

---

[42] Strong has no evidence to support his belief that the Olympic material may have originally been designed for a Barriers, aside from his feeling that the masque was too militaristic for a marriage masque. His argument partly depends on a letter, mentioned in chapter 1, which Strong incorrectly attributes to the dramatist.

[43] Stephen Orgel, *The Jonsonian Masque* (Cambridge, Mass., 1965), p. 100.

games to doe honour to these Nuptials. The *Olympian* games portend to
the Match, Celebritie, Victorie, and Felicitie. (31–38)

Many of the best and brightest young Jacobeans and, most of all,
Prince Henry found King James's pacific foreign policy shameful.
The duchess of Newcastle's sly remark that "there was no employment for heroic spirits under so wise a king as James" captures the
frustration of ardent young idealists.[44] From the viewpoint of zealous
militant Protestants, "Olympian games" on foreign battlefields were
highly desirable. This "Match" promised "Celebritie, Victorie, and
Felicitie" not only to the newly married couple but to the forces that
their marriage would revive and coalesce. The term "Victorie" is
more fitting to a cause than to a marriage and connects Beaumont's
masque to the apocalyptic vision of the Protestant ministers.

When one considers the actual scene of the main masque in light
of Strong's claims, it is a striking fact that the sorts of "games" being
envisaged are not athletic contests but chivalric joustings, since the
stage set displays "rich Armour and Militarie furniture" amid "Tents,
as if it had been a Campe" (249, 251). Strong's view is further
strengthened by Beaumont's intermixing of priests with knights, suggesting a religious dimension to the games. The performance of the
celebratory songs and dances by the priests and knights is explained
as occupying the time until Jove gives the signal for the beginning of
the games; the reason it is proper for these chivalric figures to entertain this couple is that their marriage has sanctioned a revival of the
martial arts:

> till *Joves* musicke call them to their games,
> Their active sports may give a blest content
> To those, for whom they are againe begun.
>
> (241–43)

Without the context Strong constructed, details of Beaumont's fiction, such as the revival of the Olympic games and the decision to
include priests with the knights, seem arbitrary. But once alerted,
anywhere one inspects the masque the likelihood is enhanced that he
has successfully intuited Beaumont's and Prince Henry's intention.
For example, Strong notes the failure of the prince to choose the
prime masque writer of the time, Ben Jonson, for this project. Jonson
had shown himself on previous occasions to be less than completely

---

[44] Quoted by Douglas Bush, *English Literature in the Seventeenth Century* (Oxford,
1945), p. 3.

enthusiastic about the prince's militant policies.[45] Possibly as "the king's poet" he feared alienating his royal master, whose differences both personal and political from his activist, idealistic son were notorious. On the other hand, as Norbrook points out, the willingness of the Inns of Court to mount their first joint entertainment in the Jacobean period suggests enthusiasm about the marriage and its ramifications. Beaumont would have been an obvious choice to write one of the masques because of his strong connections with the Inner Temple. But that can scarcely have been the only factor in his selection: Chapman was not a member of any of the Inns. Whoever chose Beaumont for this important assignment—perhaps Prince Henry himself—must have assumed that he had the sort of politics I have ascribed to the coauthor of *The Maid's Tragedy*. We must now consider whether the same can be said of John Fletcher when writing alone.

[45] See Strong, *Henry, Prince of Wales*, pp. 141ff., and Norbrook, "Reformation of the Masque," p. 98.

Chapter Eleven

FLETCHER'S POLITICS AFTER BEAUMONT

IN 1613 Beaumont apparently left the Bankside and the bachelor quarters he had been sharing with Fletcher—along with their jointly owned clothes, cloak, and "wench"—to marry Ursula Isley of Kent. Soon thereafter he suffered his incapacitating stroke and stopped writing. If Fletcher felt abandoned and bereft,[1] it certainly did not affect his productivity. He found many new collaborators. With Shakespeare he seems to have written two or three plays; with Massinger, about eleven; with an assortment of others, ten. He also wrote at least sixteen plays by himself.[2] To sort out the various strands of this vast output would require a volume by itself.

Here I want to concentrate on the four plays he wrote by himself that seem most overtly political. Somehow the notion persists that even if the "Beaumont & Fletcher" plays were not "Stuart propaganda," Fletcher when writing by himself was a political conservative.[3] There are indeed differences between the plays Fletcher wrote alone and those he wrote with Beaumont, but not, I hope to show, regarding kings. As in his work with Beaumont, Fletcher consistently depicted life under absolute monarchs as unendurable, suggested

[1] One piece of evidence about Fletcher's feelings at this moment may be his ninety-two-line didactic poem, "Upon an Honest Man's Fortune." It was first printed after a play, *The Honest Man's Fortune* (dated, with great precision, 1613), in which Beaumont apparently had no part and Fletcher's was small. The great length of the poem and its slight relevance to the play it follows make it unlikely that it ever served as an epilogue. It seems to have been an independent poem on the same theme as the play. The poem appears to fit this moment in Fletcher's life since it is concerned to discover how to accept life's hardest blows. It argues against the fatalism of astrologers and for a kind of Christian stoicism.

[2] I take these figures from Cyrus Hoy's persuasive studies on "The Shares of Fletcher and his Collaborators in the Beaumont and Fletcher Canon," which he published in *Studies in Bibliography* between 1956 and 1962 and on which I have relied throughout this book. G. E. Bentley, *The Profession of Dramatist in Shakespeare's Time* (Princeton, N.J., 1971), p. 275, finds Fletcher's hand in "about 69 plays." I assume this figure includes lost plays and those attributed to him for whatever reason in the seventeenth century.

[3] For example, Andrew Gurr, editor of the Revels Plays edition of *Philaster* (London, 1969), says, "Fletcher certainly would not on the evidence of his later plays have agreed with his partner's questioning of kingship" (p. lvii). As authority for such assumptions about Fletcher, Gurr cites the article by Adkins on *Philaster* cited in chapter 8 and the article by Marco Mincoff, cited below, n. 6.

that unquestioning obedience to such rulers is foolish (if in some cases also admirable, in an absurd way), and showed that tyrannicide or revolution is sometimes necessary.

THE TRAGEDY OF VALENTINIAN

The Tragedy of Valentinian (1610–14)[4] once again examines the viability and credibility of the doctrine of passive obedience as a response to political tyranny. The setting is a peaceful, sophisticated Rome in a state of moral decay and stricken with a widespread malaise. Generals lament the dissolution of the empire, soldiers complain about the humiliating life they lead, chambermaids joke about the ubiquity of bawds and panders. The cause of it all is the emperor Valentinian, a debauched monster with no redeeming features. He is an incompetent governor and so susceptible to flattery that until he experiences his slow, agonizing death by poison, he appears to believe he is an immortal. The central action of the play is the emperor's rape of Lucina, the virtuous wife of the great general Maximus. To his victim the emperor proclaims, "Justice will never hear ye, I am justice" (3.1.34).[5]

Valentinian tests whether absolute obedience is possible given the worst possible set of conditions. Instead of the weak sensualist of *The Maid's Tragedy*, this play's tyrant is Neronic; instead of the vicious Evadne, his victim is a creature of perfect virtue; instead of the immature and weak Amintor there is a brave, eloquent exponent of obedience to authority, the general Aecius. His defense of Valentinian's rule is so extensive and fervent that he is generally taken as a mouthpiece for Fletcher's political philosophy. Before the rape Aecius preaches absolute acquiescence to the outrages of Valentinian's rule and urges punishment for anyone who even murmurs disapproval. He tells his best friend, the general Maximus, who is complaining about the "wild man" (1.3.2) whom they serve,

> We are but subjects, *Maximus*; obedience
> To what is done, and griefe for what is ill done,
> Is all we can call ours: the hearts of Princes

[4] *Valentinian* first appears in the First Folio of 1647; there is no evidence of an early performance. Its ascription to Fletcher alone is based on stylistic grounds. Actors' lists from the Second Folio require a date between 1610 and 1614. Within those boundaries a later date seems more likely because Fletcher was doing most of his writing in collaboration with Beaumont until 1613.

[5] Citations in the text are from the edition of *Valentinian* edited by Fredson Bowers, in Bowers, gen. ed., *The Dramatic Works in the Beaumont and Fletcher Canon* (Cambridge, 1966–), vol. 4.

Are like the Temples of the gods; pure incense,
Untill unhallowed hands defile those offrings,
Burnes ever there; we must not put 'em out,
Because the Priests that touch those sweetes are wicked;

. . . .

. . . majestie is made to be obeyed,
And not inquired into.

(1.3.17–28)

This is one of Aecius's milder outbursts, but before permitting him
to be called the "moral commentator" in the play, as Marco Mincoff
asserts,[6] or Fletcher a servile royalist, one must note how the playwright employs this representative of absolute obedience. One is
never made to doubt his nobility or the total sincerity of his beliefs.
These attributes Fletcher exhibits most forcefully when he displays
Aecius's instant, uncomplaining acceptance of the decree for his execution by the ungrateful, insecure emperor. He is so obedient that
he kills himself when all potential executioners are too frightened to
do the deed. Fletcher doubles the effect of Aecius's idealistic suicide
by having one of his captains perform the same act to display his loyalty to his general and his emperor.

On the other hand, Fletcher also depicts the noble general as a narrow fanatic. In act 2, scene 3, his friend Maximus barely restrains
Aecius from murdering the aforementioned captain after he over-
hears him criticizing the emperor. One feels further doubts about
Fletcher's identification with Aecius's views when Valentinian's bawds
also invoke "obedience," in this case as an argument for Lucina to
sleep with the emperor:

to the Emperour
She is a kind of nothing but her service,
Which she is bound to offer, and shee'l do it;
And when her Countries cause commands affection,
She knows obedience is the key of vertues.

(1.2.90–94)

In fact, after the rape Maximus ironically makes the same point to
Aecius: "It was my wife the Emperor abus'd thus; / And I must say, I
am glad I had her for him; / Must I not my Aecius?" (3.1.287–89).
To this the loyalist replies with evident discomfiture at this reductio
ad absurdum of his deepest conviction: "no answer / Can readily
come from me" (3.1.290–91). Even more undermining of his most
cherished belief is Aecius's own aside when he suspects Maximus of

---

[6] "Fletcher's Early Tragedies," *Renaissance Drama* 7 (1964): 70–94.

planning revenge against the emperor: "nor can I blame thee / If thou breakest out, for by the Gods thy wrong / Deserves a generall ruine" (3.1.309–11). The implication seems unavoidable that, however admirable the general's honesty and firmness of character, his virtues (like Coriolanus's) are immoderate, and his political philosophy is too.

What inspired commentators like Mincoff to think of Aecius as the author's spokesman is Fletcher's harsh treatment of the tyrannicide Maximus.[7] At first glance he seems to resemble the efficient and impressive revenger Melantius of *The Maid's Tragedy*. He displays the proper distaste for Valentinian's rule; he is as cunning as Melantius at devising a safe plot to murder the emperor without bloodying his own hands; and he is armed with much stronger grounds than Melantius for vengeance. Evadne was a willing partner in her own undoing, whereas Maximus's wife, graced with every virtue, was raped. But one soon realizes that Maximus is as constricted by his conception of honor as Aecius is by his views on obedience. As soon as Maximus suspects the worst from his sobbing wife, his first reaction is to consider its effect on his reputation, and immediately he encourages her suicide:

> I am ruind; goe *Lucina*,
> Already in thy teares, I have read thy wrongs,
> Already found a *Cesar*; go thou Lilly,
> Thou sweetly drooping floure: go silver Swan,
> And sing thine owne sad requiem: goe *Lucina*,
> And if thou dar'st, out live this wrong.
>
> (3.1.156–61)

The well-trained Roman matron agrees (161). Not even the rigorous Aecius sees the absolute necessity of her immediate suicide, but Maximus answers that he would agree "if she were any thing to me but honour" (232). Survival of his wife would dishonor him, and Lucina quickly obliges by destroying herself. But her suicide is not enough. Honor requires that Valentinian must also be eradicated, and this, Maximus believes, requires the murder of his best friend Aecius because he would be a formidable obstacle to his plans. Maximus genuinely cares for Aecius, and therefore he hesitates until he devises a manner of killing him that not only will be "a safe one" for the murderer but "shall be honor" to the victim (3.3.68–69). What more can

---

[7] Ibid., p. 73: "Maximus' change from revenge to ambition . . . brings out more strongly the theme: the deterioration of his character once he succumbs to the temptation of disloyalty. From betrayal for revenge to betrayal for private gain is but a step, it is suggested."

a friend ask? Maximus skillfully engineers this by a trick worthy of
Melantius and, with Aecius out of the way, he easily manages the
murder of the emperor.

Suddenly the noble revenger realizes that he need not commit suicide, for nothing stands in the way of his becoming emperor:

> stay, I am foolish,
> Somewhat too suddaine to mine own destruction,
> This great end of my vengance may grow greater:
> Why may I not be *Caesar*, yet no dying?
>
> . . . .
>
> . . . my deare freinds pardon me,
> I am not fit to dye yet if not *Caesar*.
>
> (5.3.23–31)

The chilling note on which he concludes this soliloquy ("If I rise, /
My wife was ravish'd well" [38–39]) suggests that he has become depraved by honor, and his subsequent actions confirm this. With the
backing of his soldiers and his marriage by force to Valentinian's
widow for added legitimation ("more honour" [5.4.36]) of his tenuous claims, Maximus gains the supreme honor of the emperorship.
However, his triumph is brief, for at his inauguration his new wife
poisons him with a ceremonial wreath while a song is sung that heavily makes Fletcher's point:

> Honour that sees all and knowes,
> Both the ebbs of man and flowes,
> Honour that rewards the best,
> Sends thee thy rich labours rest;
> Thou hast studied still to please her,
> Therefore now she calls thee Cesar.
>
> (5.8.17–22)

Maximus's actions are inexcusable, and Fletcher gives him no opportunity for any final words of self-justification or penitence. For the
second time in the play a regicide has been committed; it is as clearly
legitimate as that of Valentinian.

After Maximus's soundless death, the play ends on the conventional note of stability and renewal with plans initiated for the orderly
choice of a new emperor: "*Rome* yet has many noble heires: Let's in /
And pray before we choose, then plant a *Cesar* /Above the reach of
envie, blood, and murder" (5.8.118–20). Such a placid conclusion
should not, according to Aecius, have been the upshot of a tyrannicide. In acknowledging after the rape that Maximus has ample
grounds for revenge against the unspeakable Valentinian, Aecius

confesses that he would have been willing to assist him in an assassination plot were it not for consequences to the empire—the sort invoked in *Richard II*—that would reach into future generations:

> were it not hazard,
> And almost certaine losse of all the Empire,
> I would joyne with ye: were it any mans
> But his life, that is life of us, he lost it
> For doing of this mischeife: I would take it,
> And to your rest give ye a brave revenge:
> But as the rule now stands, and as he rules,
> And as the Nations hold, in disobedience
> One pillar failing, all must fall; I dare not:
> Nor is it just you should be suffer'd in it,
> Therefore againe take heed: On forraigne foes
> We are our own revengers, but at home
> On Princes that are eminent and ours,
> Tis fit the Gods should judge us: Be not rash,
> Nor let your angry steele cut those ye know not,
> For by this fatall blow, if ye dare strike it,
> (As I see great aymes in ye) those unborne yet,
> And those to come of them, and those succeding
> Shall bleed the wrath of *Maximus*.

$$(3.3.145-63)[8]$$

In fact, Fletcher's historical source for the reign of Valentinian, Procopius, confirms the wisdom of Aecius's preachments on obedience for in that account the emperess Eudoxa enlists the help of the Vandal Gaiscric to overthrow Maximus, and Rome is left in shambles.

Instead, Fletcher turned his back on his source and chose a quiet ending that, while leaving one with an abundant sense that Maximus was ugly-spirited and morally confused, seems to permit, if not to approve openly, the tyrannicide.[9] Valentinian's unending depravities and outrages, duly dwelled upon, are the strongest argument against Aecius's political doctrines. However often he may reiterate the vir-

---

[8] Fletcher has packed into this speech many of the contemporary arguments for passive obedience: Bishop Bilson's *The True Difference between Christian Subjection and Unchristian Rebellion* (1585) on the necessity of obedience at home combined with support of armed insurrection abroad; the parcel of commonplaces that stood behind Hooker and Shakespeare on the consequences of disorder; and of course, King James's various writings on the subject.

[9] Fletcher creates a captain named Affranius to express the dead Aecius's viewpoint toward Maximus's usurpation, but his prediction that "Rome wilt grow weak with changing / And die without an Heire" (5.4.69–70) is contradicted by the ensuing action.

tue of loyalty and the importance of Valentinian's survival for the
stability of the empire, all one can see is the harm the emperor is
inflicting on Rome. The similarity to the politics of the collaborative
plays is particularly clear in a speech Fletcher gives to Valentinian. It
will be recalled that the king in *Philaster*, whom his courtiers flattered
into believing that his powers are godlike, demands that they produce
his daughter who is lost in the woods (4.4.24–54); he reviles them for
limiting him to things "possible and honest." Valentinian's response
to the announcement of the death of Lucina employs similar language. The emperor professes shock, claiming he had been led to
believe that the objects of his love are immortal:

> Why do ye flatter a beliefe into me
> That I am all that is, the world's my creature,
> The Trees bring forth their fruits when I say Summer,
> The Wind, that knowes no limit but his wildnesse,
> At my command moves not a leafe: The sea
> With his proud mountaine waters envying heaven,
> When I say still, run into christall mirrors?
> Can I do this and she dye? . . .
>
> .   .   .   .
> Why do ye make me God that can do nothing?
>
> (4.1.20–32)[10]

This experience of his limitations and the effects of a powerful poison finally convince him that, as he says in his last words, "I am mortall" (5.2.140). The play suggests that no mortal creature should have
the sort of unlimited power that the passive obedience doctrine allows. When placed within the entire sweep of the action, Aecius's
commitment to unquestioning obedience appears as an honorable
quirk, like the pacifism of well-meaning idealists in the war against
Hitler. Maximus expresses the double feeling engendered by the situation when he says to Aecius's eunuchs mourning their patron's
death, "ye have a great losse, / But bear it patiently, yet to say truth /
In justice it is not sufferable" (4.4.309–11). The attitude toward tyrannicide is not left unresolved, as Clifford Leech would have it.[11] It
is double. Suicide and revenge are shown to be right *and* wrong. Violence does breed violence, but the conscienceless tyranny of Valentinian is "not sufferable." The way of the unresisting saint is impressive but inhumane; the way of personal vengeance is egotistical and

[10] The resemblance to *King Lear* is noteworthy, especially "they are not men of their
words: they told me I was every thing" (4.6.104–5), but the pernicious effect on monarchs of flattery is a commonplace.
[11] *The John Fletcher Plays* (Cambridge, Mass., 1962), p. 115.

cruel, but somehow necessary if life is to continue. One is left with a sense not so much of an insoluble dilemma as of a genuine pluralism.

Valentinian may thus be viewed as a subtle variant on the politics of *The Maid's Tragedy*. The main difference is that Maximus is a Melantius gone bad. Lucina, Aecius, and the captain Pontius are "heroes." Maximus, while speaking the same language as the morally superior creatures, is driven by his will to achieve personal glory at any cost— even, horrifyingly, "at losse of mankinde" (5.6.53). But the play forces one to notice through ironies of situation and language that the only problem the "heroes" solve by their virtuous self-destructiveness is one Rome did not have—that of overpopulation. Although he overreaches himself and in turn becomes a public menace, it is the confused Machiavellian Maximus who purifies Rome by eliminating a tyrant and his noxious train of followers.

THE LOYAL SUBJECT

The Loyal Subject (1618)[12] is one of Fletcher's weaker efforts.[13] Nevertheless, it deserves a brief look because the doctrine of passive obedience is subjected to an even harder test than in *Valentinian*. There the ruler tyrannized over a virtuous woman; the hard-line loyalist Aecius was not directly victimized until Maximus initiated his plot. In the later play it is the "loyal subject" himself, the old Russian general Archas, whom the sovereign gratuitously humiliates, robs, tortures, even threatens to kill. Yet nothing can shake the old soldier's allegiance to duly constituted authority.

Once again the loyalist expresses himself too extravagantly and dismisses valid objections too haughtily and is proved unwise by the course of events. Such moments usually occur during arguments between Archas and his noble, impetuous son Theodore, a colonel in the army. Early in the play Theodore objects strongly to the duke's ingratitude in discharging his father from his military command. His father reproves him for his "saucy" tongue, his "disobedience," his inability to "suffer" (1.3.69, 71, 76);[14] he even threatens to draw his sword on him. One can admire Archas's loyalty while noticing that

[12] The date derived from Sir George Buc's license agrees with the evidence of the actors' list in the Second Folio of 1679. Stylistic evidence suggests Fletcher's sole authorship, and this is confirmed by Sir Henry Herbert's note of 1633. See G. E. Bentley, *The Jacobean and Caroline Stage* (Oxford, 1941–68), 3:370.

[13] For a very different evaluation of the play and of the character of Archas, see Eugene Waith, *The Pattern of Tragicomedy in Beaumont and Fletcher* (New Haven, Conn., 1952), pp. 143–51.

[14] Citations in the text are from the edition of *The Loyal Subject* edited by Fredson Bowers, in Bowers, gen. ed., *Dramatic Works*, vol. 5.

his intransigent pride drives him to claim falsely that he retired from
the army voluntarily. Nor is this the only falsehood into which he is
led by his doctrinal obedience. On one occasion the duke discovers
that Archas has been holding a large hoard of gold in safekeeping
for him. The loyal general was entrusted with it by the duke's father,
who had noticed his son's extravagant habits. When the duke enters
his house and confiscates the treasure, he takes everything in sight
since Archas disdains to reveal that some of the gold belongs to him.
Theodore sarcastically confronts his father with this disaster:

> *Theodore.* How doe you Sir? can you lend a man an Angell?
>   I heare you let out money. . . .
>   .   .   .   .
>   I know you have been rifl'd.
> *Archas.*   Nothing lesse boy:
>   Lord what opinions these vaine people publish?
>   Rifl'd of what?
> *Theodore.*   Study your vertue patience,
>   It may get Mustard to your meat.
>
>   (3.2.96–106)

Evident in his inability to admit the truth to his own son, Archas's
pride is as strong as his loyalty. When he confesses that he has also
been "rifl'd" of his daughters—that is, they have been ordered to
come to the duke's sinful court—Theodore responds with disbelief:

> *Theodore.* Toth' Court sir?
> *Archas.*   Thou art not mad?
> *Theodore.*   Nor drunke as you are:
>   Drunke with your duty sir: doe you call it duty?
>   A pox o' duty.
>
>   (3.2.117–19)

Theodore's is the definitive criticism of Archas, whose blind acceptance resembles loyalty as foolhardiness resembles courage.

Since Archas's moral defect (like Hotspur's) is the excess of a virtue
rather than its deficiency, one's admiration for him persists. Naively,
he accepts an invitation to dinner at court and stubbornly insists on
attending even after Theodore warns him that it is rumored to be the
occasion for a plot against him. Archas becomes so furious at this
imputation against the sovereign who has dismissed, insulted, and
robbed him that Theodore can only respond with scornful resignation:

> goe, like a Wood-cock,
> And thrust your neck ith' noose.

Archas. Ile kill thee, and thou speakst but three words more.
    Doe not follow me.

Exit.

Theodore. A strange old foolish fellow.

(4.4.50–54)

Archas's courage is apparent, but one can also view him as a head-strong old man in the mold of Lear. The difference is that Lear changes while Archas remains a fool, almost a caricature of loyalty. He thinks of himself as "honours Martyr" (4.5.153), but, as he recognizes in a rare moment of self-awareness, he is also "doating *Archas*" (4.5.100).

Archas reaches an unsurpassable level of dotage after his enemy puts him on the rack—the duke's animosity, it should be stressed, having no grounds but jealousy—and tortures him so fiercely that he is covered with blood. His son and some loyal soldiers, suspicious of the duke's plans, burst into the palace and rescue the old man. Instantly, he stops his rescuers from full-scale revolt and insists that they remain obedient to his oppressor:

> Is not this our Soveraigne?
> The head of mercie, and of Law? who dares then,
> But Rebels scorning Law, appeare thus violent?
> Is this a place for Swords? for threatning fires?
> The reverence of this house dares any touch,
> But with obedient knees, and pious duties.
> Are we not all his Subjects? all sworn to him?
> Has not he power to punish our offences?
> And do not we dayly fall into 'em?

(4.6.67–75)

Nothing could be more devastating to the view of Fletcher as an unthinking Tory than the delivery of these articles of faith under such circumstances. Archas then adds his most extreme distortion of the truth:

> assure your selves
> I did offend and highly, grievously,
> This good sweet Prince I offended, my life forfeited,
> Which yet his mercy, and his old love met with,
> And only let me feele his light rod this way:
> Ye are to thanke him for your Generall,
> Pray for his life, and fortune: sweat your blouds for him.

(4.6.75–81)

Carried away by his own mixture of lying, sanctimony, and stubbornness, he turns on his soldiers:

> You are offenders too, daily offenders,
> Proud insolencies dwell in your hearts, and ye do 'em,
> Do 'em against his peace, his Law, his Person;
> Ye see he only sorrowes for your sins,
> And where his power might persecute, forgives ye:
> For shame put up your Swords, for honesty,
> For orders sake and whose ye are, my Souldiers,
> Be not so rude.
> *Theodore.* They have drawne blood from ye sir.
> *Archas.* That was the bloud rebel'd, the naughty bloud,
>   The proud provoking bloud; 'tis well 'tis out boy.

                                                    (4.6.82–91)

With the soldiers transformed into insolent sinners and the duke into a forgiving Christ figure, Archas descends into absurdity. It is noteworthy that his glib lies are expressed in the easy, repetitive, obtrusively rhetorical style for which Fletcher is often chastised. Here (as is frequently the case) it is a useful vehicle for his ironic purpose.

The soldiers reluctantly and suspiciously withdraw, far from reassured and placated. Archas, however, is now exultant, for he has at last won the confidence of the duke. That he had to pay for it with his blood does not matter to him. It does matter to Theodore and his soldiers. Deciding that they have had enough of this duke's rule, they leave Moscow to join the Tartars and overthrow this tyrannical sovereign. Archas, of course, is incensed at their rebellion and mortified that his own son is the leader. He opposes the rebels, and at a word from him they surrender. He arrests his son and, in his most extreme display of dogmatic inflexibility, prepares to execute him personally. A fantastic coup de théâtre solves matters so that Archas and his family virtually own Moscow. The triumph of the obedient general is so total that the duke concludes the play by saying, "he that can / Most honour *Archas*, is the noblest man" (5.6.124–25). It is easy to see why this play was, as Sir Henry Herbert reported, "very well likt by the king" at its revival in 1633.[15] It can certainly be twisted into a "mirror to subjects": Charles could have spent his declining years collecting art had everyone responded to the play as he did. It is less easy to see how Coleridge could have made his notorious charge that Beaumont and Fletcher were "high-flying, passive-obedience Tories" on the basis of this play.[16] It is true that a twentieth-century reader has special

---

[15] Bentley, *Jacobean and Caroline Stage*, 3:370.
[16] *Coleridge on the Seventeenth Century*, ed. Roberta Brinkley (Durham, N.C., 1955), p. 656.

reasons for distrusting blind loyalty, especially from generals. But there is no need to impose modern attitudes on the play. A father who threatens on three separate occasions to kill his son for daring to suggest that he is being misused by his superior when he plainly is, a general who chastises his loyal adherents for rescuing him from unjust torture on the rack, is surely a mixed portrait. I take this play as Fletcher's response, characteristically poised and sceptical, to his sovereign's conception of how a loyal subject should act.

THE HUMOROUS LIEUTENANT

From its opening moments it is clear that Fletcher's *The Humorous Lieutenant* (1619)[17] resembles politically the plays I've been discussing. After the atmosphere of the Macedonian court is established as frivolous and licentious, one hears the complaints of some foreign ambassadors. They tell the king that although he was their ally in recent wars, he has been violating agreements and annexing some of their territories. At this point the hero Demetrius, the king's son, bursts into court—a handsome, romantic figure fresh from his sports and still brandishing a javelin. Without denying the truth of the ambassadors' claims, he justifies his country's militant, expansionist policy by asserting that true kings like his father Antigonus—as opposed to the arriviste sovereigns of the ambassadors—have the right to do what they wish:

> You call 'em Kings, they never wore those roialties,
> Nor in the progresse of their lives arriv'd yet
> At any thought of King: emperiall dignities,
> And powerfull god-like actions, fit for Princes
> They can no more put on, and make 'em sit right,
> Then I can with this mortall hand hold heaven:
> Poore petty men, . . .
>
> . . . .
>
> Must these examine what the wils of Kings are?
> Prescribe to their desires, and chaine their actions
> To their restraints? be friends, and foes when they please?
> Send out their thunders, and their menaces,
> As if the fate of mortall things were theirs?
>
> (1.1.185–206)[18]

---

[17] The date is derived from the actors' lists in the Second Folio. The attribution to Fletcher alone is confirmed by an ascription in the manuscript of the play prepared for Sir Kenelm Digby.

[18] Citations in the text are from the edition of *The Humorous Lieutenant* edited by Cyrus Hoy in Bowers, gen. ed., *Dramatic Works*, vol. 5.

A young woman named Celia who is in love with the prince exults in the "brave confidence" (1.1.199) with which he delivers his tirade, and doubtless he is to be viewed as an admirable young cavalier. But many in the theater audience must have felt that such claims for any king were excessive and presumptuous. Certainly Jacobean parliaments were unwilling to agree with their own king's view, similar to that claimed for Antigonus, that "kings are not only God's lieutenants upon earth and sit upon God's throne, but even by God Himself they are called gods."[19]

Much of the action of *The Humorous Lieutenant* may be regarded as an implicit refutation of the overblown and self-aggrandizing attitudes of Antigonus and his court. One of the most devastating comments is the glimpse given in act 2, scene 3—as harsh a piece of realism as anything in *Bartholomew Fair*—of the office of mistress of the court's sexual revels. It is operated by the bawd Leucippe, a hardworking government bureaucrat who runs an efficient office complete with a card file. She demands much of her assistants and, unlike many public servants, keeps a sharp watch on expenses. Her language has a clipped, businesslike, impersonal quality. Were she shipping prisoners to a crematorium, there would be no essential difference in her conduct or her speech:

Leucippe. . . . Where lies old *Thisbe* now, you are so long now—
Second Maid. *Thisbe, Thisbe, This*—agent *Thisbe*, o I have her,
   She lyes now in *Nicopolis*.
Leucippe.   Dispatch a packet,
   And tell her, her superiour here commands her,
   The next Mon'th not to faile, but see deliver'd
   Here to our use, some twenty young and handsome,
   As also able maids, for the Court service,
   As she will answer it: we are out of beautie,
   Utterly out, and rub the time away here,
   With such blown stuff, I am asham'd to send it.

                                                  Knock within.

   Who's that? look out: [*Exit* 1. Maid]—[*to* 2. Maid]
                    follow your businesse maid,
   There's nothing got by idlenesse: There is a Lady,
   Which if I can but buckle with, *Altea,*

                              She turnes over the Booke.

   A, A, A, A, Altea, young, and married,
   And a great lover of her husband, well,

[19] Quoted by David Willson, *King James VI and I* (New York, 1956), p. 243.

Not to be brought to Court: say you so? I am sorry.
The Court shall be brought to you then.

                                        (2.3.38–54)

The routine of the office is interrupted by the delivery of some fresh flesh—a pretty young girl with her mother. Leucippe inspects her skillfully to see whether she meets the standards:

> come ye hither maid, let me feel your pulse,
> 'Tis somewhat weak, but nature will grow stronger,
> Let me see your leg, she treads but low ith' pasternes.

                                        (2.3.66–68)

Eventually the girl's mother is paid ten crowns for her and given a cheese as a bonus, and the girl is sent off to be fitted with clothes proper for her activities.

In a *Spectator* of 1712 Richard Steele praised this scene for having "the true spirit of Comedy," but added, "tho' it were to be wished the Author had added a Circumstance which would make *Leucippe's* Baseness more odious."[20] Apparently Steele would have wished an explicit moral condemnation of the bawd's activity by some authorial spokesman. This is not how Fletcher makes judgments. He does so by dramatic irony, by silently playing off character against character, scene against scene. Thus Leucippe's office reveals the true nature of King Antigonus. As soon as he catches sight of Demetrius's beloved Celia, the king decides that he must have her. He is implacable in his pursuit, employing his efficient machinery and every kind of unscrupulous trick to gain her. Even the knowledge that his son Demetrius loves her does not deter him. Like the king in *Cupid's Revenge*, he sends his son off to war so that he may pursue her without interruption; he falsely denigrates her character to his son and even claims he has killed her in order to gain time to seduce her. Even when Demetrius responds to the news of her death by falling into a fit of melancholia, the king does not desist from pursuing her. Eventually he becomes convinced and even converted by Celia's virtue, but one cannot fail to see that Antigonus, if not a ravening animal like Valentinian, is far from the "godlike" creature of his son's early description.

The dark portrait of the king has its complement in a broadly satiric episode involving the "humorous lieutenant" and the king. In a last desperate effort to gain Celia, the king employs a magician to concoct a potion that will bewitch her into love for him. By mistake the lieutenant drinks it:

---

[20] *Spectator Papers*, ed. Henry Morley (London, 1902), p. 380–81.

He talks now of the King, no other language,
And with the King, as he imagines hourely,
Courts the King, drinks to the King, dies for the King,
Buyes all the pictures of the King, wears the Kings colors.

. . . .

Makes praiers for the King in sundry languages,
Turnes all his Proclamations into meeter,
Is really in love with the King, most doatingly,
And sweares *Adonis* was a devill to him.

                                                        (4.4.153–61)

The lieutenant's infatuation is an extended piece of horseplay that Fletcher uses to shift the play into the lighter tone with which it concludes. But the point is clear enough: kings are men, not objects for idolatry. After the potion wears off, the lieutenant tells the king that before he took the magical drink he loved him "even as much as a sober man might; and a Souldier / That your Grace owes just halfe a yeares pay to" (5.2.15–16). This is perhaps more than Antigonus deserves. Fletcher grants the king enough good qualities to permit a happy ending to the play, but also shows, contrary to what Demetrius asserts, that kings too are "Poore petty men" (1.1.191).

Leucippe's office suggests the rot at the heart of the court, but it is through the lieutenant that Fletcher depicts the ambiguous quality of some of its most unquestioned pieties. According to the general Leontius, "There fights no braver souldier under Sun" (1.1.365) than this lieutenant. His bravery, however, really springs from the time he has "served . . . under Captaine *Cupid*" (354), for he has venereal wounds that are momentarily assuaged by the action of war. In one of his forays the lieutenant receives an injury that "eas'd" him of his constant pain (3.3.21) and with it, of his courage. In fact, when healthy he appears to be something of a coward.

Just as the lieutenant's prodigious courage springs from an ignoble source, Demetrius's reckless, absurdly exhibitionistic heroism is shown to be motivated not so much by patriotism as by a desire to gain a personal reputation for honor and magnanimity. For this he receives praise as a "mirrour of noble minds" (3.7.106), but so does the lieutenant for his astounding, venereally induced feats: he is called a "mirrour of men" (3.7.11). Both "mirrors" are rather tarnished when viewed next to the shining virtues of the heroine Celia. She is one more in the line of free-spoken women derived from Marston's Crispinella and Sophonisba, but Fletcher took special pains with this particular examplar of the type. From her first entry on stage as an utterly solitary prisoner of war, thrusting her way into court by pretending to be one of the loose women who turn up there on public occasions, we are struck by a portrait that is at once full, original, and charming. With all her virtue there is nothing remote or austere about Celia. She is playful, teasing, witty, with a daring that sometimes leads her into dangerous situations and an eloquence and quick wit that extricate her from them. The sophisticated court roués cannot cope with her unique combination of traits:

> *1. Gentleman.* . . . she would make one thinke—
> *2. Gentleman.*   True by her carriage,
>   For she's as wanton as a kid to th' out side,
>   As full of mocks and taunts: I kiss'd her hand too,
>   Walkt with her halfe an houre.
> *1. Gentleman.*   She heard me sing,
>   And sung her selfe too; she sings admirably;
>   But still, when any hope was, as 'tis her trick
>   To minister enough of those, then presently
>   With some new flam or other, nothing to th' matter,
>   And such a frowne, as would sinke all before her,
>   She takes her chamber; come we shal not be the last fools.
>
>   (4.1.19–28)

It is a dangerous world she has fallen into, and her weapons are few, but she still has time to make fun to herself of the perverse spectacle she is viewing:

>   If I stay longer
>   I shall number as many lovers as *Lais* did;
>   How they flocke after me!
>
>   . . . .
>   This is the lovingst age.
>
>   (4.1.32–34, 55)

This spiritedness makes her far from defenseless; as someone remarks, those who try to win her resemble "so many whelps about an Elephant" (4.1.7). Her fearless assurance has a simple explanation, which she defiantly offers the king when, in the last of his many efforts to seduce her, he threatens to rape her: "A thousand waies my will has found to checke ye; / A thousand doores to scape ye: I dare die sir; / As suddenly I dare die, as you can offer" (4.5.63–65). Twice earlier she had hinted at this source of imperturbability, but until she has no other recourse, Celia disdains heroic rhetoric. In this respect she is almost the opposite of her lover Demetrius, who came into the play clutching his javelin and spouting noble, and as one eventually feels, irresponsible sentiments.

It is through an implicit contrast between Celia and the honor-bound cavalier Demetrius that Fletcher gives a new and positive dimension to his politics. After a brief interview in act 1, scene 1, and a tender and moving scene of parting in the second scene, the two lovers go along parallel paths, never together again until the last scene of act 4. In the interval Demetrius acts the role of the "master of courtesy" and Celia firmly and wittily repels the advances of the king and his courtiers. One learns from her asides that she comprehends how dangerous it is to be isolated in the world of the bawd Leucippe and her assistants, but she defends herself deftly, without histrionics or self-pity. Since she is so sophisticated, playful, and self-contained, the court is very slow to realize what the audience knows, that she is immovably virtuous and chaste. Finally she is driven to the explicit, emotional outburst that converts the king from lust to wonder and admiration of her character. Were it not for a special ease and fluency, this speech might have been written by Webster:

> I am reading sir of a short Treatise here,
> Thats call'd the vanitie of lust: has your Grace seene it?
> He sayes here, that an old mans loose desire
> Is like the glow-wormes light, the Apes so wonder'd at:
> Which when they gather'd sticks, and laid upon't,
> And blew, and blew, turn'd taile, and went out presently:
> And in another place, he cals their loves,
> Faint smels of dying flowers, carry no comforts;
> Their doatings stinking foggs, so thick and muddy,
> Reason with all his beames cannot beat through 'em.
>
> (4.5.28–37)

This and similar uncompromising expostulations crush Antigonus's lust and convert him into an ardent admirer of Celia's virtues. The scene ends with her kneeling because "now" he appears like a "god" (an echo of Demetrius's inflated claims for Antigonus at the play's opening), and with Antigonus insisting on her superiority to him: "Vertue commands the stars: rise more then vertue" (4.5.91–92).

At the end of the play the parallels finally intersect. The lovers are brought together, and the differences between their characters, which have been gradually revealed, are made clear. Believing his father's false report of her death, Demetrius has grieved so deeply for Celia that he nearly dies. However, as soon as she is led into his presence and he learns that she is alive, his response reveals that he like his father has not known what kind of person he has been in love with. He sees the rich clothes she now wears (provided by his father while in pursuit of her) and instantly, Philaster-like, he assumes the worst. Celia, however, does not help matters. She detects the thoughts going through his head and cannot refrain from playing with him, saying in an aside, "My maiden-head to a mote i'th'Sun, he's jealous: / I must now play the knave with him, to dye for't, / 'Tis in my nature" (4.8.53–55). Through slight hints and innuendoes she tricks him into believing she has fallen, and once he has bitten, nothing can persuade him that she "did but jest" (4.8.94). His fury becomes uncontrollable, he hurls wild accusations and insults at her, and they separate, apparently forever. When Demetrius soon learns from Antigonus how mistaken he has been, he lapses into another fit of melancholy. The general Leontius acts as a mediator, craftily brings them together, and Celia eventually forgives him.

   Most critics of this play have been scornful of this episode. Waith is especially vehement:

> The climax is achieved . . . because Celia is . . . fond of tricks. . . . She is
> at the same time a heroine . . . pure and adorable. . . . In Celia the two
> sides of her nature are developed independently and each to an extreme
> which makes the character, if not impossible, highly improbable and, in
> the last analysis, without significance. Her role of satirical trickster al-
> most cancels out her role of romantic heroine. . . . Celia, like the entire
> play, is stunningly, unashamedly factitious.[21]

Perhaps *The Humorous Lieutenant* could be acted in a manner that corroborates Waith's view, but to me such a reading misses the consistency, "significance," and sophistication with which Fletcher has endowed Celia's character. The lines that immediately follow her vow to "play the knave" provide a clear and sufficient motive for her unwillingness to defend her conduct. She perceives from a set of leading questions by Demetrius that he is "Monstrous jealous," and she asks herself in a noble aside, "Have I liv'd at the rate of these scorn'd questions" (4.8.57–58). She has lived unprotected in a dangerous court at his request, refusing jewels and even the title of queen, with nothing in her head but love for Demetrius. Why, she asks, should she dignify his jealousy by defensive replies? Waith's label of "satirical trickster" trivializes the motivation for Celia's evasive and misleading answers. The honor-obsessed warrior is too obtuse to comprehend that her answers are playful. He cannot even hear her when she confesses, in lines quoted earlier, that she has been jesting with him (4.8.94). Like many of Fletcher's heroes, Demetrius is made of grosser stuff than his mistress. His response to her proud playfulness is the final demonstration of the superficiality of his nobility. Despite

---

[21] *Pattern of Tragicomedy in Beaumont and Fletcher*, p. 154.

ample evidence to the contrary, including Celia's own protestations of innocence, he blasts her with rhetoric worthy of the battlefield (as Celia points out). Nor does he fully believe that she has survived the dangers of the court unsullied until he is assured of her preeminent virtue by his father. Thus Demetrius fails his test, but he wins the prize anyway; no one in the play is really worthy of Celia.[22]

This contrast between the virtues of Celia and those of Demetrius makes a political point that recurs in Fletcher's later work. Despite a surface note of geniality at the conclusion, the court of King Antigonus is permeated with the same sense of menace as Valentinian's. The king is converted to virtue by Celia much as Valentinian momentarily pretends to be by Lucina, but one does not hear that Antigonus has abolished Leucippe's office. Antigonus imposes his will by raw power, bribery, trickery, and even witchcraft, but Celia's strong presence represents another kind of power that makes its presence felt through a gentle tenacity and an unostentatious, total commitment to virtue. She defines what is evidently missing in even the best of the men and hence in the quality and values of their courts. If only metaphorically, these might be called "female" qualities; they appear in apolitical forms in some of Fletcher's comedies, but only in his later plays do they appear in what are called the tragicomedies.

Clifford Leech (who precedes me in admiration for this play and Celia) points out that only after Celia has fully established herself in the court of Antigonus does one learn that she is a princess and that Demetrius will be marrying a social equal.[23] My claims for Celia's political significance will become clearer after studying her soul-sister Evanthe in *A Wife for a Month*. Celia's all-but-complete identification with her is hinted at by turning one letter upside down in her true name, Enanthe.

A WIFE FOR A MONTH

Aubrey reports that in the great plague of 1625, a knight invited Fletcher to visit him in the country: "He stayed [in London] but to make himselfe a suite of cloathes, and while it was makeing, fell sick

---

[22] Philip Edwards, "The Danger Not the Death," *Jacobean Theatre*, Stratford-upon-Avon Studies 1 (London, 1960), pp. 158–77, singles out Celia's conversion of Antigonus in 4.5 to show that Fletcher's appeal was based on a "belief in eloquence as well as a delight in it" (p. 167). This is undeniably true, but there is danger of distortion in concentrating on a scene like this without also noticing that in the more important confrontation with Demetrius, Celia is as reluctant as Cordelia to employ her eloquence. Fletcher's art is often subtler and quieter than is usually allowed.

[23] *Fletcher Plays*, pp. 73–74.

of the plague and dyed."[24] A year earlier he had written what was apparently his last unaided play, *A Wife for a Month*.[25] It has a curiously retrospective quality, as though Fletcher were recapitulating much of his life's work. In the opening scene a chorus of three courtiers laments the influence on the king of a flattering Machiavellian counselor. The heroine, who is in love with a young courtier, must withstand the sexual advances of a cruel, sensual king. Before the masque celebrating the wedding of the virtuous couple, a clamorous group of citizens attempts to crash the gate. On the wedding night there are prolonged scenes of sexual teasing before the couple is left alone, and then comes yet another of Fletcher's agonizing scenes in which a marriage is not consummated. A revolution dislodges the tyrant and permits a happy outcome. At times it seems as if *A Wife for a Month* is meant to recall (at least) *The Maid's Tragedy*, *Thierry and Theodoret*, *Valentinian*, and *The Humorous Lieutenant*. And at the center is the heroine Evanthe, who is as similar to the Enanthe ("Celia") of *The Humorous Lieutenant* as their names.

Once again Fletcher explores the effects of political tyranny on private lives. The absolute king Frederick is the "fountaine of all honours, place and pleasures" whose "will" and "commands" are "unbounded" (1.1.48–50).[26] He acts as though he is above the law, and the few virtuous courtiers can only mutter impotent ironies against the state of affairs. No matter how great the outrage, his subjects acknowledge the king's right to "tye up mens honest wills and actions" (4.2.45). Even when the hero Valerio experiences the most extreme physical and psychological torture from the king, he like Amintor and Aecius takes for granted "that reverent duty that I owe my Soveraigne, / Which anger has no power to snatch me from" (3.3.54–55). It is passages like these, ripped from context, that give Fletcher the reputation for championing passive obedience. But no one who considers the play as a whole could come to that conclusion.

To King Frederick—married, it is relevant to mention, to an admirable, virtuous lady—it seems virtually a usurpation of his kingly prerogative for someone to dare to love a woman on whom he has designs:

[24] *Brief Lives*, ed. Anthony Powell (New York, 1949), p. 54.

[25] The date of 1624 and the attribution to Fletcher alone are based on Sir Henry Herbert's license of May 27, 1624, according to Bentley, *Jacobean and Caroline Stage*, 3:422–23. Waith, *Pattern of Tragicomedy in Beaumont and Fletcher*, p. 15, shows that the historical setting owes something to *The Historie of Philip de Comines*, translated by Sir Thomas Danett in 1596.

[26] Citations in the text are from the edition of *A Wife for a Month* edited by Robert K. Turner for Bowers, gen. ed., *Dramatic Works*, vol. 6.

Frederick. You have private Visitants, my noble Lady,
 That in sweet numbers court your goodly vertues,
 And to the height of adoration.
Evanthe.   Well Sir,
 There's neither Heresie nor Treason in it.
Frederick. A Prince may beg at the doore, whilst these feast with ye;
 A favour or a grace, from such as I am,
 Course, common things—

                (1.2.141–47)

To gain the love of someone whom the king lusts after is regarded as a kind of treason, hence punishable by death, in this case with a special twist. In a love poem to Evanthe that the king seizes, Valerio expresses the wish that

> *To be your owne but one poore Moneth, I'd give*
> *My youth, my fortune, and then leave to live.*

                (1.2.91–92)

The king cruelly grants his wish. Valerio is to be married to Evanthe immediately, but as the title indicates, after a month of marriage he will be executed and Evanthe married again under the same conditions.

As in *The Maid's Tragedy*, what Fletcher is primarily concerned to show is the victims' responses to their oppression. As one would expect from a descendant of Amintor, Valerio accepts the king's cruel edict with noble resignation:

> Envy could not have studied me a way,
> Nor fortune pointed out a path to honour,
> Straighter and nobler, if she had her eyes:
>
> . . . .
>
> I would not have my joyes grow old for any thing.

                (1.2.214–23)

This is almost too jaunty; he revels in his plight as if he had learned the evils of long life from A. E. Housman:

>   who would live long?
> Who would be old? 'tis such a wearinesse,
> Such a disease, that hangs like lead upon us;
>
> . . . .
>
> Beside, the faire soules old too, it growes covetous,
> Which shewes all honour is departed from us,
> And we are earth againe.

                (2.5.23–31)

Indifference to death and the meaninglessness of it are frequent themes for noble, lyrical setpieces in Fletcher's plays. But one must listen to them closely and notice their context, because at times one may detect an immoderate, extravagant note. Such is the case with the title figure Memnon in Fletcher's *The Mad Lover*, when through dizzying verbal acrobatics in the second act he obliterates the distinction between life and death. When he speaks that way, he sounds mad. In this play the queen also offers arguments for the advantages of death as she desperately tries to cheer up Evanthe before her tragic wedding:

> What pleasure's there [i.e.,in death]? they are infinite
>> *Evanthe*;
> Onely, my virtuous wench, we want our sences,
> That benefit we are barr'd, 'twould make us proud else,
> And lazy to look up to happier life,
> The blessings of the people would so swell us.
>
> (2.2.61–65)[27]

This Shelleyan vision of death is meant to be consolatory, not mad, but Fletcher suggests that the queen's attitude is not the whole truth. The heroine Evanthe, for one, noble as she is, does not embrace the prospect of death with Valerio's glib, cavalier nonchalance. Clifford Leech observes that for "Fletcher's characters there is simply the life with each other, offering for a brief while its own prizes and dangers. In *A Wife for a Month* Valerio and Evanthe are promised a marriage that a month will terminate: they rejoice, because this is only to constrict in some measure all that lies within their range of hope."[28] But this is to take at face value Valerio's desperate effort to think positively about their tragic plight. Evanthe's first response is to weep (1.2.227) and then to consult the queen on how to mitigate the king's

---

[27] There is a very similar speech about the unimportance of death in the Fletcher and Massinger collaboration, *The Double Marriage* (Arnold Glover and A. R. Waller, eds., *The Works of Francis Beaumont and John Fletcher* [Cambridge, 1905–12], vol. 6, act 2, pp. 347–48). Written a few years earlier (ca. 1621) and also placed in a historical setting derived from Comines, it is in some ways a companion piece to *A Wife for a Month*. Most commentary concentrates on the difficult circumstances referred to in the title, involving the hero Virolet, that force him to cast aside his loving, heroic wife in order to marry again. However, this is only one of a series of situations in which he is portrayed as a weak blunderer, far less masculine (despite his name) than his "masculine" (act 1, p. 327) first wife Juliana and his Amazonian second wife Martia, as she is significantly named. The contrast between the two vigorous "incomparable women" (act 4, p. 380) and the inept, incompetent male resembles that between Demetrius and Enanthe and between Valerio and Evanthe.

[28] *Fletcher Plays*, p. 111.

sentence. Before the play is over, one sees that Evanthe is as coura-
geous as her lover but not at all in love with easeful death.

Until the end of the play, *A Wife for a Month* seems to be painting a
progressively darker picture, compared with which a concluding stoic
bloodbath of noble suicides would appear relatively positive. Valerio
is not even allowed the simple tragic fate of physical fulfillment and
a rapid honorable death, as the king's cruel sentence had determined.
Under the influence of the devilish advisor Sorano, the conditions of
the marriage are altered. Just after the wedding in act 3 Valerio
learns that he is forbidden to consummate the marriage on pain of
Evanthe's death, nor may he reveal the true reason for his failure.
This leads to one of the most harrowing and skillfully managed
scenes in Fletcher's vast oeuvre, equaled only by the similar situation
between Amintor and Evadne in *The Maid's Tragedy*. Unlike the earlier play, this one fully informs the audience of Valerio's dilemma.
Thus, throughout the cunning prolongation of the rituals that pre-
cede their seclusion in the bedroom, one's apprehension, fed by Valerio's, mounts. Finally the couple is alone and, instead of Evadne's
blunt, harsh refusal, one hears Valerio's pathetic evasions and lies.

In these days of bedroom-centered drama, the wedding night "fiasco" is a frequent subject for dramatic entertainment, sometimes pathetic, more often comic. What makes Fletcher's scene special as well
as characteristic of his work at its best is that so much is happening
simultaneously. Valerio is a man doomed to death, and he desperately desires a bride who innocently but unabashedly expresses her
desire for him. Moreover, he must resist her caresses to safeguard
her life, for their wedding chamber is under surveillance. The villainous Sorano has warned Valerio that "you will finde about ye / Many
eyes set, that shall o're-looke your actions" (3.2.116–17).

In light of Fletcher's reputation—and practice—it must first be
stressed that this scene has none of the lewd or cheap jokes that the
situation makes possible; while at moments gently comic, it is at all
times tasteful and moving. Nor does he develop the scene in a way
that could be described as merely "theatrical." Valerio's initial pose is
that of an idealistic, platonic lover who does not wish to sully their
love by descending to the basely physical. Evanthe disposes of this
desperate ploy as though she has read Donne's "Ecstasy" and Mar-
vell's "Coy Mistress," with the sexes reversed:

Valerio. May not I love thy minde?
Evanthe.   And I yours too,
   'Tis a most noble one, adorn'd with vertue;
   But if we love not one another really,

And put our bodies and our mindes together,
And so make up the concord of affection,
Our love will prove but a blinde superstition:
This is no schoole to argue in my Lord,
Nor have we time to talke away allow'd us.

(3.3.174–81)

As Valerio persists in his specious if sometimes brilliant academic argument against consummating their union, Evanthe gradually grows quieter, answering in terse, dignified, but hurt tones. Finally she asserts that he finds her unattractive and loves someone else. Valerio is driven from acting to lying; he has to blurt out, "I am no man" (3.3.231). Gradually Evanthe takes in the significance of this confession, and with great grace and tact accepts her fate:

Come, you have made me weep now,
All fond desire dye here, and welcome chastity,
Honour and chastity! do what you please Sir.

(3.3.257–59)

The scene is at once painful and fascinating, voyeuristic but restrained and tasteful. Fletcher exploits all facets of the complex situation he has concocted, even making Evanthe mutter, in an aside in the midst of her suffering, about the inherent absurdity of the pitiable situation in which she and Valerio are trapped, " 'Tis hard to dye for nothing" (3.3.238). From this candid, wry remark, it is apparent that virtuous conduct and resignation are not Evanthe's only traits.

About Evanthe's character the two most important critics of this play disagree. Waith believes that the pattern of all Fletcher's tragicomedies and of *A Wife for a Month* to an unusual degree is "Protean": "The theme is once more the triumph of honor . . . but the characters who represent the abstract poles of Fletcher's opposition do not remain constant." Thus he asserts that Fletcher violated decorum in the creation of Evanthe, who is "far . . . from the conventional portrayal of the chaste heroine."[29] Clifford Leech regards Evanthe's conduct as natural and finds her "within the framework of the play and within the theatrical type to which she belongs . . . more shrewdly and vitally drawn than any other in the tragicomedies of Fletcher."[30] I agree with Leech but feel he might have made his case stronger had he defined more precisely the "theatrical type to which she belongs." She is, in fact, another—the last—of Fletcher's many portraits modeled after Marston's Crispinella and Sophonisba. Unconstrained by narrow con-

---

[29] *Pattern of Tragicomedy in Beaumont and Fletcher*, pp. 163, 167.
[30] *Fletcher Plays*, pp. 104, 106.

ceptions of what a heroine should be, Fletcher makes these women speak without inhibition; more than their male counterparts they are capable of the highest heroism.

Fletcher further deepens Evanthe's portrait in the fourth act. First, she resists the subtle arguments of the "learned bawd" Cassandra, her maid, who has been employed by the king in his behalf. Then the king tries a dangerous new tactic. He reveals that he knows that Valerio has not yet consummated the marriage and claims that her husband had feigned impotence to save his own life. Evanthe's interest suddenly quickens. She is shocked at Valerio's lack of spirit, at the indifference toward her that such cowardly self-regard suggests. The king's cunning lies kindle her resentment; he increases the pressure by claiming that Valerio even inspired her maid to act as his bawd. Evanthe's faith wobbles; momentarily she even contemplates avenging herself by accepting the king:

> Evanthe.   But I shall fit him.
> Frederick. All reason and all Law allowes it to ye,
>   And ye are a foole, a tame foole, if you spare him.
> Evanthe. You may speake now, and happily prevaile too,
>   And I beseech your Grace be angry with me.
> Frederick. I am, at heart.—She staggers in her faith,   [Aside.]
>   And will fall off I hope, Ile ply her still.
>
>   (4.3.171–77)

There is strong plausibility to the king's lies, and Evanthe's momentary impulse to vengeance is consistent with her passionate, "masculine" spirit; she is not a simple allegorical image of chastity. Then the king, sensing victory, pushes his case too hard. He suggests that Valerio himself had been acting as a bawd to gain her for the king. Evanthe has a highly emotional personality, but as seen from her aside in the midst of her wedding night anguish (" 'Tis hard to dye for nothing"), Fletcher conceived her as having an intelligence that is always at work. She sees now that she is being tricked:

> Follow'd thus far? nay then I smell the malice,
> It tasts too hot of practis'd wickednesse,
> There can be no such man, I am sure no Gentleman:
> Shall my anger make me whore, and not my pleasure?
> My sudden unconsiderate rage abuse me?
> Come home againe, my frighted faith, my vertue,
> Home to my heart againe.
>
>   (4.3.183–89)

She bursts out in wild fury at Frederick's vicious innuendoes and returns to the role of "masculine" heroine: "This little Fort you seeke, I shall man nobly, / And strongly too, with chaste obedience / To my deere Lord, with vertuous thoughts that scorne ye" (4.3.202–4).

It is in such an aggressive and angry mood that this complexly drawn heroine approaches the hapless Valerio, in every way a gallant and estimable figure but less vital and less defiant than Evanthe. When the evil Sorano had shown him a ring signifying the "Kings will" (3.2.59), he obeyed, lamenting here and elsewhere the futility of opposing "the mighty wills of Princes" (3.2.125). By contrast Evanthe says directly that there are commands that ought not to be obeyed:

> *Evanthe.*   Did you command him?
> *Frederick.* I did in policy to try his spirit.
> *Evanthe.* And could he be so dead cold to observe it?
>
> (4.3.128–30)

Evanthe is so indifferent to the king's prerogatives that she even warns that she will take bloody vengeance against him:

> Victorious *Tameris* nere won more honour
> In cutting off the Royall head of *Cyrus*,
> Then I shall do in conquering thee.
>
> (4.3.205–7)

Fletcher's "masculine" heroines do not subscribe to patriarchal myths and do not reflexively drop their swords when the king's name is invoked.

After Evanthe hears the false claim that her husband has been feigning impotence to protect his life, she angrily criticizes him for his apparent cowardice. The honorable but relatively phlegmatic Valerio manages to interject the information that it was her life he was protecting, not his. Instead of being mollified by his revelation, Evanthe becomes even more furious:

> And was not I as worthy to dye nobly?
> To make a story for the times that follows,
> As he that married me? what weaknesse, Sir,
> Or dissability do you see in me,
> Either in minde or body, to defraud me
> Of such an opportunity? Do you think I married you
> Only for pleasure, or content in lust?
> . . . .
> Had I been my *Valerio*, thou *Evanthe*,

> I would have lyen with thee under a Gallowes,
> Though the Hangman had been my *Hymen*, and the furies
> With iron whips and forks, ready to torter me.

(4.5.34–52)

Righteous indignation is one of Fletcher's most frequent occasions for high rhetoric. Often it sounds factitious or overly facile; sometimes, apparently, it is meant to. But here is a prime instance, I would claim, of the propriety, even the necessity of such language. Behind Evanthe's angry protestations is a series of actions that justify her assured, straightforward claim that martyrdom "with iron whips and forks" would have been easy for her. On their wedding night she had imagined herself as Valerio's Pygmalion; here she sees herself as an ideal version of Valerio. She is the nobler, the more "masculine" spirit, as her admiring husband acknowledges:

> I wonder at ye,
> You appeare the vision of a Heaven unto me,
> Stuck all with stars of honour shining cleerly,
> And all the motions of your minde celestiall;
> Man is a lumpe of earth, the best man spiritlesse,
> To such a woman; all our lives and actions
> But counterfeits in *Arras* to this vertue.

(4.5.67–73)

Through Evanthe's ire, one now realizes that she is, like Marston's Sophonisba, a "wonder of women" and, like her, the "just shame of men."[31] Evanthe's example shows Valerio that he was supine in obeying the king, that his evasive actions on their wedding night sprang from a condescension toward her strength and dignity—that his attempt at heroism was a "scurvy curtesie" (4.5.58). This revelation of Evanthe's true stature enraptures Valerio, and in a tone of endearment and amused admiration he urges her to

> Chide me againe, you have so brave an anger,
> And flowes so nobly from you, thus deliver'd,
> That I could suffer like a childe to heare ye,
> Nay make my self guilty of some faults to honour ye.

(4.5.74–77)

But even here, at her moment of godlike grandeur, Fletcher does not lose control of his realistic conception of Evanthe's character. He shows that she can see herself, can hear the passionate excess in her tone and the calculated exaggeration in Valerio's praise: "Ile chide no

[31] *The Plays of John Marston*, ed. H. Harvey Wood (Edinburgh, 1934–39), 2:63.

more, you have rob'd me of my courage. / And with a cunning patience checkt my impudence; / Once more forgiveness! [*She kneels*]" (4.5.77–79). They are totally reconciled and prepared at last to consummate their marriage when a guard interrupts them to take Valerio to his execution.

This scene concludes the fourth act. Up to this point the play appears to be heading toward a tragic ending. Suddenly a happy resolution is effected. Alphonso, Frederick's older brother, whom one sees intermittently consumed by a melancholia that has disqualified him from rule, is cured of his malady by the (somehow) curative powers of a poison administered by Sorano to kill him. Once recovered, Alphonso is placed on the throne by a bloodless revolution, and the lives of Evanthe and Valerio are saved. In context this turn of events is less implausible than it sounds. Throughout, the unhappy fates of the melancholic Alphonso and the tyrannized lovers are carefully juxtaposed and paralleled. Suddenly, inexplicably, all begins to go well for the virtuous, apparently because of the intercession of "Heavens high hand" (5.1.22), whose inscrutable scheme makes as much sense here as it does in *The Winter's Tale*.

The point I would stress is that once again Fletcher shows the forcible overthrow of an immoral king. As in Melantius's plot in *The Maid's Tragedy*, the forces of good obtain the "keyes" (5.3.270) to the kingdom's power. The virtuous captain of the castle forthrightly expresses the anti-passive obedience convictions at the heart of the play's politics: "Though I am the Kings, I am none of his abuses" (5.1.29). It will be recalled that in *The Maid's Tragedy* Melantius had justified his disobedience by saying to the new king, "Thy Brother, / Whilst he was good, I cald him King," but because of his vile actions "I have flung him off with my allegeance" (5.2.39–49). According to Hoy and others Fletcher wrote those lines; these by the captain express the same sentiments, with several important verbal echoes:

> I fling off duty
> To your dead Brother, for he is dead in goodnesse,
> And to the living hope of brave *Alphonso*,
> The noble heire of nature, and of honour,
> I fasten my Allegeance.
>
> (5.1.42–46)

A dozen years later and with no pressure from Beaumont, Fletcher's solution to tyrannous rule remained unchanged.

But there is a difference. A collaborative play with Beaumont would probably have ended with the new king stressing the dangers to the commonwealth of a king with Frederick's temperament. Here, instead, Fletcher makes Alphonso seek out the heroic Evanthe: "Is this the Lady that the wonder goes on?" (5.3.336). She is the inspirational center of political resistance. Contrary to Charles Lamb's opinion, there is nothing "strained or improbable" about her virtue.[32] She is by turns angry, defiant, playful, and reflective; she desires life and physical satisfaction but is indifferent to death. One can grant that she is "protean" and yet see a core from which her diverse actions stem. Evanthe embodies all that is often called "feminine" but raises those qualities to a level of fully human greatness. Through her Fletcher rescues the term "honor" from its vulgarization by the base and literal-minded, extending it beyond the male "counterfeits in *Arras*" (4.5.73) who pass for virtuous. To be truly honorable is a state to be wondered at, something "celestiall" (4.5.70).

In his last years Fletcher saw that resistance to tyranny was not by itself enough. One can detect even in work written during the Beaumont years a recognition of a "female" element in scenes generally attributed to Fletcher, and eventually he seems to have conceived the "female" as a force to shore up the rotting foundations of centuries of patriarchal rule. It was unusual in the early seventeenth century to use the terms "male" and "masculine" as metaphors, although, curiously, it was common usage among Fletcher's Leicestershire connections. The countess of Huntingdon was a great beauty, but her many admirers' greatest praise was for her "masculine" qualities. Her own husband in a letter to his son mentions her "masculine understanding."[33] Lord Falkland says in his elegy on her that she was "soe Masculine, men must allow / That most had lesse of their owne Sex [than she]."[34] Thomas Pestell goes farthest in this direction, claiming in one of his poems about her,

> had shee ben a man, and *Homer been*
> Alyve; hee wou'd have writt his workes agen
> Of two less-glorious halfes; framinge one peice
> Mixinge his *Iliads* in his Odysses.
> And without fixtion storyinge her alone
> *Achilles* and *Ulisses* joyn'd in one.[35]

This, one may recall, was the kind of language in which Celia / Enanthe was praised in *The Humorous Lieutenant*:

[32] "Specimens of English Dramatic Poets," *The Works of Charles and Mary Lamb*, ed. E. V. Lucas (New York, 1903–5), 4:329n.

[33] *HMC (Hastings)*, 2:70–71.

[34] The text is from Kurt Weber's *Lucius Carey, Second Viscount Falkland* (New York, 1940), p. 288, l. 41.

[35] *The Poems of Thomas Pestell*, ed. Hannah Buchan (Oxford, 1940), p. 89, ll. 71–76.

Demetrius. . . . where got'st thou this male spirit?
   I wonder at thy mind.
Celia.   Were I a man then,
   You would wonder more.
Demetrius.   Sure thou wouldst prove a Souldier,
   And some great Leader.

(1.2.16–19)

Celia's answer is correct: in the world of Fletcher's plays there seem to be more female "male spirits" than male ones.

FLETCHER AND "COUNTRY HUMANISM"

At this stage in his career, Fletcher also created a flawless male hero in *The Island Princess* (1619–21) named Armusia, some of whose virtues would have been called "female" by the roaring boy cavaliers of the seventeenth century: "Honest, / Perfect, and good, chaste, blushing-chaste, and temperate, / Valiant, without vaineglory, modest, stayed."[36] A figure like Armusia would have been out of place in the court of King James, but there was nothing obsolete about the values of this latter-day Red Cross Knight. In his study of English education, *Scholars and Gentlemen*, Hugh Kearney traces a direct conflict between the imported, Italianate "court humanism" of Castiglione and Sir Thomas Elyot and what—alluding to Hans Baron's widely-used term "civic humanism"—Kearney labels "country humanism":

> [There] are two contrasting ideals of what a humanist education should be, the one drawing its inspiration from the values of the Italian courts, the other from the city states of Strasburg, Geneva, Basle and Zurich. One was lay, the other clerical. One looked to the court, the other to the country. One stressed the values of display, magnificence and sexual prowess, the other the virtues of restraint and godliness.[37]

Kearney illustrates this countervailing brand of "humanism" through an anti-Castiglione treatise on education by Laurence Humphrey titled *The Nobles* (1563). Humphrey, a Marian exile and "probably the most important single person at Oxford in his lifetime" (p. 43), based his position primarily on the Bible rather than the classics and directed his work to a noble, courtly audience. He urged courtiers to

[36] George Walton Williams, ed., in Bowers, gen. ed., *Dramatic Works*, vol. 5, 5.2.111–13. For fuller treatment of this amusing and subtle play see my "John Fletcher as Spenserian Playwright: *The Faithful Shepherdess* and *The Island Princess*," *Studies in English Literature* 27 (1987): 285–302.

[37] (Ithaca, N.Y., 1962), p. 43. Subsequent page references in the text refer to this edition.

use as models neither Castiglione's ambitious, worldly politician nor the swashbuckling cavalier who "licentiously roams the street in ryot . . . with wavering plumes, hanged to a longside blade and pounced in silks . . . haunting plays, feats, baths and banqueting" (p. 41). Courtiers should pattern themselves after the Marian exiles or better still, the "crest, the fame and type of nobility, without whom nothing is noble in this inferior circle below the moon," Christ himself (p. 39). To Laurence Humphrey a gentleman should above all be godly. He should nurture that attribute foreign to most nobles, humility, which Humphrey places above temperance, modesty, and continence in his hierarchy of the moral virtues. This sort of emphasis was familiar enough in Puritan moral tracts for the middle class. Humphrey is noteworthy in insisting on the same virtues in nobles. His direct influence on some of them reminds one that the appeal of Puritanism often crossed class lines, that some nobles (for example, Fletcher's friend and patron, the earl of Huntingdon) organized their households on Puritan principles and out of moral revulsion absented themselves from court as much as possible.

By the time of the closing of the theaters in 1642, Puritanism virtually constituted a counterculture, hostile to the poetry, painting, and papistry of the court of King Charles and his French Catholic queen. But by then, in the words of Petronius that Christopher Hill aptly quotes, "ubique naufragium est"[38]—there was shipwreck everywhere; the rift was irreparable. Referring to an earlier moment around 1630, P. W. Thomas wrote, "There were it seems two warring cultures. But it is more accurate to talk of a breakdown of the national culture, an erosion through the 1630's of a middle ground that men of moderation and good will had once occupied."[39] In the 1620s, however, at the end of Fletcher's career, one can still find people who adhered to the Puritan viewpoint without becoming narrow-minded, vituperative Prynnes. Holding to "country" views consciously or not, they could attend court, go to the theater, even patronize playwrights (as the earl of Huntingdon did), and yet refuse to whore after the strange gods of Renaissance courtly magnificence.

It is with Thomas's "men of moderation" that I would place the Fletcher of his later plays. Figures like Evanthe, Enanthe, and Armusia embody all the moral virtues advocated by Laurence Humphrey, but the plays they inhabit, while firmly critical of courtly manners, morals, and politics, never degenerate into hectoring sermons.

---

[38] *Milton and the English Revolution* (New York, 1979), p. 11.

[39] "Two Cultures? Court and Country under Charles I" in *The Origins of the Civil War*, ed. Conrad Russell (London, 1973), pp. 168–93.

The uncompromising insistence on individual freedom is moderated by a civility, a generous "female" wit that understands and excuses the posturing of Demetrius, the weakness of Valerio, the fraudulence of the "island princess," Quisara. Fletcher's life and the Jacobean era ended in the same year. Soon, as Matthew Arnold perceived in his essay apotheosizing Lord Falkland, it became difficult in the midst of the "generall ruine"[40] to detect anyone occupying the middle ground.

[40] *Valentinian*, 3.1.311.

THE KING'S MEN AND THE POLITICS OF
BEAUMONT AND FLETCHER

BEAUMONT AND FLETCHER are the vast unexplored Amazonian jungle of Jacobean drama. For the textual, linguistic, and literary scholar, their gigantic folio offers many difficult challenges. For the director, at least a few plays of their plays in addition to *The Knight of the Burning Pestle* deserve to be assimilated into the present repertory of Jacobean plays on academic stages, notably *Philaster* and *The Maid's Tragedy*. And for the historian, there is much to ponder. As we have seen, Beaumont and Fletcher had good and sufficient reasons, both private and public, for being critical of king and court. But why would they have written plays that risked life and limb? Why would the supposedly cautious and canny King's Men have been willing to present the sorts of plays I have described? Why would the Master of the Revels have selected these plays for court entertainment, and why would the king and his court have attended them and asked for more?

A famous incident in the House of Commons in 1610 suggests an answer to these questions. In 1607 a professor of civil law at Cambridge, Dr. John Cowell, published a book called *The Interpreter* that made extreme claims for the extent of the king's prerogative: "Of these two, one must needs be true, that either the King is above the Parliament, that is, the positive laws of the kingdom, or else that he is not an absolute king."[1] In another passage, which the lawyer, man of letters, and M.P. John Hoskins singled out for objection in the Commons, Cowell wrote about subsidies, "Whereas the Prince of his absolute power might make laws of himself, he doth of favor admit the consent of his subjects therein, that all things in their own confession may be done with indifferency."[2] It is no surprise that members of the Commons were offended by opinions, as Sir Edwin Sandys put it, to "the disreputation of the honor and power of the common law."[3] What is fascinating is the king's reaction. The monarch, who was constantly claiming that a king was "the supremest thing upon earth,"[4]

[1] David Willson, *King James VI and I* (New York, 1956), p. 261.
[2] Wallace Notestein, *The House of Commons 1604–1610* (New Haven, Conn., 1971), p. 294.
[3] Ibid.
[4] Willson, *King James VI and I*, p. 243.

supported the Commons' objections, saying that the civilian "hath been too bold in some things with the common laws of the Realm."[5] Of course, James was speaking hypocritically because at the moment when Cowell's book was being criticized the extravagant king was in desperate need of financial support from Parliament. Thus poor Cowell was prosecuted by Sir Edward Coke and convicted, and his book was burned with the king's full concurrence for *supporting* the king's own deeply held views on the extent of regal powers. Unfortunately for Cowell, his patron Archbishop Bancroft was too ill to protect him in his hour of need, but it was rumored that Bancroft was able to strike the deal whereby Cowell's book was burned but its author saved from imprisonment.[6]

While it was certainly safer to cast doubts on the prerogative from the shelter of the House of Commons than from the public stage, the Cowell incident suggests how things worked in Jacobean England. Certainly the king was very powerful, but his powers were far from unlimited, as Beaumont and Fletcher imply in *Philaster*. There, one may recall, a courtier forthrightly tells the king that he should be obeyed only when he acts justly, that is, according to the law, after which the king concedes that his power is finite (4.4.45–50). Many thrones, dominations, and princedoms for various reasons also possessed power in the kingdom: M.P.s, judges, peers, soldiers, handsome young men and their sisters and cousins and aunts. Few opposed regal absolutism out of idealistic motives, but the effect, nonetheless, worked something like a system with checks and balances.

Thus the only possible answer to my questions about how a critical drama was possible: the atmosphere in Jacobean England was more open, perhaps more chaotic if not exactly tolerant and forgiving, than is generally described. It is astonishing what the unpredictable king permitted to go unpunished; it is astonishing what his subjects sometimes dared say directly to him.[7] This does not mean that the Globe Theater and Blackfriars need be imagined as academies for the promulgation of radical ideas, or that one should now look at the plays of Shakespeare for a hitherto unsuspected radical political dimension. The remote and nearly mythical "romances" he wrote before and after the advent of Beaumont and Fletcher, with their superficial similarities to the work of the younger men, subsumes politics into a larger vision that provides glimpses into the mystery of

[5] Notestein, *House of Commons*, p. 296.

[6] Ibid., p. 297.

[7] See my article " 'The Comedians' Liberty': Censorship of the Jacobean Stage Reconsidered," *English Literary Renaissance*, 16 (1986): 123–38, for examples.

things. But regular performances by the King's Men of plays like *The Humorous Lieutenant* and *Valentinian* suggest that the company felt free to offer plays from various points of view on issues with political implications. Their willingness to take on daring plays like Fletcher and Massinger's *Sir John van Olden Barnavelt* (1619), which was produced against the bishop of London's wishes, and Middleton's notorious *A Game at Chess* (1624) may be seen as a matter of course, the outcome of a situation where anything was possible if one's noble protector was powerful enough to blunt or overrule the Master of the Revels,[8] or if one knew how to distribute *douceurs* in the proper palms in Whitehall.

Politics is only one area in which the plays of Beaumont and Fletcher, sprawling in their vast bulk across King James's reign, can help us to learn more about that greatest of times. But just as Beaumont's place in the "Poets' Corner" is unmarked and Fletcher's burial spot in Southwark Cathedral is unknown, the "biceps Parnassus" lies largely ignored on a back lot of Jacobean literary history. We will never see the Age of Shakespeare clearly without taking into full account their brilliant, dissident art.

[8] See Margot Heinemann, *Puritanism and Theatre* (Cambridge, 1980), pp. 166–69.

THE DATE OF BEAUMONT AND FLETCHER'S
THE NOBLE GENTLEMAN: CA. 1611

THERE IS a larger difference of opinion about the date of *The Noble Gentleman* than about any other play in the Beaumont and Fletcher canon.[1] Some view it as one of Fletcher's latest works, ca. 1625/6. G. E. Bentley takes this position in *The Jacobean and Caroline Stage*, 3:387–91. Others, among them Cyrus Hoy in "The Shares of Fletcher and His Collaborators in the Beaumont and Fletcher Canon," *Studies in Bibliography* 11 (1958): 94–95, largely on the basis of internal, linguistic evidence, would place it among Beaumont's earliest work, ca. 1605/6, with later revisions by Fletcher. Baldwin Maxwell in *Studies in Beaumont, Fletcher, and Massinger* (Chapel Hill, N.C., 1939), pp. 147–65, presents data for a somewhat early date (1609) and a somewhat late one (1619–21) and prefers the earlier.

The earliest mention of the play is in a license by Herbert for its performance on February 3, 1625/6, some five months after Fletcher's death. Its first appearance in print was in the First Folio of 1647. The play's prologue refers to its having been in fashion "some twenty yeare agoe," and some (notably Hoy) have used this to date the play twenty years before Herbert's license, hence 1606. Bentley, 3:388–89, claims that since the prologue also appears in the second quarto of *Thierry and Theodore* (1649), it is of "doubtful" value as a dating aid. However, the latest editor of *The Noble Gentleman*, L. A. Beaurline, points out, "the prologue and epilogue to *Thierry* were inserted in the second issue of Q2, and an inserted epilogue was also borrowed, this from Shirley's *The Changes* (1632). Similarly the epilogue to *The Noble Gentleman* reappears, again on an inserted fold, in Q2 1649 of *The Woman Hater*. . . . Therefore, it seems likely that the other plays were the borrowers and ours the lender; hence I presume the prologue was written for *The Noble Gentleman*."[2] But as Beaurline rightly insists, this still means that the play text as we have it, including the pro-

---

[1] This is a much-altered version of my note in *Notes and Queries* 24 (1977): 137–140. In it, I argued for a 1606–10 date, but as a result of my altered views on censorship I now feel that a somewhat later date, which all my evidence suggests, is more likely.

[2] Fredson Bowers, gen. ed., *The Dramatic Plays in the Beaumont and Fletcher Canon* (Cambridge, 1966–), 3:115.

logue, could have been written at any time from the period of the licensing date of 1625/26 to the printing date of 1647. Hence, the prologue cannot be used as evidence for the date of the play.

Baldwin Maxwell, believing on subjective, stylistic grounds that he detects Beaumont's hand, suggests a pre-1613 date. Since he feels that the Arabella Stuart material prevents a post-1610 date, the presence of Beaumont requires a pre-1610 date. Maxwell also detects a few internal references that suggest a date around 1619–21. One of these is the announcement by the title figure's wife that her husband plans to leave town to show off his new honors at his home:

> This Gentleman, the Lord of Lorne, my husband,
> Will be gon downe to shew his play fellowes,
> Where he is gay.

> (5.1.86–88)

Maxwell shows that this could refer either to a contemporary lord of Lorn or to a figure in a Child ballad, in which case it has no value for dating. The contemporary lord converted to Catholicism, left Scotland, and fought for the king of Spain, for which he was denounced as a traitor in 1619 but pardoned in 1621. A contemporary invective against him said, "Now Earl of Guile and Lord for-Lorn thou goes, / Leaving thy native prince to serve his foes."[3] Since the Noble Gentleman is planning to leave town, a tenuous parallel exists between the situations. However, the Child ballad seems much closer to the situation in the play. It refers to a steward who falsely assumes the title of lord but is unmasked. Maxwell notes a more telling piece of internal evidence when the title figure advises his cousin Cleremont to send his wife to court. Cleremont responds, "Sir, I had rather send her to *Virginia* / To help propagate the English nation" (1.1.90–91). Since the point of this exchange is that the court is even worse than Virginia, Dyce's citation of efforts (10:116n) (among them a pamphlet of 1610) to confute "scandalous Reports" about life in the colony is precisely on the mark. But there are earlier passages in Jacobean drama about wives in Virginia. Among others, Middleton's *The Roaring Girl* of ca. 1610 has the heroine putting off an importunate suitor by saying, "Take deliberation, sir; never choose a wife as if you were going to Virginia" (2.2). Thus Maxwell's recital of efforts made between 1619 and 1621 to stock Virginia with women is less than decisive. In

[3] Quoted by Alexander Dyce, ed., *The Works of Beaumont and Fletcher* (London, 1843–46), 10:182n.

any case, it is a single, isolated reference and, as Maxwell himself admits, might well have been inserted into a revival for topical interest.

In his edition of the play L. A. Beaurline proposes a terminus a quo of 1623, arguing that it alludes to Villiers's rise, climaxing in a dukedom in that year. He sees the play as commenting on "the undeserved and preposterous honours granted by the king" (p. 116n). For some reason Beaurline finds it "unlikely" that the Arabella material "would have been tolerated" but believes that a farcical, inevitably highly offensive representation onstage of the most powerful man in the kingdom, the king's beloved Buckingham, would have been allowed. In fact, the play does not show the award of titles by the king but a patently unconvincing pretense of such awards by some courtiers to a particularly stupid gull. What are felt to be "preposterous" are the aspirations of the title figure; the court is shown to be in responsible hands. In short, no persuasive evidence has been discovered to confirm the notion that the play dates from late in Fletcher's career, near to the time of Herbert's license of 1625/6.

This is not surprising because Fletcher's late plays differ radically from *The Noble Gentleman*, and I begin my argument for a relatively early date by noting its high degree of resemblance to certain plays by Fletcher (with or without Beaumont) that are reliably dated in the 1608–13 period. It was Fletcher's habit to seize upon a theme, a genre, or a situation and to write in succession a cluster of similar plays. The most obvious of such groupings would include the three famous collaborations on regal intemperance, *Philaster* (1608–10), *The Maid's Tragedy* (1610), and *A King and No King* (1611); the two Roman tragedies, *Bonduca* (1609–14) and *Valentinian* (1610–14); and the two plays about fratricide, *Thierry and Theodoret* (ca. 1617) and *Rollo, Duke of Normandy* (1617?). Another such is a group of comedies that have as a major theme the sovereignty of women in marriage. These are *The Coxcomb* (1608–10), *The Scornful Lady* (1608–10), *The Woman's Prize* (1611), and, I would add, *The Noble Gentleman*.[4] The similarities and interconnections among these plays are numerous; I shall confine myself to their relationship to *The Noble Gentleman*.

The Coxcomb shows a witty wife who secretly cuckolds her stupid husband, the title figure. The wife describes her husband as one

---

[4] Authority for the dates relevant to my argument: *Coxcomb*: Chambers, *Elizabethan Stage*, 3:223; *Scornful Lady*: Maxwell, *Studies in Beaumont, Fletcher, and Massinger*, pp. 17–28; *Woman's Prize*: Maxwell, ibid., pp. 29–45. Fletcher wrote another play using this theme, *Women Pleased*. It was performed between 1619 and 1623, but Bentley believes (3:431–33) it was written earlier. In any case, the play is a romantic tragicomedy, far different in tone and treatment from the group I am describing.

so sweetly temper'd,
That he would make himselfe a naturall foole,
To do a noble kindnesse for a friend.

(5.3.165–67)[5]

As E.H.C. Oliphant first pointed out in *The Plays of Beaumont and Fletcher*,[6] the wife of the title figure in *The Noble Gentleman* describes her husband in the same terms:

hee's the sweetest temper'd man for that
As one can wish, for let men but goe about to foole him,
And hee'l have his finger as deep in't as the best.

(5.1.228–30)

She remorselessly fools this "coxcomb," as she frequently calls him, aiming in thus mastering him to act as a model for all wives. In this and many other ways, Mme. Mount Marine resembles the redoubtable wife in Fletcher's *The Woman's Prize, or the Tamer Tamed*. Ostensibly a sequel to *The Taming of the Shrew*, it shows Petruchio's new wife Maria completely subjugating him before agreeing to act like a conventional wife. In detail as well as in overall pattern, the kinship with *The Noble Gentleman* is perceptible. To list a few of many examples, in both plays women wear the "breeches" and are described as "Amazons" unwilling to sacrifice their freedom. In each there is a servant named Jaques. Each plays "May Games" with her husband.

    The Scornful Lady (1608–10) also has many resemblances in situation, character, and language to *The Noble Gentleman*. The heroine is a domineering woman who for four acts humiliates a suitor she calls a "coxcomb" but loves. Both plays have old servants—Savill in *The Scornful Lady* and Jaques in *The Noble Gentleman*—who try to prevent young wastrels from dissipating their inheritance but eventually themselves become seduced by the attractions of a luxurious life. In both there is a reference to the Cleve Wars, not in itself a precise dating aid, but there is another reference that, I submit, anchors *The Noble Gentleman* to this cluster of datable plays. At the beginning of act 3, the Noble Gentleman's cousin responds incredulously when told that his kinsman has been made a duke. He suggests that he must have received some lesser honor, such as being made "Some leane Commander of an angry Block-house / To keepe the Fleamish Eele-boats from invasion" (3.1.9–10). In *The Scornful Lady* a servant tells a rejected suitor:

---

  [5] Irby B. Cauthen, ed., in Bowers, gen. ed., *Dramatic Works*, vol. 1.
  [6] (New Haven, Conn., 1927), p. 186.

> Good Captaine, or whatever title else,
> The warlike Eeleboats have bestow'd upon thee,
> Goe and reforme thy selfe: prethee be sweeter,
> And know my Lady speakes with no such swabbers.

(3.1.85–88)

One hears once more of eel boats in act 5 of *The Honest Man's Fortune* (firmly dated 1613). A servant speaks disparagingly of a sea captain's reputation:

> . . . they say h'as been at Sea, a Herring-fishing, for without doubt he dares not hale an Eel-boat i'th'way of War.
> 2. [*Second Servant*]. I think so, they would beat him off with Butter.[7]

I have been unable to discover precisely what is being referred to in these passages, but it would seem to be about a fishing war between the English and Dutch in the first or second decade of the seventeenth century, when the English coast apparently had to be protected against incursions by Flemish fishermen in improbably pugnacious—this would be the point of the joke—eel boats. It does not seem to me necessary to know precisely the referent in order to find the continual mention of this topic a dating aid. Clearly, the eel boats provoked talk at a certain moment—they are mentioned in three plays with clear links to each other. Since the limits to the dates of two of the plays are definite, I believe this confirms a date for *The Noble Gentleman* that previous considerations make likely.

One other independent approach leads to the same time frame. Broad and farcical as *The Noble Gentleman* may appear, its distortions and exaggerations are based in the political and social realities of the Jacobean period. Nothing is more characteristic of the reign of King James than the profligate awarding of honors, but one may distinguish stages in the practice. It was not until 1615, according to Lawrence Stone in *The Crisis of the Aristocracy*, that James decided upon "a radical change in policy, to a system of direct cash sale of titles by the Crown."[8] In *The Noble Gentleman* the title figure spends vast sums of money, five thousand crowns in one case, in a vain effort to obtain some sort of title or office, but the possibility of gaining one by cash payment is never raised, not even by the venal courtiers who hover around him. This line of argument can fix the date even more sharply. In 1611 James established and widely publicized the avail-

---

[7] Arnold Glover and A. R. Waller, eds., *The Works of Francis Beaumont and John Fletcher* (Cambridge, 1905–12), 10:270.

[8] (Oxford, 1965), p. 103.

ability of the title of baronet, obtainable fairly easily for £1,095.[9]
M. Marine, the "Noble Gentleman," is a gullible fool, but he is from
an old and wealthy family; he could easily have met the qualifications
and afforded the cost of the title. Throughout the play his aspirations
are treated as a joke, an impossible dream. By 1615 there were
ninety-three baronets. Once titles were for sale the joke would become progressively more pointless. Thus the closer to 1611, the more
efficacious the primary joke of the play would be.

[9] Ibid., pp. 82–97.

THE EVIDENCE FOR BEAUMONT'S STROKE:
THOMAS PESTELL'S ELEGY

An Elegie I made on Mr. Francis Beaumont,
dying 1615–16 at Westminster

Unto thy ever-loved memory,
And o'er thy hearse, this weeping Elegie
Shedds hee, who to restore thee, as thou wert
Once a full perfect man, would spend his heart;
5   And't were a blest fate, if such things as I,
To make thee live, might but by myriades die.
Yet fond Philosophie will prate, and dare
Tell us mens souls alike and equall are.
O, 'tis an odious lie, made out of pride;
10   Thine was as large as halph the world beside:
And as old wives imagine to this day,
The moon to starrs each month is clipt away,
Whence heaven is fill'd; if thy most ample witt,
Or just so much, God took and parted it
15   To dramms and grains, the purest and the best
Would furnish fortie colledges at least
(I think); the refuse I am sure would bee
Too good for th'Inns a Court and Chancerie.
'Tis true there be some able witts alive,
20   (Though very fewe), about a fowr or five;
But which of theise is natural and free,
Not prentise to long art and industrie;
Which, with mere labour, all that they can doo
Is *patching* up an old drie bobb or two
25   To make a lord laugh, or some lady gaye
A bracelett or a jewell cast away?
But (which pure Nature only did refine)
A braine that could conceive so quick as thine,
And be delivered so without all paine,
30   Ile never looke to meet the like againe.
All such sleight sylly things as I might steale
Witt, that thou threwst away at every meale

(When first I knew thee), with good husbandrie,
Able to serve us till the day we die.
35   The Jesuits that trace witt and subtiltye,
And are mere cryticks in Divinitie;
Who to the soadring a crackt cause allow
Sett fees for every new distinction; thou
By a clean strength of witt and judgment wert
40   Well able to confound, if not convert.
Have we not cause then to lament thee dead?
Death, I acknowledge thee the supreme head
Over all persons: God haes given thee sway
In thy two kingdomes of the earth and sea.
45   I knew thee mighty; but I thought thou wert
More wise, and less maliciouse then thou art.
For, being re-advis'd his death will show
To be a foolish and a spitefull blow.
For was it wisedome in a rage to kill
50   Him, for the very last words that his quill
Lett fall, instructing ladies how their lives
Are best preserv'd, with no[e] preservatives;
Since he well knew, if this way were denied,
Thou hadst a thousand entrances besides.
55   Alasse, he wrote it in none hate to thee:
His frequent wishes for thy company,
And, when thou cam'st, embraces, gave good proof
He ever lov'd and lik'd thee well enough.
How comes it with thy friends so angrie growne
60   Thou art, and tak'st pett; letting such alone
Whose every writing gives a foule offence,
And all their deeds defie thine excellence?
Looke in that place where thou didst last contrive
His death: they swarme as bees about the hive;
65   Which do disgrace (for theise no lawyers be)
And staine that needfull, noble facultie,
The sinews of our state, to which they grow
As heresies, or as diseases doo;
Atturneys, punies, clerks, solicitors,
70   Encamping and uniting all their force
'Gainst thee: their gunns are bouncing inkhorns, and
Their armour skins of beasts; their penns a stand
Of pikes and launces; and their watch-word Fees;
With buckram knapsacks fill'd with pilferies.

75 Yet is their language worse than mutinie,
Drowning thy dradd name in obscuritie
By talke of leases, states, assurances,
Possessions, tenures, and recoveries,
Lives, and three lives; which suff'ring, look to see,
80 Shortly thy state adjudg'd a nullitie.
Then thou art dead in law, and nothing lacks
But roubing thee in calve-skinns balm'd in waxe.
If thou beest sensible of wrong, then mend
This geare; and like a ravening storke descend
85 Among theise froggs, whose hideous number crall
And cover ore the land; and now they fall
To building castles, and to fortifie
In each fatt place, like a new monkerie.
Do but enquire, as you travell still,
90 Of everie faire house upon everie hill,
And everie one will tell thee, here does live
Such a law-driver, nine times under-shreive;
And there dwells such a one, solicitour
To such a lord, that was not long before
95 A petitefogger, sprouted from a clark's
Mann's boy that wypt boots; yet such wretched sharkes,
Such things not worth the thinking on as theise,
In spight of thee, still grow in wealth and ease.
I should believe, but that you canst not see,
100 And art impartiall, they had bribed thee.
Sure thou wilt shortly, though you give them scope
Awhile, lett in the Devill or the Pope,
And make a skuffle: or is't policie
In thee to lett them waxe and multiplie,
105 And (like ranke weeds) ore-topping other men,
Possesse the land themselfs alone; and then
This dragon-tongu'd fraternitie (as they
That sprung of teeth) shall one another slaye?
Thy follie thus excus'd, I yet must judge
110 Thou slewst him for a spitefull secret grudge,
'Cause those quick lines from his live Muse did passe
Have marble shedd and everlasting brasse
Over three ladies, which still fresh shall be,
And live to thy disgrace in memorie.
115 This did so vexe thee, Death, that thou were faine
To hire an apoplexe, to shend his braine,

Till thou couldst come thyselfe, and hinder so
That sprightly nectar which from it did flow;
And yet his puissant witt was nere so drie,
120 But even in midst of most infirmitie
It crown'd his last worke with so faire an end,
'Twould puzzle the best witts alive to mend.
And now, although his life on earth be done,
Thou hast gain'd nothing; he haes; it's begunne
125 In Heaven more glorious; wher that sacred head,
'Mongst Saints and Angells, is canonised;
And men shall henceforth, when they mean to frame
A wittie poem, invocate his name
The new *Saint Francis*; and those fewe that are
130 Able to lead their lives so regular
(Though ne'er in all points so exact) as hee
Shall a new order of *Franciscans* bee.[1]

[1] From *The Poems of Thomas Pestell*, ed. Hannah Buchan (Oxford, 1940), pp. 71–74. Buchan, p. liv, seems to have missed the point that ll. 115ff. describe a stroke: We hear . . . of that melancholy that hung on Beaumont for about three years before his death, seeming to paralyse him. He longed for death, and Pestell states quite definitely that he wrote nothing at all after he had finished the elegy on Lady Penelope Clifton." The poem makes it plain that Beaumont's melancholy was the result of the apoplexe."

INDEX